BIG LIES

Also by Joe Conason

*The Hunting of the President: The Ten-Year Campaign
to Destroy Bill and Hillary Clinton*
(with Gene Lyons)

JOE CONASON

BIG LIES

The
Right-Wing
Propaganda Machine
and How It Distorts
the Truth

THOMAS DUNNE BOOKS ✷ ST. MARTIN'S PRESS
New York

THOMAS DUNNE BOOKS.
An imprint of St. Martin's Press.

www.stmartins.com

Library of Congress Cataloging-in-Publication Data

Conason, Joe.
    Big lies : the right-wing propaganda machine and how it distorts
the truth / Joe Conason.— 1st ed.
        p. cm.
    ISBN 0-312-31560-0
    1. United States—Politics and government—2001– 2. United
States—Politics and government—1993–2001. 3. Propaganda,
American. 4. Conservatism—United States. 5. Right and left
(Political science) I. Title.

E902.C365 2003
973.931—dc21

                                                    2003049196

First Edition: September 2003

10 9 8 7 6 5 4 3 2 1

For Elizabeth,

and in memory of my mother

Contents

Introduction   1

1 Limousine Liberals and Corporate-Jet Conservatives   13

2 Peroxide Paradox: The Blonde Misleading the Blind   29

3 Male Cheerleaders and Chicken Hawks   52

4 Déjà Voodoo, All Over Again   74

5 Why Dick Armey Joined the ACLU   89

6 Private Lives and Public Lies   109

7 Tokens of Their Esteem   128

8 Crony Capitalism, Infectious Greed, and the Way the World Really Works   146

9 Faith, Charity, and the Mayberry Machiavellis   171

10 "Dead or Alive" — Or Maybe Just Forgotten   190

Notes   213
Acknowledgments   233
Index   235

BIG LIES

"In all those things which deal with people, be liberal, be human."

—Senator Prescott Bush, of Connecticut,
quoting President Eisenhower in the
Congressional Record, February 18, 1955

INTRODUCTION

Is the United States of America liberal or conservative? So effectively has right-wing propaganda dominated political debate in this country for the past two decades that the question hardly seems worth discussing. Almost without thinking, the majority of Americans—including many who describe themselves as liberal or progressive or left of center—would probably answer "conservative."

In my opinion, they would be wrong. But right or wrong, such dull conformity is a warning sign for the world's most enduring democracy. If only one political perspective is heard clearly, there can be no robust debate and no meaningful democratic choice. At a time when highly partisan and extremely reactionary Republicans control every branch of government, our country needs full, fair, and uninhibited debate that encourages participation—not a loud, monotonous drone that breeds apathetic surrender.

Conservatives enjoy their virtual monopoly over the nation's political conversation, of course. They paid a lot of money for it and they intend to keep it. They dominate the national debate not because their ideas are better (or more popular), but because they have more resources and a vast, coordinated infrastructure that has been built up during three decades. They also tend to dominate because—unlike the supposedly liberal mainstream media—conservatives are perfectly willing to stifle opposition. Liberal opinion is hard to find in conservative newspapers and liberal voices are rarely heard on conservative talk radio.

This kind of political imbalance also pervades the "objective" and comparatively nonpartisan media, which too often fall into line under the intense, unrelenting pressures from the right. Conservatives are quite proud of their ability to intimidate mainstream media executives, so cowed by the fear of being labeled *liberal* that they bend over backward to placate conservatives. The result is that the most familiar political voices are on the right, and they make so much noise that it sounds as if practically everyone agrees with them. The buzz of conservative cant creates an illusion of consensus.

In a book devoted to debunking myths about liberalism (and conservatism), it seems appropriate to begin with the notion that America, and Americans, are fundamentally conservative.

To stake their claim, conservatives can roll out their favorite colored map, with its vast acreage of "red states." They can turn up the volume on talk radio and cable television, where reactionary opinion consumes almost all the airtime. They can boast about the Republican Party's domination of government. They can even point to all the Democratic politicians, from Mario Cuomo to Bill Clinton to the 2004 presidential aspirants, who avoid the *liberal* label, and snicker at the little band of elected officials who wear it proudly. Finally, and most convincingly, they can cite survey data gathered over the past quarter century that shows, with great consistency, about 18 percent of Americans identifying themselves as "liberal."

Yet the propagandists of the right are still too quick to brand America "conservative." Despite decades of angry denigration of liberalism, the American people continue to uphold the same ideals that have always been identified with the progressive tradition, from Thomas Jefferson and Benjamin Franklin to Martin Luther King Jr. and Robert Kennedy. Americans believe in fairness, equality, opportunity, and compassion; they reject social Darwinism and excessive privilege.

What do liberals stand for? Their adversaries constantly accuse them of elitism, political correctness, immorality, socialism, communism, even treason. These are standard-issue lies from the right-wing propaganda arsenal. Liberalism is an American philosophy that encompasses a broad variety of ideas—yet is probably more coherent than the current brand of conservatism, which ranges from atheist libertarianism to theocratic fundamentalism.

The most basic liberal values are political equality and economic opportunity. Liberals uphold democracy as the only form of government that derives legitimacy from the consent of the governed, and

2

they regard the freedoms enumerated in the Bill of Rights as essential to the expression of popular consent. Their commitment to an expanding democracy is what drives liberal advocacy on behalf of women, minorities, gays, immigrants, and other traditionally disenfranchised groups.

Liberals value the dynamism and creativity of democratic capitalism, but they also believe in strong, active government to protect the interests of society. They understand that markets function best when properly regulated, and they also know that unchecked concentrations of private power encourage environmental pollution, financial fraud, and labor exploitation. Liberals see a broad social interest in ensuring real opportunities and decent standards of living for everyone, while requiring basic responsibility from everyone.

Those who regard such ideals as naïve today should remember that America in the twentieth century was built on liberal policy, from the Progressive Era through the New Deal, the Fair Deal, the GI Bill, and the Great Society. The modern economy—a private enterprise system that relies on government safeguards against depression and extreme poverty—is the legacy of liberal leadership, from Theodore Roosevelt and Woodrow Wilson to Franklin D. Roosevelt and Lyndon B. Johnson. (And more recently Bill Clinton, who erased Republican deficits that were sending the economy into a spiral of recession and began to pay down the national debt.) Liberal policies made America the freest, wealthiest, most successful, and most powerful nation in human history. Conservatism in power always threatens to undo that national progress, and is almost always frustrated by the innate decency and democratic instincts of the American people.

If Americans have a common fault, however, it's our tendency to suffer from historical amnesia. Too many of us have forgotten, or never learned, what kind of country America was under the conservative rule that preceded the century of liberal reform. And too many of us have no idea whose ideas and energy brought about the reforms we now take for granted.

If your workplace is safe; if your children go to school rather than being forced into labor; if you are paid a living wage, including overtime; if you enjoy a forty-hour week and you are allowed to join a union to protect your rights—you can thank liberals. If your food is not poisoned and your water is drinkable—you can thank liberals. If your parents are eligible for Medicare and Social Security, so they can grow old in dignity without bankrupting your family—you can thank liberals. If our rivers are getting cleaner and our air isn't black with pollution; if our wilderness is protected and our countryside is still green—you can thank liberals. If people of all races can share the same public facilities; if everyone has the right to vote; if couples fall in love and marry regardless of race; if we have finally begun to transcend a segregated society—you can thank liberals. Progressive innovations like those and so many others were achieved by long, difficult struggles against entrenched power. What defined conservatism, and conservatives, was their opposition to every one of those advances. The country we know and love today was built by those victories for liberalism—with the support of the American people.

Whether they now describe themselves as liberal or not, most Americans remain strongly progressive in their views about taxation, health care, education spending, Social Security, environmental protection, and corporate regulation. In fact, despite conservative political advances in recent decades, survey evidence gathered by pollsters of all persuasions suggests that Americans are still more liberal than conservative.

The best way to test that assertion is to shear away the current stigma attached to the L-word itself, and examine popular attitudes about specific issues. For more than fifty years, from Harry Truman's surprise presidential victory in 1948 to Bill and Hillary Clinton's failed reform effort in 1994, a signature liberal cause has been to provide every American, regardless of income or social status, with affordable health care. Many liberals support universal coverage funded by the national government, like the systems that protect all citizens in Europe and Canada.

The conservative position is equally clear, if not from their rhetoric then from their actions. They and their corporate allies abhor national health insurance. They spent millions to thwart the ambitious Clinton plan of 1994—and have fought every incremental step toward universal health care, including Medicare and Medicaid. (Those same conservatives now claim to be the protectors of the popular Medicare program while scheming to dismantle it.)

According to nearly every survey taken during the past decade, Americans favor the liberal side of this debate, supporting universal health coverage by very wide margins. The level of support for national health insurance ranges between 60 percent and 85 percent in various major polls. In October 1999, an NBC News/*Wall Street Journal* poll found that 67 percent supported a federal guarantee of health insurance coverage for every American. Between 59 percent and 72 percent backed universal, guaranteed coverage in CNN/*Time* surveys from 1993 to 1995. And a Louis Harris poll in 1994 showed that 86 percent of respondents believed the federal government should provide universal health insurance for all Americans. Smaller but still respectable majorities—from 60 percent in a 1990 *Los Angeles Times* poll to 51 percent in a 1998 Zogby poll—backed a Canadian-style single-payer system when that question was asked.

Liberalism's most enduring domestic achievement is the Social Security system, another popular program that conservatives have always opposed and undermined. Created by Franklin D. Roosevelt, the patron saint of liberalism, Social Security embodies American values of community and fairness. Despite enormous publicity campaigns in recent years by right-wing organizations questioning its solvency and urging its privatization, public support for Social Security as a mandatory system of public pensions remains adamant. Asked whether people should or should not be required to pay into the Social Security system in a March 1999 NBC/*Wall Street Journal* poll, 70 percent answered "should be required." And in a March 2000 ABC News/*Washington Post* poll, 67 percent responded that financing of Social Security should take priority over cutting taxes.

During the midterm elections in 2002, several Republican congressional candidates were forced to abandon the Bush privatization proposal. In fact, the same politicians suddenly pretended that they had never heard of privatization. Asked how they prefer to save the system, a substantial majority of American voters favors raising payroll taxes on the most affluent.

Most Americans echo the liberal concern that the tax system favors the wealthiest few. Responding to a March 1999 Fox News poll that asked registered voters what bothered them the most about the tax system, 21 percent said the large amount they pay, 26 percent said the complexity of the tax system—and 46 percent said they were most troubled by the suspicion that some rich people get away without paying their fair share. People are especially wary of the Bush administration's overwhelming desire to cut taxes for the richest, tiniest minority of its supporters. A Gallup poll in January 2003 found widespread suspicion about the latest Bush scheme to remove all taxation on stock dividends as yet another sop to the rich.

Despite their professed suspicions about overweening government, Americans have consistently told pollsters by margins of two to one that they prefer public spending to tax cuts. That view hadn't changed as of late November 2002, when 69 percent of respondents in a CBS/ *New York Times* survey said they would have preferred devoting the federal budget surplus to Social Security and Medicare. Only 23 percent were happy that the surplus had been squandered on the 2001 Bush tax cut.

Similar figures gathered by every reputable polling organization reiterate the same themes. Americans consistently and indeed overwhelmingly support environmental regulation, consumer protection, spending on infrastructure and education, increasing the minimum wage, extending unemployment benefits, providing food stamps, and nearly every other liberal priority and program. (The sole important exception to this rule has been welfare, but most Americans also believe that generous child-care and health benefits should be provided to help welfare recipients enter the workforce.) Substantial majorities support stricter environmental regulation—precisely the opposite of the antigreen, conservative minority.

The results of recent elections likewise subvert the idea of a conservative majority. No conservative presidential candidate has won a majority of the popular vote since 1988. The most recent presidential election showed a clear popular majority for the center-left and left-of-center candidates: Al Gore and Ralph Nader. The Green Party candidate devoted much of his campaign to attacking Gore and the Democrats—but their views on national issues were much closer than either of them was to George W. Bush, the Republican corporate conservative who was ultimately awarded the presidency by partisan Florida bureaucrats and the Supreme Court.

The combined Democratic and Green vote in November 2000 exceeded 51 percent, a numerical victory made even more impressive by the mammoth financial advantage of the Republicans. The Bush campaign outspent Gore and Nader combined by nearly $60 million. (The other conservative in the race, rightist commentator and former Reagan aide Patrick J. Buchanan, squandered almost $40 million to garner less than 0.5 percent of the vote.)

Rush Limbaugh indirectly acknowledged the significance of the Gore plurality by trying to erase it. Having declared that America "is not a liberal country, is nowhere near a liberal country," the talk jock was asked by a rare dissenting caller why more Americans voted for Gore than for Bush. "You know," Rush replied, "I would bet you that *if we counted* all the absentee ballots in California, I will bet you that George W. Bush won the popular vote." That was only true in the alternate reality of right-wing talk radio.

Now conservatives prefer to forget or dismiss the disputes of 2000; they have declared that the midterm election two years later proved their ideological majority. But when all the votes were counted, the national stalemate in Congress remained nearly the same in 2002 as before—again, despite enormous spending advantages enjoyed by the GOP, a docile press that has promoted Bush's favorable ratings every day since the terrorist attacks of September 2001, and a political strategy that succeeded in associating the President and his party with the national struggle against foreign enemies. Even so, only the terrible loss of Paul Wellstone—who was eight points ahead of his Republican opponent when his plane crashed in northern Minnesota—allowed the Republicans to win a single-vote majority in the Senate.

The continuing schism between progressive public opinion and conservative political domination is an indictment of the way we conduct and finance our elections. Yet liberals still face a vexing question: If so many Americans endorse progressive ideas, why are so few willing to call themselves liberal? Why is the L-word anathema to politicians, including undeniably liberal Democrats? Why are liberals constantly on the defensive? Why do self-identified conservatives outnumber liberals by ten or twenty percentage points in national surveys?

Here is one answer. After decades of relentless disinformation from the right, Americans associate the word *liberal* with a series of negative stereotypes: spendthrift, immoral, unpatriotic, "politically correct," and elitist, among others. Right-wing demagoguery has convinced more than a few people that liberals are essentially no different from Communists or terrorists. Without real Communists around in sufficient number to frighten anyone, the right focused and intensified its attack on liberalism in recent years. The effect of this campaign, bolstered by hundreds of millions of dollars from tax-exempt conservative foundations, has been devastating.

Demonizing liberals is a conscious strategy of the Republican right, where such demagoguery is not only a political style but a career path. It's a vicious technique that dates back to Joe McCarthy and the early Nixon, and it hasn't changed much since then. As a conservative media analyst boasted on Fox TV not long ago, their aim is to make *Democrat* and *liberal* synonymous with *socialist*, *Communist*, and *Marxist*. Republican strategist David Horowitz urges a form of conservative political warfare based on identifying liberal Democrats with left-wing terrorist sympathizers and totalitarians. Ann Coulter is even more simple-minded: "I think it's time to drop the infernal nonsense about liberals being well-intentioned but misguided," she wrote in a

2002 column. "I will say that there is only one thing wrong with liberals: They're no good."

She's entitled to her banal sputtering, of course. She's even entitled to make millions of dollars by polluting the airwaves and bookshelves with mindless diatribes. What is long overdue, however, is a response commensurate with these right-wing attacks. What is needed, more than ever, is an answer to conservative propaganda that holds the right accountable for its lies and hypocrisy.

The right prefers to demonize liberals and set up fights with "politically correct" straw men rather than debate with real progressives. (That is why, for example, the bully boys and girls of the right-wing media almost never confront a labor leader on television; such a debate would instantly destroy the stereotype of the liberal "elitist.") Stereotypes and caricatures are the most important kind of message delivered by the conservative media. By "defining" and discrediting their opponents, they can substitute invective for argument and images for facts. The technique is unscrupulous and almost foolproof. It's the big lie, repeated and repeated until the truth is obliterated and the lie is legitimated.

Whether the right-wingers who create and disseminate this vicious propaganda actually believe it is unimportant, although I suspect that the smarter conservatives know very well when they are lying. What matters is that their lies have spread unchallenged by facts for so many years.

Are liberals unpatriotic, a favorite conservative canard? No. The record of loyalty (and military service) among liberals equals that of conservatives. Do liberals despise the work ethic? No. Liberals defend the interests of working Americans against the fake populism of corporate conservatism. Don't liberals always tax and spend the economy into ruin? No. The numbers prove that liberal Democrats have been the most competent, fiscally trustworthy stewards of the economy for the past seven decades. Aren't liberals determined to restrict freedom in the name of political correctness? No. In fact, liberals have been the most consistent defenders of the Bill of Rights for the past century.

Isn't *liberal* a synonym for *immoral?* No. Liberals do preach less about "family values," but they're just as likely as conservatives to honor those values.

To debunk conservative mythology about liberals is inevitably unflattering to the right. As might be expected, the most vocal liars often turn out to be hypocrites as well. Comparisons that involve patriotism and morality, for example, are incomplete without examining some unpleasant facts about certain prominent individuals. But conservatives have been making ugly accusations about their adversaries for a long time, without hesitation or regret. If they don't enjoy hearing the truth about themselves for a change, I offer no apologies. They've asked for it many times over.

This book confronts the biggest lies deployed by conservatives against liberals, progressives, and Democrats. Its purpose is not to defend every liberal position or politician. (It also isn't intended to disprove every right-wing myth, some of which are so widely disbelieved as to be irrelevant—such as the Bush administration's insistence that its goals include cleaner air and water.) It doesn't suggest a conspiracy against liberals, or argue that Democrats haven't brought any of their problems on themselves. And it shouldn't be taken as a blanket indictment of Republicans or conservatives.

That last point is of special importance to me. The spiteful, malignant discourse that became so common during the Clinton era has done lasting damage to democratic participation and civility in our political system. Although as a matter of literary convenience I frequently refer to *conservatives* and *Republicans,* I certainly don't believe that every conservative or every Republican is responsible for the offenses discussed in these pages.

Unlike Rush Limbaugh or Ann Coulter, I also don't believe that my political adversaries are uniformly "no good," or un-American, or greedy, or bigoted, or stupid. I shouldn't have to say this, but I know from personal experience that generosity, compassion, and wisdom cross all partisan and ideological boundaries. I married into a family that includes Republican conservatives who happen to be among the finest people I have ever known. My wife's grandfather is an unrepentant right-winger who likes to tweak me with editorials from the *New York Post* and Internet jokes about dumb Democrats. He is also a true patriot and a gentleman who has treated me with kindness from the first day we met, despite my obnoxious opinions. I would much prefer an atmosphere that encourages friendship rather than hatred among Americans, regardless of ideology and party.

Unfortunately, I don't think there's much chance of that happy outcome until liberals learn to hit back hard. The classic American hero is the underdog who wins respect by fighting back against a bully. Sometimes the bully just limps away to nurse his wounds. Sometimes the bully wises up and mends his ways. Occasionally, the underdog and the bully become best friends.

But the underdog who dares to fight back is always better off.

1

LIMOUSINE LIBERALS AND CORPORATE-JET CONSERVATIVES

"Tax-cutting Republicans are friends of the common man, while liberals are snobbish elitists who despise the work ethic."

One of the most successful themes of conservative propaganda is the notion that the right, not the left, represents everyday working Americans. Conservatives claim to speak for the silent majority, and depict liberals as silly, affluent elitists who despise the work ethic. Promoting envy and resentment of "limousine liberals" is the right-wing version of class warfare. It's an updated, socially acceptable substitute for the traditional prejudices used by the most unsavory right-wingers to distract people from voting in their own interest.

There is no point in denying that limousine liberals exist or that they can be obnoxious — but any trouble they cause is far outweighed by the depredations of another remote and arrogant elite: corporate-jet conservatives. Recent revelations of that set's incomprehensible greed and callousness make the limo liberals seem like saints. And unlike any clique of left-wing movie stars, they're a real problem.

At the turn of the last century, Theodore Roosevelt denounced such people as "malefactors of great wealth." A hundred years later, there are two very important differences: the rich have indeed gotten far richer — and the President of the United States is not their foe but their front man.

For that job, George W. Bush possesses excellent qualifications of personality and temperament. He's a rich guy who enjoys masquer-ading as a regular guy, and he honestly hates the clever types from New York, Washington, and Los Angeles who consider him dumb and vulgar. Ignorant but certainly not stupid, he's an unusually talented politician. He shmoozes and chats at county fairs and fat-cat feasts with an ease that always eluded his father. Moreover, although most voters realize that he will first take care of the wealthy—the oilmen and the corporate lobbyists—they like him anyway. He seems charm-ing, approachable, caring, and playful. His drawling gaffes sound un-pretentious and real. And he can perform for hours at a time, in front of perfect strangers whose background is entirely different from his own.

Bush is a modern master of pseudopopulist style. What that style blurs is the profound Republican cynicism toward the same people he embraces and cajoles.

The difference between policies and photo opportunities was illus-trated on August 5, 2002, when Bush visited Somerset County, Penn-sylvania. The White House had arranged an inspirational moment with the nine coal miners who had just escaped a nearly fatal catas-trophe. After three suspenseful days, the men had emerged alive from the flooded Quecreek mine shaft. Their courageous grit, their com-mitment to survive together, and the Herculean effort to save them had captured the sympathetic attention of the nation.

So several days after their deliverance, the President showed up to put his arms around the heroes and smile for the cameras. In slightly mangled English, he hailed them and their indefatigable rescuers for "showing our fellow citizens that by serving something greater than yourself is an important part of being an American." The entire epi-sode, he said, "really defines kind of a new spirit that's prevalent in our country, that when one of us suffer, all of us suffers."

It was a wonderfully uplifting story, except for the part that actually involved the Bush administration. The miners' narrow escape from drowning would have been impossible without round-the-clock tech-nical assistance from officials of the Mine Safety and Health Administration. But several months before his visit to Somerset County, the President had proposed slashing the already inadequate budget of that small federal agency.

The humble miners knew nothing of that; they were naturally dazzled by the President's warm praise. Although his administration's indifference to safety enforcement displayed greater compassion for owners than workers, such details weren't permitted to interfere with the happy publicity. It was the summer of corporate scandal, with several Bush friends and contributors in very bad odor. Being seen with ordinary heroes could do the President much good and no harm.

Back in Washington, he had named a coal industry executive to oversee mining safety and health — a man who publicly boasted about trimming away the regulatory improvements devised by Clinton's appointees. There would be fewer inspectors and less rigorous mine inspections, no new rules concerning ventilation and accident investigation. It was particularly telling that the White House would seek a 6 percent reduction in the mine safety budget when coal-mining fatalities had increased from twenty-nine in 2000 to forty-two in 2001. The Quecreek accident that almost killed those nine men might well have been prevented by more rigorous regulation. Without the federal regulators who played a major part in their rescue and whose jobs were threatened by the Bush budget, they would surely have died.

In all likelihood, the President is well insulated from such unpleasant realities of right-wing governance, and always will be. His regular-guy-from-the-heartland shtick obscures a background of extraordinary privilege and a lifetime of business and political favors.

Bush belongs to the real elite. Yet he appears far more comfortable playing the role of commoner than his father, whose taste for pork rinds always seemed out of character. George W. used to say that the big difference between them is that his father went to Greenwich Day School in that tony Connecticut suburb, while he attended San Jacinto High School in dusty Midland, Texas. He didn't mention that after one year, he left public education behind to attend exclusive prep schools in Houston and Massachusetts, leading inexorably to his Yale matriculation as an underachieving "legacy."

George W. is the kind of "regular guy" who burns through millions of other people's dollars in failed businesses, drinks too much until early middle age, dodges an insider-trading scandal, picks up a major-league baseball franchise, and eventually finds himself in the Oval Office as commander in chief of the world's only superpower, thanks to a justice appointed to the Supreme Court by his father.

He likes to talk about helping the average taxpayer. *Average* is the word he used in his 2003 State of the Union message to mislead the public about the effects of his tax cut, saying that "ninety-two million Americans will keep, this year, an average of almost a thousand dollars more of their own money." Doesn't that sound as if Bush is saying each of those 92 million citizens would find a $1,000 check from the Treasury in the mailbox? It does, but the truth is that wealthy taxpayers like Bush himself would get many thousands of dollars, while everyone else would get a few hundred dollars (except for those at the bottom, who would get no tax break at all).

There is, however, a meaningful way to calculate the average effects of the Bush plan: The fortunate 1 percent at the top will receive an average annual tax cut of about $45,000. The less fortunate 20 percent in the middle of the income distribution will have their taxes cut by an average of $265. The least fortunate 60 percent at the bottom will get an average annual tax cut of $95.

It all depends on what the meaning of *average* is.

Vice President Dick Cheney and White House political adviser Karl Rove used similar semantic deceptions to sell the dividend tax cut. "The fact is that fifty-four million Americans own stocks that pay dividends," insisted Cheney, who is certainly among them. He didn't remember to subtract from that number about 19 million people whose stocks are in retirement accounts and therefore already exempt from immediate taxation. Rove went further when he insisted that "45 percent of all of the dividend income goes to people with $50,000 or less incomes, family incomes. Nearly three-quarters of it goes to families with $100,000 or less family income." Unfortunately, those are invented statistics. (If true, Rove's figures would indicate a much more equitable distribution of American wealth than now exists.) About 47 percent of dividend income goes to families making less than $100,000 a year—and those families would receive less than 30 percent of the benefits from Bush's plan.

Incidentally, the tax bill that Bush signed in 2001 provided him with a sweet windfall. An estimate based on his presidential salary and his 1999 tax return shows that he and Laura Bush can expect their total tax bill to be reduced by as much as $267,000 between 2002 and 2006. According to Citizens for Tax Justice, their annual tax reduction will grow annually, reaching $100,000 in 2006. If the cuts are made permanent, as Bush has proposed, their gains could be much greater—and none of those figures includes their potential gain from the abolition of the estate tax or reductions in dividend and corporate income taxes.

Voters who regard George W. Bush as a regular guy may also be deluded enough to accept his transparent arithmetical deceptions about the "average" taxpayer. Most of them live in the reddest of Republican states, whose taxpayers are least likely to benefit from Bush's 2003 tax proposals: states like Mississippi, Louisiana, West Virginia, Arkansas, Alabama, Kentucky, Oklahoma, South Carolina, Montana, Idaho, and Tennessee, where more than a third of the taxpaying families will get nothing at all.

Right-wing populism is an illusion that hides a fundamental fact of American politics: With very few exceptions, conservative Republicans promote the narrow interests of a tiny minority of our wealthiest citizens. Liberal Democrats, again with certain exceptions, defend the broad interests of working and middle-class Americans. Over the past three decades, as economic inequality has intensified, that partisan and ideological divide has become ever more polarized.

While conservatives may demur, the empirical evidence is beyond serious dispute. The stratification of America's political economy in recent decades has been mapped by three distinguished political scientists: Princeton's Nolan McCarty and Howard Rosenthal, and their colleague Keith T. Poole of the University of Houston (who holds a chair endowed in the name of former Enron chairman Kenneth L. Lay). Among the organizations that have published research papers by these three nonpartisan academics is the very conservative American Enterprise Institute. Their studies and others have established that growing class polarization between the two major parties has coincided with increasing income stratification in American society. Using a complex computerized map graphing congressional voting patterns over the past century, the three professors have found precisely the same polarization between the parties on Capitol Hill. With increasing consistency, Democrats support legislation that helps the middle class and the poor, while Republicans protect their affluent constituency.

In other words, that little Monopoly plutocrat in the top hat is back with a vengeance, grasping bags marked with dollar signs. He's still a Republican, he has a lot more money now, and he has probably become a patron of the Heritage Foundation or the American Enterprise Institute—like "Kenny Boy" Lay (Enron Corporation, but you knew that). He is likely to be a Fortune 500 CEO or a Forbes 400 heir as well as a major Bush fund-raiser—like Maurice "Hank" Greenberg (American International Group insurance), Robert Wood "Woody" Johnson IV (Johnson & Johnson heir), or Lee Bass (Bass family oil interests). He may have flown Bush around the country on a corporate jet during the 2000 primaries—like Heinz Prechter (American Sunroof) or Alex Spanos (A. G. Spanos real estate). He would surely take a call from Tom DeLay or Bill Frist when they need to funnel money to a candidate or sponsor negative advertising—like Carl Lindner (American Financial Group, Chiquita Brands) and Sam Wyly (Maverick Capital, Green Mountain Power). His priorities are faithfully reflected by conservative think tanks and Republican politicians, and he is assuredly not one of the little guys.

To deflect attention from this plutocratic elite, the right deploys a barrage of abusive verbiage about the alleged elitism of the left. Somehow those clichés remain perpetually fresh, at least in the minds of those who scream them. There are "limousine liberals" and "Hollywood liberals" and "eastern establishment liberals" and "liberal eggheads" and "liberal academics" and "privileged liberals" and "upper-class liberals" and "Upper West Side liberals" and "Harvard boutique liberals" and "liberal snobs"—as well as "liberal elitists" and, of course, "elitist liberals."

It is an old theme that can be traced back to Joe McCarthy's vituperative assaults on the "striped pants" Democratic diplomats and liberal intellectuals from Yale and Harvard. (People who read and think often arouse suspicion on the far right.) It gathered greater force when Richard Nixon vented his enduring resentment of the Kennedy family, which eventually mutated into an attack on his "elitist" opponent George McGovern, a prairie Democrat who was nothing of the kind. It persists in Rush Limbaugh's daily tirades against Hollywood liberals and the "rich Democrat presidential candidates," a "bunch of vastly wealthy multimillionaires" trying to disguise the fact that they, too, are "elitists."

However deeply Nixon felt his alienation from what he perceived as a hostile eastern liberal establishment (and the Jews he saw lurking there), his complaints were rooted as much in his own social insecurities as in any political philosophy. He was once, after all, a partner in a big Manhattan law firm. His few close friends were all millionaires, and his campaigns were financed by corporate fat cats with suitcases of cash. But Nixon's skillful exploitation of class, cultural, and racial resentments brought him the support of "hard hat" labor and middle-class Americans who felt threatened by radical students and rioting blacks.

Republicans who learned their political tactics from Nixon, such as the Bush family, know that if they had to rely solely on the people whose interests they actually represent, their share of the electorate would be tiny. With coded racial appeals having fallen out of favor, they have turned increasingly to what sounds like class envy. By attacking left-leaning actors and movie directors with lavish lifestyles, New York City newspaper publishers, college professors, and other figures remote from "normal Americans," conservative propaganda encourages resentment against such people and their politics. Such sniping is meant to prove that liberal Democrats are spoiled, insincere, and out of touch with ordinary people.

In *Slander*, Ann Coulter goes further. She insists that Democrats "actually hate working-class people" and that "all conceivable evidence supports the theory that liberalism is a whimsical luxury of the very rich—and the very poor, both of whom have little stake in society." Why the very wealthy would have little stake in the society that enriches and idolizes them is an assertion she leaves unexplained, like so many others in her screed. But she expatiates at length on her view that conservatives are "aggressively anti-elitist," the only true friends of the little folk for whom liberals feel only contempt. She supports this assertion by noting archly that four of the wealthiest U.S. senators happen to be liberal Democrats.

The stereotype that Coulter exploits was discredited in late October 2002—after the most liberal member of the Senate died along with his wife, daughter, and three staff members in a tragic airplane crash. "Most liberal" scarcely does justice to Paul Wellstone's outstanding progressive politics. It was the late senator's commitment to working people, along with his engaging personality and tireless crusading, that earned him the affection of farmers, machinists, meatpackers, nurses, teachers, firefighters, veterans, shopkeepers, and office clerks in his adopted home state. The diminutive former college professor was devoid of snootiness or superiority. Even his most right-wing senatorial adversaries could not help respecting and liking him, as they admitted in the days following his death.

Across the ideological divide, his stricken colleagues and constituents poured forth eulogies for an honest, self-deprecating, empathetic man. Among those closest to him was Senator Pete Domenici, a hard-bitten old conservative from New Mexico who wept openly on television, so choked with grief for Paul and Sheila Wellstone that he couldn't speak.

In the year before his death, Wellstone was preoccupied with preventing Bush's proposed cuts to the Mine Safety and Health Administration. His wife was from Kentucky and he had traveled throughout Appalachia, meeting and learning from miners. The Senate hearings he chaired on coal-mining regulation attracted few reporters and no television cameras. And the colleagues with whom Wellstone worked most closely on that issue happened to be two other Democratic senators named Kennedy and Rockefeller.

Paul Wellstone grew up modestly in a family of Russian Jewish extraction. Politicized by the sixties New Left and the civil rights movement, he was an intellectual and in some respects a radical. He was also a person of integrity and authenticity whose constituents regarded him as a "regular guy." Joining the self-important club known as the U.S. Senate didn't change him much.

According to the affectionate obituary in the Minneapolis *Star Tribune*, his hometown paper, Wellstone remained democratic in character and conduct as well as theory: "He was famous for talking not just to the customers of the cafes he loved to frequent, but for going into the kitchen, talking up the dishwashers and fry cooks, urging them not only to vote for him but also to demand more for themselves. He befriended U.S. Capitol security guards and brought them home to dinner. But he remembered names and family members of Minnesotans at all levels, as people who waited to shake his hand every year at the State Fair found out."

The modest, middle-class Wellstone was certainly an exception in the Senate, where there are too many millionaires on both sides of the aisle. Conservatives delight in pointing at Ted Kennedy and Jay Rockefeller, among others, mocking their populist sympathies as inherently incompatible with personal wealth and family prominence. But that argument is illogical and meaningless, except for what it reveals about the narrow minds of those who make it.

If it is morally right and good for America to lift families out of poverty with a minimum wage increase or an earned income tax credit, why would those policies be less valid when advocated by a millionaire? And why wouldn't a millionaire or a billionaire who loves

America advocate what's best for all the American people? Quite a few enlightened men and women of wealth have sought to help the poor and the middle class. That has often meant abandoning their narrow, immediate material interests. Yet somehow conservatives cannot imagine that a person who has enjoyed abundance, privilege, and education might adopt any worldview other than icy selfishness.

Western history is replete with examples of the well born and well heeled siding with "the people" against the interests of their own class. This illustrious tradition can be traced all the way back to the role of the brothers Tiberius Sempronius Gracchus and Gaius Sempronius Gracchus, both Roman statesmen during the second century B.C. The Gracchi were heirs of a noble family who sacrificed their lives fighting for land reform and public welfare as tribunes of the plebeians. A short list of the Americans who belong in the same category would include some of this nation's greatest leaders: Thomas Jefferson, James Madison, Theodore Roosevelt, Eleanor and Franklin D. Roosevelt, John F. Kennedy and Robert Kennedy. Not every fortunate son is as blinded by privilege as the offspring of the Bush family.

No doubt there are frightful liberal snobs to be found in Manhattan, Malibu, and Cambridge, just as there are appalling conservative snobs lurking in Houston, Greenwich, and Virginia's horse country. Like any other human trait, excessive attitude cuts across political, geographic, economic, and ethnic boundaries. Having grown up in one of Connecticut's most exclusive and conservative suburbs, Ann Coulter could be expected to know that her own beloved WASP Republicans are hardly free of snobbery—and she probably does, despite all her tiresome harping on the "veiled class bigotry" of liberals.

The essential fraudulence of such right-wing populism could be glimpsed in *Cigar Aficionado*'s profile of Rush Limbaugh. Interviewed for the luxury magazine by a fellow epicure, the radio talker felt free to drop any pretense of resembling the middle-class "ditto-heads" who worship him. Although his trademark theme is the polarizing struggle between "us" (conservative, hardworking middle Americans) and "them" (liberal Democrat elitists), the private Rush is actually a ridiculous snob in matters of wine, cigars, hotels, and all the other pleasures of upper-bracket life. Unlike the late Wellstone, Rush Limbaugh wouldn't ever show up for lunch in the kind of cheap restaurant that set up a "Rush Room" where diners could listen to his broadcast.

He informed *Cigar Aficionado* that his favorite Bordeaux is Château Haut Brion '61, although he allowed that he would settle for the '82 vintage. (For those who may not know—perhaps including the typical Limbaugh fan—a bottle of the exceedingly rare 1961 Haut Brion retails for around $2,000. That isn't much to a "regular guy" who earns upward of $20 million a year.)

Name-dropping wine vintages is standard if unsophisticated snob behavior. Still, for a xenophobic rabble-rouser from Missouri, Limbaugh's cultural aspirations are very refined. Much as he professes to dislike big city liberals and perfidious foreigners, he loves living in New York City "for its culture and restaurants." He doesn't vacation at Disney World or Six Flags with his fans, either. When this man of the people takes a few days off, he prefers Paris, San Francisco, or London—and whenever he pops over to London, he stays at the Connaught, one of the oldest, priciest, snootiest joints in town. What he buys in London, Paris, and Saint Maarten are Cuban cigars, regardless of legal embargos and the vileness of Havana's Communist dictatorship. As a cigar snob, he doesn't let principle get in the way of a superior smoke.

Limbaugh shares the tastes and prejudices (as well as the restaurants and hotels) of the same elite that he denounces on the airwaves. But he is no more inconsistent than his friend Coulter. She claims to prefer the wholesome atmosphere of Kansas City, where the "real Americans" live—but not so long ago she moved from Washington to Manhattan, a place she supposedly despises. With satellite communications and the Internet, there is no professional reason why Limbaugh and Coulter can't live anywhere they like. Despite their populist posturing, both prefer Sodom-on-Hudson to the red-state heartland (although Coulter has again moved, to Miami).

The elitist values of the right are expressed in policies as well as personalities. Strip away all the pompous moralizing—along with such loony sideshows as teaching creationism in schools—and the basic program of conservative Republicanism turns out to be quite simple: cut taxes and gut government. This translates easily into attractive slogans. Everyone hates paying taxes. Nobody likes the government telling them what to do.

Concealed beneath the slogans, like the fine print in a credit-card contract, are schemes to milk and bilk the regular guys. The taxes to be cut are those that affect the very wealthiest people in society, even as their share of national income is rising more rapidly than at any time in the nation's history. The regulations to be repealed are those that protect defenseless families from the predators of the marketplace. The minimum wage, for example, has long been a target of Congressional conservatives, who apparently believe that slave labor is what the American economy needs most. Or consider the proposal from the Bush Labor Department to deregulate overtime pay for white-collar workers. Secretary Elaine Chao has devised the most radical changes in the Fair Labor Standards Act since the advent of the 40-hour work week. If enacted, her proposals would exempt employers from paying overtime to hundreds of thousands, possibly millions, of workers earning more than $22,000 a year.

Nothing provokes as much dissembling among conservatives as the topic of taxation. They have misled the public about the intentions and effects of Republican tax policy for more than twenty years, dating back to the first months of the Reagan administration. Advertised as broad tax relief that would lead to reduced deficits and a supply-side miracle of growth and opportunity, the Reagan scheme didn't work out that way. Only years after the disaster had taken shape did Reagan's budget director David Stockman reveal its true causes and hidden purpose.

In a candid interview with the *Atlantic* magazine and later in his own disillusioned memoir, Stockman described Reagan's broad tax cuts as a "Trojan Horse" to reduce the top income tax rate paid by the wealthiest families. Working families saw their tax burden continue to rise, while the rich enjoyed tax breaks on capital gains, personal investments, estates, depreciation, and profits. Under Reagan's plan, a family earning $30,000 a year would suffer a slight increase in taxes, while a family with an annual income of $200,000 would enjoy a tax cut of 10 percent. There were even some special tax breaks for the owners of oil leases.

Stockman admitted that the White House had cooperated with business lobbyists to affix all manner of corporate tax indulgences to the Reagan supply-side tax legislation. "The hogs were really feeding," he recalled pungently. "The greed level, the level of opportunism, just got out of control." (The same herd of swine returned to gorge themselves repeatedly after George W. Bush entered the Oval Office, with consequences that the nation will endure for at least a decade.) Stockman confessed that supply-side economics was nothing but the old "trickle-down theory" dressed up as a revolutionary new idea.

By reversing Reaganomics and raising the top rate on income a couple of percentage points again in 1993, Bill Clinton infuriated the Republicans. (It was still around half the historical postwar peak of 70 percent.) That did nothing to hurt the average taxpayer, but for conservatives it represented an unforgivable offense. Such Clintonian initiatives routinely enraged them, particularly after they won control of Congress and thought they would be devising economic policy. The Republicans wanted to abolish the minimum wage. Clinton increased it twice. The Republicans wanted to abolish or restrict the earned income tax credit, although Ronald Reagan himself had supported this form of assistance to the working poor. Clinton nearly doubled the number of families helped by it. Thanks to his progressive reforms, the taxes of most working families fell during the nineties. With targeted cuts such as the earned income credit, the $500 child credit (a progressive measure supported by most Republicans as "profamily"), and tuition credits for higher education, he slashed the federal tax burden on moderate-income families to the lowest level in more than three decades.

For the rest of his presidency, Clinton had to fight off attempts by

Newt Gingrich and congressional Republicans to repeal the fairest aspects of his economic plan. The financiers behind Gingrich weren't exactly regular guys. They were more typically investors like Pittsburgh billionaire Richard Mellon Scaife, who spent millions in his "Arkansas Project" vendetta against the Clintons, and New York stockbroker Richard Gilder, an owner of the Texas Rangers baseball franchise with George W. Bush.

Despite Gingrich's efforts, the desire of America's wealthiest for lower taxes still awaited fulfillment when Bush entered the White House. The centerpiece of the Bush campaign was a tax-cutting plan that clearly favored the rich—and he had lost the popular vote to Al Gore by half a million votes (and to Gore and Ralph Nader combined by nearly three and a half million votes). That expression of popular will didn't matter, however, when the new President pushed the most regressive tax legislation in almost a century through Congress. Taking account of all its features, Bush's first tax bill provided very little relief for the "regular guy," meaning anyone in the middle 60 percent of the taxpaying population. After the President and congressional Republicans had reserved 43 percent of the cuts for 1 percent of the taxpayers, there just wasn't much left for families making less than $75,000 a year.

And there was nothing in the bill at all for the bottom 20 percent, who owe little or no federal income tax. Those people fall into the category mocked as "lucky duckies" in an extraordinary November 2002 *Wall Street Journal* editorial, which demanded higher taxes on the working people who are least able to pay. It noted disapprovingly that a family subsisting on $12,000 a year—or roughly the minimum wage—pays income taxes of about 4 percent, and suggested that those "lucky duckies" should be paying more, without noting that they already pay much more, proportionately, in regressive payroll and sales taxes than high-income families.

As the nation's most ardent advocates of supply-side economics, the *Wall Street Journal*'s editorial writers must have noticed that public enthusiasm for tax cuts is disappearing. According to them, families that are barely feeding their children should be soaked—if only so that they, too, will rebel against high taxes. Those conservatives respect the work ethic so much that they want to drive the lowest-paid workers even deeper into poverty.

When the Treasury Department mailed out the first tax "rebate" checks during the summer of 2001, almost 40 percent of the nation's least affluent taxpayers got nothing, or a minuscule amount. Others received full rebates, which turned out to be early tax refunds that would soon disappear in the market crash. The real Bush bonanza awaits the rich in later years, when more than half of the scheduled cuts will benefit the top 1 percent. His repeal of the estate tax likewise promises to create a new aristocracy of wealth. Exactly how much George W. and his four siblings will benefit from estate tax repeal we may never know, but the amount is assuredly in the tens if not hundreds of millions.

Not content to reward the nation's wealthiest individuals and families, the Bush administration also sought enormous retroactive tax refunds for large, highly profitable corporations such as General Electric and IBM. Dozens of these corporations were already paying little or nothing in income taxes. The White House "economic stimulus" proposal of 2002 included rebating more than $7 billion to those large companies—with as much as $250 million in the package for Bush's friends at Enron. Bush's Treasury Department spent considerable effort protecting big corporate and individual tax evaders, while failing to revive the national economy.

His first Treasury Secretary, Paul O'Neill, resisted European initiatives to shut down the multinational corporations' foreign tax havens. His minions at the Internal Revenue Service implemented new rules designed to permit corporations to write off billions of additional dollars, without even seeking the approval of Congress. Then O'Neill was fired in the fall of 2002 and replaced as Treasury Secretary by John W. Snow, chief executive of the CSX Corporation, a man who had displayed perfect understanding of the Bush philosophy of taxation. Under his stewardship, CSX avoided paying any corporate income taxes on nearly a billion dollars in pretax profits between 1998 and 2001. Instead of paying its share, the transportation conglomerate collected $164 million in tax "rebates" from the Treasury.

Meanwhile, Charles Rossotti, chief of the Internal Revenue Service, tried to tell Congress in November 2002 that the nation's fattest cats are cheating his agency—and Americans who dutifully pay their taxes—with increasingly sophisticated scams. Rossotti wanted to testify that the IRS needs thousands more enforcement agents because it is "steadily losing the war with tax cheats, especially the wealthiest and most sophisticated among them." He would have pointed out that an investment of $2 billion in law enforcement could net more than $70 billion in lost tax receipts annually. But the White House ordered Rossotti, a candid man who was about to resign after five years of laudable public service, to keep his mouth shut. The Bush administration isn't about to start chasing its tax-evading friends and supporters all over the Bahamas and the Cayman Islands. That is the real American elite—and by this government they are considered untouchable.

All the conservative hype about liberal elitism is a distraction from such embarrassing realities. It's a rhetorical trick, designed to fleece angry suckers as smoothly as three-card monte. While everyone screams at the Hollywood limousines, the corporate jets depart on schedule for those tax havens in the Caribbean.

PEROXIDE PARADOX: THE BLONDE MISLEADING THE BLIND

"Liberals control the media and misuse their influence to promote left-wing policies."

Is any cliché in American public discourse quite as stale as "liberal media bias"? Probably not, unless it's "tax-and-spend liberal." Is there a literate adult living in this country who hasn't heard or read that dull, deceptive phrase literally hundreds or even thousands of times? Not unless said person resides permanently in a wilderness beyond range of all TV, radio, newspaper delivery, and the U.S. Postal Service. Have any of the American media's real problems—increasing corporate concentration, diminishing public service, and the narrowing spectrum of political discussion—attracted a fraction of the attention devoted to this tedious grievance? No.

For decades, nobody with the slightest interest in politics has been able to avoid the right's ranting about "liberal bias." Conservatives complain so habitually and so monotonously about their exclusion that usually nobody notices the relative scarcity of liberal voices. It's more than a bit paradoxical that so many conservatives appear in so many publications and on so many broadcasts—all insisting that their point of view isn't heard in the media.

To sustain this palpably ridiculous argument, the right-wingers deny reality with great vehemence. They protest too much, and then they protest some more. Consider a typical paragraph from *Slander*, a book in which Ann Coulter laments at great length how "the left's media dictatorship" has kept the truth and light of conservatism from a benighted public: "Newspaper editors, TV executives, and publishers could simply refuse to hire or publish conservatives. They could jam liberalism down our throats on every television broadcast, morning show, late-night comedy program, and large-circulation newspaper and magazine in the country."

Coulter's highly visible career illustrated how fatuous and dishonest that complaint was long before *Slander* came out. (Her name calls up more than two thousand references on the Lexis database—a huge number by any reckoning—during the ten preceding years.) Since its publication there has been little chance of avoiding her. The passage above appeared under the imprint of Crown Publishers, a division of Random House, whose release of *Slander* with a substantial marketing budget and nationwide promotion marked Coulter's escape from the right-wing ghetto of Regnery Publishing.

Slander rolled out on the *Today* show, whose anchor Katie Couric is compared in its pages to Hitler's mistress. That triumph of tasteful merchandising was followed by a live shot on ABC's *Good Morning America*, a dozen appearances on the NBC cable affiliates (including eight *Hardball* dates), five on CNN (of which four were on *Crossfire* in prime time), at least six on Fox News, plus reams of reviews, interviews, and profiles in nearly every American publication, supplemented by endless hours of radio chat. (Obviously, Coulter's success also owes much to her charm, sophistication, and personal warmth. Of her gracious host Couric, the author later said, "I think that a lot of people really hate her, and I was just the first one to pop her.")

Where is the evidence that liberals in the media have tried to suppress Coulter's ideas or the primitive emotions that she presents as ideas? Even left-leaning Phil Donahue, who hosted her on his MSNBC show (since canceled), felt obliged to wish her well in the most obsequious terms. "God bless her," he said a few weeks later. "I hope she makes a zillion dollars and the book flies out of the store, which apparently it is."

In fact, the "liberal media" as defined by Coulter provide her with abundant opportunities to promote herself and her writing. But there have been two well-documented schemes to deprive Coulter of an audience. In both cases, the villains who tried to silence her were affiliated with right-wing institutions.

HarperCollins, the publishing subsidiary of Rupert Murdoch's News Corporation, which distributes many titles pleasing to its conservative boss, canceled *Slander* late in 2001. Her editor at Harper-Collins had died, and no amount of hectoring could persuade the company to continue with the Coulter project he left behind. Several months later Crown Publishers bought her book. According to her worldview, of course, both Crown and its parent company, Random House, are "liberal," and they have indeed published a wide variety of writers from Gore Vidal and Norman Mailer to Jesse Jackson and . . . Katie Couric. (They also happen to be owned by the German media conglomerate Bertelsmann.)

Before HarperCollins dumped Coulter, the censorious management of the *National Review* had already seized the opportunity to smother her. America's leading conservative magazine dropped her column from its online edition after she made an infamous recommendation for dealing with Islamist terror: "We should invade their countries, kill their leaders, and convert them to Christianity." Comporting herself after her dismissal with characteristic dignity and intellectual rigor, Coulter responded by taunting *National Review* editors Rich Lowry and Jonah Goldberg as "girly boys." (It's a tough playground at Ronald Reagan Junior High.) In *Slander*, Coulter doesn't mention the *National Review* episode.

What's wrong with this picture? America's most visible right-wing propagandist is fired without warning by William F. Buckley Jr.'s venerable magazine. Her book is killed abruptly by Rupert Murdoch's publishing house but later picked up by a liberal, European-owned Manhattan firm. She embarks on a triumphant promotional tour through the studios and newsrooms of the same "liberal media" establishment excoriated in that book. She continues to lament the squelching of innocent conservatives by scheming liberals.

The mainstream newspapers that sit atop Coulter's fictional leftist "propaganda machine" all treated *Slander* quite gently. The *New York Times* gave it to cultural critic Janet Maslin, who mildly criticized its "insult slinging" and "sarcastic overkill" but was too awed by its thirty-six pages of footnotes to determine whether any of them were accurate. Maslin missed the astounding error about her own paper in *Slander's* last-page peroration, where Coulter indicts the snobbish *Times* for waiting two days to cover the racing accident that killed NASCAR idol Dale Earnhardt. The morning after the accident, in fact, a story on Earnhardt's demise appeared on page one, under the byline of Robert Lipsyte, one of the paper's most distinguished reporters. (With her customary chutzpah, Coulter denied that this was a mistake — but after the Daily Howler Web site and others exposed the Earnhardt error, Crown corrected it in subsequent editions.)

Meanwhile, in the *Los Angeles Times* — repeatedly identified by Coulter as a mainstay of the liberal media monopoly — her book's friendly reviewer was Andrew H. Malcolm, former deputy communications chief for the Bush-Cheney 2000 campaign. Both Malcolm and the paper's editors failed to mention his campaign job, even as he touted *Slander* for exposing alleged press bias against Bush.

While the mainstream press sucked up, perhaps the most cogent analysis of the Coulter phenomenon appeared in a *Commentary* review by the nonconservative magazine's managing editor, Gary Cohen. He didn't even pretend to conceal his scorn. Brushing aside the footnotes that festoon this "piece of agit-prop," he observed that it "pretends to intellectual seriousness where there is none." Cohen dismissed the constant refrain about liberal media bias as jejune exaggeration, and he mocked the author's injured pose: "Coulter is a strange hybrid — part partisan polemicist, part entertainer, all carefully calculated act. And she pulls it off with aplomb, playing the role of the angry, excluded conservative while reaping the rewards of being a blonde-maned, mini-skirted celebrity." Cohen deftly dismisses her manufacturing of sham outrage for personal gain and political advantage.

Coulter is only the latest to work this scam, which employs many people and sells hundreds of thousands of books. An equally meretricious and huge bestseller was Bernard Goldberg's *Bias*, the work of a disgruntled former CBS correspondent. Leaving aside Goldberg's evident grudge against his old colleagues, his claims about liberal slanting on the networks and in newspapers were swiftly exploded by more careful researchers. His central "proof" of bias is that conservatives are more often labeled in the media than liberals — because journalists regard liberalism as normal and conservatism as deviant. Typically, Goldberg offered no research to confirm this observation.

Put to the empirical test by Geoffrey Nunberg, a Stanford professor of linguistics and research scientist, Goldberg's assertions proved to be totally false as far as major newspapers are concerned. Using a database that includes the twenty top American daily newspapers, Nunberg tested the *Bias* hypothesis with the names of ten "well-known politicians, five liberals and five conservatives." To his surprise he found that the average liberal had "a better than 30 percent greater likelihood of being given a political label than the average conservative does." Barney Frank, the gay Democrat from suburban Boston, was called liberal more than twice as frequently as Dick Armey, the fundamentalist Republican from suburban Dallas (who once called Frank "Barney Fag" on the House floor) was labeled conservative.

Goldberg also insists that conservative celebrities, such as Tom Selleck and Bruce Willis, are labeled more often than their liberal counterparts. Again Nunberg found him to be completely wrong. Barbra Streisand and Rob Reiner were identified by their ideology four times more often than Selleck or Willis.

The Stanford professor did some additional research of his own. "In the newspapers I looked at," he wrote in *The American Prospect*, "the word 'media' appears within seven words of 'liberal bias' 469 times and within seven words of 'conservative bias' just 17 times — a twenty-seven-fold discrepancy. Now *there's* a difference that truly deserves to be called staggering. . . . Certainly critics on the left haven't been silent about what they take to be conservative bias in the media, whether in the pages of political reviews or in dozens of recent books. But the press has given their charges virtually no attention, while giving huge play to complaints from the right about liberal bias." Those numbers show that the media are slanted in favor of critics like Goldberg, which helps explain why his book sold so well despite its intellectual vacuity.

Blubbering about liberal control of the media is a trick every professional conservative can perform, like a grifter working an old but reliable con. Among self-respecting rightists, however, this bogus grievance has been an inside joke for many years. Most of them can keep a straight face and avoid snickering when some boob starts griping earnestly about "liberal media bias." (The boob is usually a struggling cable TV host—someone like Jerry Nachman or Mike Barnicle—who hopes to ingratiate himself with the right and lure a few more viewers to watch his show.) Sophisticated conservatives know better, but occasionally one of them blurts out the truth.

Back in 1995, the witty and sometimes candid conservative commentator Bill Kristol confessed that his movement had little reason to complain. "I admit it," Kristol told the *New Yorker*. "The liberal media were never that powerful, and the whole thing was often used as an excuse by conservatives for conservative failures." (Evidently Kristol, who edits the *Weekly Standard*, still hasn't let his coeditor, Fred Barnes, in on the joke. Barnes continues to solemnly flog "liberal bias" in their magazine and on Fox News Channel.) Rush Limbaugh made a similar point after the midterm election, when he gloated over Democratic complaints about right-wing talk radio. "There's been a massive change in media in this country over the last fifteen years," he said. "Now it's 2002 and the traditional liberal media monopoly doesn't exist anymore."

So what is the grousing all about? Complaining constantly about bias serves to intimidate journalists, enforce demands for favorable coverage and privileged access, and ultimately, to maintain the overpowering influence that conservatives now enjoy. As long ago as 1992, partisan conservative Rich Bond, a former chairman of the Republican

National Committee, explained that charges of liberal bias were just maneuvers in a cynical game. "There is some strategy to it [bashing the liberal media]. I'm a coach of kids' basketball and Little League teams. If you watch any great coach, what they try to do is 'work the refs.'" To "work the ref" means to yell and scream about the unfairness of every penalty so the referee will think twice before blowing the whistle. As Bond put it, "Maybe the ref will cut you a little slack on the next one."

Conservatives have learned to "work the ref" so diligently that their exclusion is one of the most widely discussed topics in the media — with them doing most of the talking. Liberal bias is a perennial favorite on the cable circuit, a daily staple of talk radio, and an easy story for newspaper columnists who have nothing else to say. It is a subject that essentially has its own cable outlet, like money or sports or food, in the form of Fox News Channel. Yet the conservatives still demand pity as media outcasts. This paradox raises an obvious question: if liberals actually dominate the media, why do they spend so much time and effort publicizing their ruthless suppression of their adversaries?

Actually, there are two reasons why conservative media criticism inundates any competing noise from the left. Neither has anything to do with the merits of the argument.

The supposedly liberal media are far more sensitive to charges of bias from the right than from the left, as should be obvious from the ubiquitous appearances of Ann Coulter, Bernard Goldberg, and other conservative critics. Liberal and leftist analysts of the mass media write lots of books, too, but their work receives little or no attention from the mainstream media. (While two recent bestsellers by Ralph Nader and Michael Moore criticized the mainstream media, that wasn't the main topic of either book.)

Even more important than the inherent media bias in favor of conservatives is the huge financial advantage lavished on right-wing propaganda over the past twenty years by major funders. The largest and most notable, which work closely together, are the Smith Richardson, John Olin, Sarah Scaife, and Lynde and Harry Bradley foundations.

Coordinating their expenditure of hundreds of millions of dollars, the directors of those four foundations (along with many others) have underwritten a formidable infrastructure of think tanks, magazines, publishing grants, media programming, and academic research, all of which promote conservative ideas. The imbalance has been exacerbated by the reluctance of liberal foundation executives to match the ideological zeal and singular focus of conservative philanthropy. The result is that there are currently three national organizations producing media criticism on the right—and only one performing a similar function on the left.

The original organ of right-wing media criticism is Accuracy in Media, created during the seventies as an instrument of Richard Nixon's vendetta against the press, and overseen ever since by the now elderly and rather weird Reed Irvine. His simplistic attitude toward the mainstream media is summed up on his Web site: "They admit they're anti-business, pro–big government, anti-family and anti-religion." Irvine no longer gets as much attention as in his prime, partly because he has become a merchandiser of eccentric ideas. (He fervently believes that former Independent Counsel Kenneth Starr intentionally covered up the "murder" of Vince Foster, the Clinton White House deputy counsel who committed suicide in July 1993.) Yet AIM has survived and thrived, partly thanks to Richard Mellon Scaife, the equally strange Pittsburgh billionaire who became notorious for his crusade to destroy the Clintons.

For a decade or so, the Media Research Center, chaired by L. Brent Bozell III, has overshadowed AIM. The belligerent, red-bearded Bozell, a nephew of William F. Buckley Jr., scarcely pretends to be anything more than an instrument of the Republican Party's conservative leadership. (His father was the coauthor, with Buckley, of *McCarthy and His Enemies*, a book-length defense of the Wisconsin demagogue, and ghostwriter of the late Barry Goldwater's *Conscience of a Conservative*.) According to Bozell, the only Republican who ever gets undeservedly favorable coverage is John McCain. After more than fifteen years in business, Bozell's operation has grown large, diversified, well connected, and well financed. It bills itelf as "the nation's largest and most sophisticated television and radio monitoring operation, now employing 60 professional staff with a $6 million annual budget."

Smaller and less openly partisan, but still plainly oriented toward corporate conservatism, is the Center for Media and Public Affairs, a Washington think tank that pours out copious streams of data allegedly proving media bias against businesses and other institutions. Its most often quoted product is "The Media Elite," a 1990 study alleging that liberal journalists twist news coverage.

S. Robert Lichter, the center's founder and president, is a former fellow at the conservative American Enterprise Institute. To raise seed money for the center, Lichter relied on direct-mail endorsements from such right-wing idols as Ronald Reagan, Pat Buchanan, and Pat Robertson. Lichter has gradually worked toward broader acknowledgment of his organization's impartiality, by associating himself with nonpartisan academics and institutions. But the probusiness agenda remains easily visible beneath his group's "independent" veneer.

Both AIM and the Media Research Center openly support Republican and conservative campaigns and causes, while Lichter's nominally nonpartisan outfit pursues similar goals with a greater degree of subtlety. All three have received millions of dollars in grants and subsidies over the years from the four major conservative foundations listed above.

Criticizing the media from the opposite perspective is the relatively small, underfunded Fairness and Accuracy in Reporting, whose political orientation is closer to Ralph Nader than to the Democratic Party. The unsophisticated Democrats simply have no organ of media advocacy as partisan and aggressive as Bozell's and Irvine's. In fact, they have none at all.

While FAIR offers carefully documented critiques of both mainstream and conservative media, it is disadvantaged in competition with its right-wing counterparts. A simple statistical calculation that is among the right's favorite techniques for measuring bias easily proves the point, and explodes the right-wing myth about the media.

Both Ann Coulter's *Slander* and Bernard Goldberg's *Bias*—the twin bestsellers brimming with allegations of media prejudice against conservatives—rely heavily on the Lexis-Nexis service. To demonstrate that mainstream media organizations favor liberals and denigrate conservatives, they simply punched such terms as *right-wing* or *left-wing* into the mammoth database. The crude statistics retrieved by Coulter and Goldberg in this fashion can easily be twisted. Leaving that aside for the moment, however, the same method can be used to determine which media critics get more ink and airtime. The technique is simple. Punch in Media Research Center, Accuracy in Media, Center for Media and Public Affairs, and Fairness and Accuracy in Reporting—and then add up the number of hits for the right and the left.

Before examining those numbers, it is worth recalling what Rush Limbaugh had to say about this subject several years ago. Limbaugh knew beyond doubt that his critics at FAIR had an unfair advantage in the media, or so he claimed. "The Media Research Center has been around for years, and every two weeks they put out a newsletter . . . in which they document factual errors and bias of the mainstream press," he began. "Never, ever is this stuff reported. The mainstream press never reports what the Media Research Center is saying. But they will, without checking, report whatever leftist media attack dog groups are saying." The attack dog he meant was FAIR, of course.

The truth is precisely the opposite of what Limbaugh said. Those simple Lexis searches demonstrate that the conservative media critics enjoy an overwhelming supremacy in the major media. During the three years that ended on December 1, 2002, Accuracy in Media notched 370 Lexis hits. The Media Research Center outpaced AIM considerably with an impressive 1,040 hits, while the Center for Media and Public Affairs ranked first with 1,441 hits. That adds up to 2,851 total hits for the right—or five times as many as FAIR scored during the same period.

On its Web site, the Media Research Center boasts, "Many media outlets—radio, television and print—regularly feature MRC guests on their programs, quote MRC spokespeople in their articles, and cite

MRC research in their stories." That's very nice, of course, but then where's the liberal bias?

When conservatives are challenged to prove their case, they invariably cite the Center for Media and Public Affairs studies that purport to show that most journalists voted for Bill Clinton in 1992 and 1996. It was the first resort of conservative columnists who dredged up those same studies once more in December 2002. The short answer is, so what? Even if most reporters voted for the Democrat in those elections, why would that necessarily prove anything about the political bias of their newspapers? As anyone who has worked in an American newsroom knows, decisions about what goes into a newspaper are made not by reporters but by editors.

Every one of those editors serves at the pleasure of the publisher, who reads the paper carefully. And most American newspaper publishers, like most corporate chieftains in every industry, are and always have been Republican and conservative. For some reason, no one complains about the "conservative bias" of newspaper owners. No one insists that any of those conservative publishers surrender their positions to liberals for the sake of "balance."

How ownership actually influences the political stance of the media can be glimpsed every four years, when newspapers endorse presidential candidates. The latest trends show movement to the right, not the left, even among relatively liberal publishers such as the Gannett newspaper chain.

Gannett allows each local paper to determine its own political endorsements. In the 2000 presidential election, forty-one of the chain's dailies backed Al Gore, thirty-seven backed George W. Bush, and twenty made no endorsement. That lineup marked a shift toward the Republicans from 1996, when forty-five Gannett papers endorsed Bill Clinton, twenty-eight chose Bob Dole, and twenty-four made no endorsement.

The negligible Democratic edge in the Gannett group was completely wiped out by the overwhelming Republican preference among all American newspapers. A week before Election Day 2000, the newspaper trade magazine *Editor & Publisher* hired a professional survey firm to poll the nation's newspaper executives—that is, the management that controls what goes into the papers. There was no doubt about the result.

"The nation's newspaper editors and publishers strongly believe the Texas governor will beat Al Gore in Tuesday's election for president," the magazine reported. "By a wide margin, they plan to vote for him themselves. And, to complete this Republican trifecta, newspapers endorsed Bush by about 2-to-1 nationally."

That deserves repetition for emphasis: The nation's newspaper editors and publishers voted for Bush themselves, and their papers overwhelmingly endorsed him. Of all daily newspapers, 48 percent went for Bush, while only 23 percent chose Gore. (The rest picked another candidate or didn't endorse.) Newspapers with circulations of under 50,000 chose Bush by a margin of almost three to one; middling papers with circulations under 100,000 chose Bush by five to three; and papers of over 100,000 circulation picked Bush by five to four. According to the pollster's analysis, the newspapers that backed Bush represented 58 percent of the total national circulation, while those backing Gore only had 42 percent.

Editor & Publisher summed up its poll results with an obvious question. "One has to wonder: whatever happened to the so-called 'liberal press'?" The obvious answer is that the liberal press has never existed. There are some liberal newspapers, although they are dwarfed in number and circulation by conservative newspapers. The trend favors Republicans. Bob Dole won many more endorsements than Bill Clinton did in 1996, but not by a margin as impressive as that Bush achieved in 2000.

As for reporters, their attitudes are more complex than conservatives will admit. The most recent study, conducted in 1998 by David Croteau, a sociology professor at Virginia Commonwealth University working with survey experts, polled hundreds of reporters in the Washington-based national press corps. It found that most reporters identify their own politics as "centrist." Reporters covering the capital tend to be somewhat less diverse than most Americans on economic questions such as health care and taxes, and somewhat more liberal on social issues such as abortion and gay rights.

To anyone who has spent much time with Washington journalists, those results were not exactly shocking. There is no abundance of hard-core liberals or leftists lurking in the capital's newsrooms. Most Washington reporters, contrary to the romantic image of the investigative journalist, travel in herds. Political instincts in the typical newsroom tend to be safely conformist. (This conformity can be observed up close, as in Alexandra Pelosi's Bush campaign film, *Journeys with George,* or from a distance, as in the shifting tides of journalistic preference that swept from Bill Bradley to John McCain to George W. Bush in 2000.) Radicalism, dissent, and unorthodox thinking aren't compatible with a successful career in newspapers or broadcasting. So journalists generally reflect the same spectrum of viewpoints as any other group of college-educated, upper-middle-income, urban and suburban Americans.

If publishers and editors are largely conservative, and reporters are mostly centrist, then what about the pundits who directly influence public opinion and political discussion? Those Republican editors — who are hired and fired by even more conservative publishers — choose the reporters who get columns, and also decide which syndicated columns to publish. The unsurprising result is a much larger pool of conservative writers, who appear in many more newspapers than liberal writers do. For years the most widely syndicated columnists in America have been George Will, the dyspeptic Tory featured on ABC's *This Week,* and Cal Thomas, the religious right pundit and former vice president of Jerry Falwell's Moral Majority.

Conservatives have sprawled across most of the acreage on the nation's op-ed pages for well over a decade. An independent study conducted in 1990 listed seven syndicated columnists whose writing appeared regularly in more than a hundred newspapers with a combined circulation of more than 10 million readers. Four of the seven were conservatives: George Will, James J. Kilpatrick, William Safire of the *New York Times*, and *National Review* founder William F. Buckley Jr. Only one, Ellen Goodman, could be classified as liberal.

Before that study came out, the editor of *Policy Review*, the monthly journal of the Heritage Foundation, had already candidly assessed the opinion landscape. "Journalism today is very different from what it was ten or twenty years ago. Today, op-ed pages are dominated by conservatives," said Adam Meyerson. "We have a tremendous amount of conservative opinion, but this creates a problem for those who are interested in a career in journalism after college. . . . If Bill Buckley were to come out of Yale today, nobody would pay much attention to him. He would not be that unusual . . . because there are probably hundreds of people with those ideas [and] they have already got syndicated columns."

Nothing much has changed, except that the opinion environment is even less diverse. In 1999, syndication statistics compiled by *Editor & Publisher* showed that the four top-ranked columnists were all on the right or extreme right: George Will, Robert Novak, Cal Thomas, and Focus on the Family president James Dobson (who threatened to bolt the Republican Party several years ago because of its left-wing excesses). According to the stats, each of those top four writers appeared in about 500 newspapers. Of the top fourteen columnists, whose work then appeared in 250 dailies or more, nine were conservative, three were liberal, and two were centrist.

How far the media have turned to the right can be judged from the disparate treatment meted out to Democrats and Republicans. Several books have been written about the dogged pursuit of Bill and Hillary Clinton by the "liberal media," from the creation of the White-water "scandal" by the *New York Times* and the *Washington Post* to the symbiotic relationship between network news reporters and Independent Counsel Kenneth Starr, to the dogged sexual inquisitions sponsored by *Newsweek* and the *Los Angeles Times*.

Ralph Reed acknowledged that reality when he was invited to lunch with the *L.A. Times* editors in 1996. "I'm probably less of a media basher than probably some in our community because my sense is that it's probably never as good as you think and it's never as bad as you think," the former Christian Coalition director said amiably. "I think if you look at the way Clinton's been treated, for example, I think you'd be hard-pressed to say that the personal liberal ideological views of most reporters . . . have somehow led to a free ride for Bill Clinton."

For eight years, the nation's largest mainstream news organizations devoted substantial resources to bringing down a Democratic administration. Investigative units at ABC News and NBC News chased scandal stories so zealously that they became virtual adjuncts of the prosecutors and conservative groups attacking the White House. The enmity between the Clintons and the "liberal media" still remains legendary in Washington.

That same enmity infected the coverage of Democratic nominee Al Gore during the 2000 presidential election. False stories designed to ruin Gore's reputation, including phony and distorted quotes, found their way from the Republican National Committee to the conservative media and seeped into the mainstream press. Hostility spanned the ideological spectrum, from the *Washington Times* to the *New York Times*.

For more than three years, influential figures in the press shaped a story line about Gore as an insincere, dissembling caricature of a politician. Facts that didn't support this narrative disappeared from the "liberal media's" stream of consciousness, just as falsehoods that did were maintained in circulation long after they had been exposed.

A couple of examples indicate the pattern. Reporter Roger Parloff proved in the *American Lawyer* magazine in May 2000 that there had been no Democratic "fund-raiser" at the Hsi Lai Buddhist temple in 1996, but his diligent digging left no impression. Pundits and reporters alike continued to refer to the mythical fund-raising event as if it had actually occurred as described in Republican press releases. And Karen Tumulty of *Time* magazine — who first wrote about the Gores and *Love Story* — explained more than once that Al Gore had never tried to claim a greater role as the inspiration for the popular novel and movie than what author Erich Segal had confirmed to her. Tumulty's explanation had no effect on Maureen Dowd or any of the other journalists who never corrected their nasty, demeaning columns about that phony tale. When Gore's early legislative work to promote expansion of the Internet was affirmed by experts from Vinton Cerf to Newt Gingrich, that didn't matter, either. Instead, a phony quote that had the Vice President asserting he had "invented" the Internet persisted in journalistic folklore, courtesy of the Republican National Committee.

No such scornful scrutiny was applied to George W. Bush during the 2000 campaign. His prevarications about his past were glossed over or ignored by the "liberal media" outlets that excoriated Gore. On the very day that Bush announced his presidential candidacy, he told *NBC Nightly News*, "I've never lived in Washington in my life." That remark, intended to portray him as a populist outsider from the heartland, was blatantly false. Bush had lived in northwest Washington for eighteen months as a paid adviser to his father's 1988 presidential campaign. There were other more serious distortions and omissions, concerning his service in the Texas Air National Guard and his concealed arrest for drunk driving.

"While Washington was deadlocked, he passed a patients' bill of rights," Bush's campaign advertising claimed. What had really happened in Texas was that as Governor, he vetoed one such reform bill and backed away from his threat to veto another two years later because the legislature was poised to override him. Under intense pressure from consumers and labor, he did permit some reforms to occur. But his claim of authorship was entirely fraudulent. He could falsify his Texas record, as he did in the debates more than once, in the serene expectation that he would escape accountability. Some newspapers duly noted his "exaggerations," but nobody in the media described them as blots on his personal character.

Bush also lied unashamedly and repeatedly about his economic proposals, notably about how he planned to pay for his scheme to "privatize" Social Security. He claimed that his plans would allow hundreds of billions of dollars in new domestic spending and a trillion-dollar-plus tax cut without increasing the deficit. He promised to give a trillion dollars in Social Security revenues to workers for investment in private accounts, while simultaneously insisting that there would be no benefit cuts or tax increases — which both he and his advisers knew was impossible. In one of several *New York Times* columns demonstrating with simple arithmetic that Bush's numbers were fake, Paul Krugman remarked that "reporters have failed to call Mr. Bush to account on even the most outrageous misstatements, presumably for fear that they might be accused of partisanship."

In real life, the kind of bogus accounting indulged in by the Bush campaign for propaganda purposes can lead to criminal indictments.

In campaign politics, however, it's business as usual — particularly for a Republican presidential candidate covered by a cowering "liberal" press corps. Speaking of creative accounting, Bush's curious business career at shady Harken Energy and allegations of insider trading there were either ignored during the 2000 campaign or noted briefly in long profiles. (That changed two years later during the wave of corporate financial scandal, when those subjects took on new relevance.)

The *Boston Globe* was the only mainstream news outlet that thoroughly investigated Bush's Vietnam era stint in the Texas Air National Guard, although every news organization in the country had exhaustively covered Clinton's draft dodging. During the month between late September and late October 2000, when Gore's solid postconvention lead evaporated, even newspapers that endorsed Gore promoted Bush on their front pages. According to an exhaustive study by the Project for Excellence in Journalism, the nation's most important media outlets favored Bush with twice as many positive stories as Gore during that critical period.

That pattern has continued since the very first days of Bush's controversial arrival in the Oval Office. In stark contrast with their instantaneous hostility to Clinton, the "liberal" Washington press corps gave Bush the longest honeymoon ever. Within a few months, the servility of the media had become so appallingly obvious that the *Washington*

Post editors finally offered an explanation on May 6, 2001. In a long article on the Style section's front page, correspondent John Harris confessed: "Are the national news media soft on Bush? The instinctive response of any reporter is to deny it," he wrote. "But my rebuttals lately have been wobbly. The truth is, this new president has done things with relative impunity that would have been huge uproars if they had occurred under Clinton. Take it from someone who made a living writing about those uproars."

James Warren, then Washington bureau chief of the *Chicago Tribune*, offered a harsher assessment after the annual White House Correspondents Association dinner turned from satirical roast to presidential love fest. "It was the perfect example of all the sucking up to Bush that's been going on every day in this town since he was elected," growled Warren, whose paper endorsed Bush in November 2000. "We have been effectively emasculated. . . . So far, we've made a virtue out of his shortcomings."

Almost two years after the presidential election, with Bush still riding a wave of national support and media promotion following the September 11 attacks, the truth about the mainstream press hostility to his Democratic opponent finally emerged. "I think that Gore is sanctimonious and that's sort of the worst thing you can be in the eyes of the press," admitted *Washington Post* reporter Dana Milbank in August 2002. "And he has been disliked all along and it was because he gives a sense that he's better than us." Florida Republican Joe Scarborough, a hard-line conservative who now has his own MSNBC show, was stunned by the treatment of the Democratic candidate. "I think, in the 2000 election, [the media] were fairly brutal to Al Gore," Scarborough told *Hardball* host Chris Matthews in November 2002. Former Bush White House aide James Pinkerton made the same point on Fox News. "Look," he said, "the problem with Gore is, nobody [in the press] really likes him." Of course, reporters aren't supposed to "like" any candidates; they're supposed to provide fair coverage of all candidates.

In August 2002 the authoritative, scrupulously nonpartisan daily column on the ABC News Web site known as The Note decried the constant media abuse of Gore, after a particularly mean story about his wife, Tipper, proved to be entirely false. Among the "facts of life in '02 Washington," its editors noted, is that "Al Gore is regularly treated unfairly by the press corps at large. . . . Al Gore might have, like most humans, some flaws, but hasn't this unfair coverage gone on long enough?"

As Gore observed before he announced that he would not run for president again, the negative coverage of Democrats and liberals by the national press corps is heavily influenced by relentless pressure from conservative media. Yet when right-wingers complain about the media, they persist in pretending that the huge and ever louder conservative megaphone doesn't exist. Coulter scarcely mentions the right-wing media, and Goldberg ignores it as well. That isn't easy, considering the enormous propaganda resources at the right's command.

With a few exceptions—such as National Public Radio's politically balanced programming—the tenor of the nation's talk radio programming ranges from right to extreme right. Atop the tower of babble sits Rush Limbaugh with an audience of 15 to 20 million a week. At Limbaugh's heels is Sean Hannity, with more than 10 million. Then there's Dr. Laura Schlessinger, the Old Testament moralist—but even she is comparatively moderate in a field that includes Michael Savage, who thinks homosexuality is a plot to destroy "the white race," and G. Gordon Liddy, who once instructed his listeners on the proper way to shoot a federal agent. (It is amazing that the "family-oriented" and multicultural Disney Company promotes the kind of race hatred broadcast by the aptly named Savage.)

Among the top ten radio hosts are several apolitical talkers but not a single liberal. Talk radio jocks are such reliable Republican parrots that the White House communications office invited more than fifty of them from around the country to broadcast directly from the White House lawn on October 30, 2002, a week before Election Day. Eminent members of the Bush administration—from Defense Secretary Donald Rumsfeld and Homeland Security chief Tom Ridge to presi-

dential counsel Karl Rove and vice presidential adviser Mary Matalin—were wheeled out for soft interviews with the eager jocks.

Conservatives enjoy several other vast stretches of uncontested ter-
rain in the national media, including the *Washington Times*, the capital daily subsidized by the Reverend Sun Myung Moon's Unification
Church; the *Wall Street Journal* editorial page, one of the most widely
circulated opinion sources in the country; the *New York Post*, a tabloid
that also gets considerable national circulation; United Press International, the wire service that is now also owned by the Moon conglomerate; Richard Mellon Scaife's Pittsburgh *Tribune-Review*; Pat
Robertson's Christian Broadcasting Network, along with several smaller
religious right cable outlets; the *Weekly Standard*, *National Review*,
and finally the tarnished jewel in the Republican crown, Rupert Murdoch's Fox News Channel.

Run by former GOP media consultant Roger Ailes, Fox insists that
its coverage is neutral even as it shamelessly shills for Republican candidates and causes. The conservative writer Andrew Sullivan loves the
channel but disdains the pretense: "Fox News is obviously biased toward the right. It's simply loopy to pretend otherwise. Ailes' attempt to
deny the bleeding obvious is just pathetic . . . It's embarrassing, and
undermines their credibility on everything else."

Credibility isn't what the Ailes acolytes are seeking. Fox anchor Brit
Hume, a former contributor to the *American Spectator* magazine, is
so comfortable with his network's notorious bias that he joked about
it with Don Imus shortly after the Republican victory in the November
2002 midterm elections. "It was because of our coverage that it all
happened," Hume wisecracked. "We've become so influential now
that people watch us and they take their electoral cues from us. No
one should doubt the influence of Fox News in these matters."

The influence of conservative media and pressure groups has affected other broadcasters as well. For instance, the programming
lineup on NBC, CNBC, and MSNBC is slanted powerfully to the
right. Former Nixon White House aide John McLaughlin has had not
one but two time slots on the network for many years. The *Wall Street*

Journal editorial board had its own weekly program on CNBC, hosted by Stuart Varney, until "editorial differences" led to its cancellation. Far-right ideologue Alan Keyes and conservative pundit Laura Ingraham were awarded their own programs, both of which also flopped. Other right-wing personalities featured on the NBC channels have included Oliver North, Bay Buchanan, Pat Buchanan, Robert Novak, Lawrence Kudlow, Jerry Nachman, and the majority of McLaughlin's regular guests on *The McLaughlin Group*. (The only liberal ever to host his own program on NBC cable without a conservative for "balance" was Phil Donahue.)

Then there's Don Imus, the radio personality whose show is featured on MSNBC in the morning. The obnoxious "I-man" is in a class by himself. His penchant for racist invective has led him to refer to a black female journalist as "a cleaning lady," and to another black writer as a "quota hire." He has mentioned that he picked one of his producers to write "nigger jokes." While Imus has tended to favor Republicans and mock Democrats, he may or may not be a conservative — but he certainly isn't an example of "liberal bias."

In October 2002, the chief executive of the General Electric Company, which owns NBC, made a remarkable statement on Fox News Channel. He suggested that MSNBC producers were scrambling to imitate Roger Ailes. "I think the standard right now is Fox, and I want to be as interesting and as edgy as you guys are," said Jeffrey Immelt in an interview with Fox host Neil Cavuto. (The GE chief's famed predecessor Jack Welch was a strong Republican partisan, mentioned in 2000 as a possible running mate for George W. Bush and widely suspected of pressing for favorable treatment of the Republicans on Election Night 2000.)

On ABC News, executives seek some balance between moderate liberals and conservatives. But ABC also hired executive news producer Dorrance Smith straight from the communications office of the first Bush White House. (In 2000, having departed ABC, Smith turned up in Florida, working for the Bush-Cheney campaign.) ABC features John Stossel, the only network correspondent permitted to produce hour-long specials with a blatant political bias. A rigidly ideological conservative, Stossel has been caught more than once airing serious distortions. There is no liberal correspondent on any network who is permitted to promote his own bias in a similar manner.

The surest sign of the mass media's partisan shift toward the right is the changing attitude of conservative groups toward the Fairness Doctrine. That discarded federal regulation, once a favorite of Accuracy in Media and other right-wing organizations, used to force broadcasters to balance the political viewpoints they aired. In practice, conservatives used the rule to combat what they regarded as "liberal bias." Today, however, radio stations that feature Rush Limbaugh or Sean Hannity on airwaves licensed by the public would have to give equal time to liberal and moderate programming. Unimaginable, isn't it? That's why the same groups that used to support the Fairness Doctrine now oppose it as an infringement on the First Amendment. They're not so worried about fairness anymore.

The conservative media are highly partisan and strongly Republican, unlike the more diverse mainstream outlets they pillory as "liberal." The networks, from CBS to PBS, carefully alternate liberal and conservative, Democrat and Republican. So do the mainstream newspapers and magazines, which feature right-wing columnists in their pages. But the conservative press would never publish a liberal equivalent to George Will, William Safire, William F. Buckley, Jr., James Glassman, John Tierney, Michael Barone, Charles Krauthammer, Robert Samuelson, or any of the right-wing writers whose opinions are highlighted regularly in the "liberal" press.

The funniest aspect of this ongoing argument is the wanton abandonment of market principles by conservatives who find them too inconvenient to apply here. Ann Coulter points to the rise of Rush Limbaugh and Fox News—and the sales of conservative books—as proof that Americans are fed up with liberal bias in the news media. She and other conservatives seem to believe that mainstream news outlets have an obligation, despite the First Amendment, to promote the right. But the audience for prime-time news on CBS, NBC, and

ABC still dwarfs Fox's by an order of magnitude. If viewers are furious about liberal bias, they can easily change the channel from liberal Dan Rather to conservative Brit Hume. Very few of them do.

Despite their blather about the market, few of the conservative outlets are profitable. The *Washington Times*, the *New York Post*, the *Weekly Standard*, and the *National Review* would all be defunct if they had to depend on circulation revenue and advertising sales. Their mainstream competitors thrive as profitable businesses, with billions in stock capitalization. Conservatives simply cannot accept the verdict of the media market. They demand ideological welfare handouts from the mainstream, and too often get them.

What conservatives really hate most is a fair fight, which brings out their inner wimp. In the spring of 2001, when CNN revamped the tired format of *Crossfire* and introduced fiery liberal Democrats James Carville and Paul Begala to the lineup, Republican leaders started muttering about a boycott. An informal directive to avoid *Crossfire* leaked out from the office of the Senate Republican leadership, perhaps in an effort to intimidate the aggressive new hosts or the CNN management.

Conservatives aren't really worried about liberal bias, because they know that it doesn't exist. They just prefer a fixed fight.

3

MALE CHEERLEADERS AND CHICKEN HAWKS

"Conservatives truly love America and support the armed forces, while liberals are unpatriotic draft dodgers."

Of all the pernicious claptrap emitted by right-wing propagandists, none is more offensive than smearing liberals and Democrats as unpatriotic. The portrayal of a liberal elite that despises its own country has allowed conservatives to appropriate the flag, the national anthem, and other national symbols — the heritage of every American — as their movement's private property, and to misuse those symbols for narrow partisan purposes. To the extremists, anyone who doesn't pledge allegiance to the Republican platform is a "traitor."

Rank-and-file reactionaries out in the red-state hinterland may believe this tripe, but the Republican insiders know better. Living in major cities like New York and Washington, they can't avoid knowing liberals who have proudly served in the military, revere the Constitution and the flag, and share the values of liberty and democracy — who are, indeed, just as patriotic as any conservative. That knowledge only makes their promotion of this slanderous myth more shameful.

Like so much rightist cant, "liberals hate America" is a slogan designed to confuse and inflame the ignorant. And like many another successful frame-up, this one grossly exaggerates a small fact. On the far left there does exist a handful of annoying academics and activists — typified by Noam Chomsky and Ramsey Clark — whose ideas about America and the world haven't changed much since the seventies. Their politics hark back to a period when the criminal excesses of the Cold War in Indochina, Latin America, and southern Africa had alienated many young Americans from our country. The overwhelming majority of those young people never contemplated any kind of unpatriotic act, and those who remained active in politics took up the challenge of democratic reform.

As for the remnant of ultraleftists, whether they love America or not is for them to say. What they surely detest—as they would be the first to affirm—is American liberalism. That's what conservatives always forget (or pretend to forget) when quoting left-wing literature to prove that liberals hate and blame America.

Distinguishing fringe factions from the progressive majority is essential to wiping away the "anti-American" smear against liberals. It is a task complicated by the fact that, as a matter of constitutional principle, liberals consistently uphold the civil liberties of radicals at both ends of the spectrum. It's simple for conservatives to look patriotic by threatening dissenters or amending the Constitution to ban obnoxious behavior like flag-burning. But what could be more fundamentally American and patriotic than the liberal commitment to defend *all* of the freedoms symbolized by the Stars and Stripes?

The relentless disparagement of liberal patriotism by right-wing ideologues is an attempt to punish that commitment to free speech, and an abandonment of traditional American values of fair play and civic decency. There is nothing truly conservative about the conservatives' compulsion to divide the nation for their own political gain. There is nothing patriotic about perverting the natural love of country into suspicion, bitterness, and hostility. (Strangely, many of the conservatives who seek to inflame hatred against their liberal neighbors would describe themselves as devout Christians—but then some of our most jingoistic warmongers also claim to be true disciples of the Prince of Peace.)

In an earlier era there were Republican statesmen, such as the senators who initiated the censure of Joseph McCarthy, who considered such smear tactics contemptible. To those outraged colleagues, McCarthy's strategy betrayed real patriotism by falsely impugning the loyalty of innocent Americans for momentary personal advantage. The senators who finally stood up against their fellow Republican did so because they realized that his unfounded accusations of disloyalty were eroding national unity, constitutional authority, and intellectual freedom—and assisting America's real enemies.

Many Americans of all persuasions still recognize that challenging an opponent's patriotism is low and thuggish, but others unfortunately don't. It presents an easy way to win an argument, or an election. That's why some of the most aggressive right-wingers can't resist the temptation to identify liberals, progressives, and Democrats with "the enemy," whoever that may happen to be at the moment. Everyone who reads, watches television, or listens to the radio has been exposed repeatedly to such venal accusations. So pervasive is the mythologizing about "anti-American" and "treasonous" liberals that to cite specific examples almost seems redundant.

During the months preceding the war in Iraq, conservatives used the same sleazy tactics to disparage liberals, progressives, and Democrats. Liberals who preferred inspections to invasion were denounced as unpatriotic. Democrats (and Republicans) who saw through the administration's disinformation and fumbling diplomacy were called appeasers. And the usual Republican suspects sought to paint all critics with the same smear brush, as if patriotism demanded mindless obedience to whatever spin might emanate from the Pentagon.

In their zeal to take partisan advantage of the war, Republican propagandists ignored the real complexities of the national debate over Iraq. The argument ranged across a spectrum that included left-leaning "hawks" such as House Minority Leader Gephardt, *New Yorker* editor David Remnick, and Paul Berman, author of *Terror and Liberalism*; and such prominent right-wing "doves" as Patrick Buchanan, Texas Republican Representative Ron Paul, and Doug Bandow of the Cato Institute. Everyone who questioned the war didn't share Chomsky's hostility to American power, and everyone who supported the war didn't agree with Bush's unilateralism. The truth about Iraq was complicated. So was the political lineup on either side of the war debate. But for the purpose of defaming Democrats and liberals, the right-wing bullies must keep their ideological categories simple.

Since September 11, 2001, rhetorical bullying by the self-appointed sentinels has become shrill and continuous: Ann Coulter snarls that liberals must be threatened with execution to deter them from becoming "outright traitors." Andrew Sullivan warns against the "decadent enclaves" of East and West Coast liberals "mounting a fifth column"— a term that means a group of secret sympathizers with the enemy— in the war on terrorism. (He later blames "liberal culture" for the disloyalty of the young Californian who joined the Taliban.) The *New York Post* columnist Steve Dunleavy denounces "liberals, whom I regard as traitors," for daring to quote the Constitution in defense of civil liberties.

The modern mini-McCarthys are always eager to form a mob, to trample anyone who resists their immediate partisan objectives. When Vermont's Jim Jeffords went independent and Democrats regained control of the Senate in early 2001, the right found a new target to replace Bill Clinton, their perennial favorite. The conservative hit squad went after Tom Daschle.

At first they denounced the soft-spoken South Dakotan as an "obstructionist" with no agenda except to thwart President Bush. This was a ridiculous overstatement, but not a slur. By the end of the year, however, the campaign against Daschle turned hard and dirty. Newspapers all over his home state suddenly published full-page advertisements with photos of Daschle and Saddam Hussein and a headline shrieking "What do these two men have in common?" The ads were sponsored by American Renewal, a group affiliated with religious right broadcaster James Dobson that works closely with White House political director Karl Rove. Their ostensible reason for aligning Daschle with Saddam was the Democrat's opposition to oil-drilling in the Alaskan wildlife reserve (an opinion long shared by most Americans).

What disturbed many observers was that those Daschle-bashing ads appeared at a time when nearly every Democratic elected official in the country had affirmatively answered the President's call for bipartisan unity against terrorism. But the blitz mounted by the Dobson outfit in South Dakota was actually part of a carefully coordinated partisan scheme to make Tom Daschle into a negative symbol. "It's time for Congressional Republicans to personalize the individual that [sic] is standing directly in the way of economic security, and even national security," advised a "talking points" memorandum issued to Senate Republicans by political consultant Frank Luntz. "Remember what the Democrats did to Gingrich? We need to do exactly the same thing to Daschle."

Within weeks after Congress returned from the holiday recess, Republican leaders resumed their mugging of Daschle, feigning terrible offense at mild remarks he had made about the progress of the war against al-Qaeda and the imperative of capturing Osama bin Laden and the Taliban mullahs. Representative Tom Davis of Virginia, chairman of the GOP's congressional campaign committee, ranted that Daschle's "divisive comments have the effect of giving aid and comfort to our enemies by allowing them to exploit divisions in our country." Tom DeLay called Daschle's comments "disgusting."

The Democratic leader shrugged off DeLay and Davis with a thin smile. He wouldn't be provoked, even when Trent Lott refused to repudiate the insinuation of treason against him on national television, and instead seemed to endorse it. "How dare Senator Daschle criticize President Bush while we are fighting our war on terrorism?" cried the Republican leader.

Daschle should have pounced on that invitation to compare their respective patriotic credentials, which would hardly have been flattering to Lott—and would have exploded a widespread delusion about liberals and conservatives. The flag-flapping, ultranationalist Republican had not only avoided the draft with student deferments, he had spent the early years of the Vietnam conflict waving pompoms as a cheerleader at Ole Miss. The thoughtful but determined Daschle, who rarely spoke about his own military service, had served three years in the Air Force after college as an intelligence officer in the Strategic Air Command.

It was John Kerry, not Daschle, who addressed the Republican leaders in the manner they deserved. At a Democratic dinner in New Hampshire, the senator from Massachusetts stood up and said, "Let me be clear tonight to Senator Lott and to Tom DeLay. One of the lessons that I learned in Vietnam—a war they did not have to endure—and one of the basic vows of commitment that I made to myself, was that if I ever reached a position of responsibility, I would never stop asking questions that make a democracy strong. . . . Those who try to stifle the vibrancy of our democracy and shield policies from scrutiny behind a false cloak of patriotism miss the real value of what our troops defend and how we best defend our troops."

Kerry received a standing ovation from the New Hampshire Democrats. Thus encouraged, he repeated his roasting of the Republican leaders at a press conference the following day. As a Vietnam combat veteran who earned three Purple Hearts, a Bronze Star, and a Silver Star in two Navy tours—and who later founded Vietnam Veterans Against the War—Kerry had ample stature to challenge the character assassins.

What the Daschle episode revealed was how routinely Republicans and conservatives resort to the kind of hyperbole that was once heard only from extremists and bigots. The Kerry speech electrified his audience because, like so many liberals, they were tired of listening to conservatives blast away at their patriotism unanswered. At long last, someone had fired back.

Manipulating patriotic fervor to taint liberals is a tactic that right-wingers have resorted to repeatedly in our nation's history. Joe McCarthy indicted both FDR and Truman for "twenty years of treason." The deranged, alcoholic demagogue finally imploded in 1954 during his destructive vendetta against the U.S. Army. He was just becoming a major national figure in 1950, however, when he showed up in San Diego to endorse Representative Richard Nixon for the Senate, and announce a showdown "between the American people and the administration Commiecrat Party of betrayal." During that campaign, Nixon earned his lifelong nickname of "Tricky Dick" for sliming the liberal Democrat and staunch anti-Communist Helen Gahagan Douglas as "the Pink Lady."

Almost forty years later, when the Cold War was ending, those same themes reappeared in a slightly different form. In 1988 George Herbert Walker Bush updated the ugly contrivances of his mentor Nixon to win the presidency. Whispering into Bush's ear during that campaign was Lee Atwater, a dirty trickster whose instincts would have pleased the worst of Nixon's henchmen. In an echo of McCarthy's favorite trope, Bush repeatedly berated Michael Dukakis as a "card-carrying member" of the American Civil Liberties Union. (Years later, after the ACLU joined Republicans and conservatives in a lawsuit against the McCain-Feingold campaign finance reform bill, the venerable defender of the Bill of Rights no longer appeared quite so subversive.) To Bush, the American flag served as a stage prop, to be used for the ritualized flogging of the Democratic nominee.

More than ten years earlier, as Governor of Massachusetts, Dukakis had vetoed a bill requiring students to recite the Pledge of Allegiance. He did so because the state's highest court and the Attorney General had both advised him that the statute was unconstitutional. Such mundane facts didn't faze Bush, who turned the Dukakis veto into the inflammatory centerpiece of his stump speech and recited the pledge everywhere he went. Predictably, Bush's most rabid supporters veered into overkill — as when Utah's Senator Steven Symms concocted a slanderous story that the Democratic nominee's wife had once burned the American flag at an antiwar demonstration.

By vilifying Dukakis for his alleged lack of patriotism, Bush also articulated his party's malignant view of the opposition. Nearly every speech scourged the Democrat with what Bush called "the L-word." His snide invective conveyed an unsubtle message about the supporters of "the liberal Governor": Liberals won't say the pledge. Liberals won't salute the flag. Liberals don't love America.

Despite Atwater's premature death from brain cancer in 1990, his destructive spirit animated Bush's reelection campaign. During the final weeks of that race, the President and his surrogates went after Bill Clinton as a "draft dodger." They defined Clinton's Vietnam dissent and his reluctance to serve as a test of character that demonstrated his unfitness for the presidency. It was fine to be a fortunate son like George W. Bush or Dan Quayle, to whom an "honorable" method of evading Vietnam's perils was awarded like a graduation gift. It was unacceptable, however, to be a self-made young man from a lower-middle-class family like Clinton, who didn't want to fight in a war he believed was terribly wrong.

"I have a different concept of public service and service to the country," the elder Bush, a decorated World War II veteran, told Rush Limbaugh in September 1992 as they discussed Clinton and Vietnam. The talk jock's own somewhat undignified means of avoiding the draft—a medical deferment for a persistent inflammation on his backside—went unmentioned during that inspirational chat. So did the fact that none of George Bush's four sons served in the war that their father had vocally supported.

Deep in the archives of the State Department, Bush political appointees rummaged through Clinton's old passport files, searching for incriminating details of his travels abroad while studying at Oxford. During one of their debates, the President demanded that the young Democratic nominee tell what he had done during a 1969 student trip to Moscow. "It is absolutely germane to the voting public to know precisely why Bill Clinton traveled to the heart of enemy territory at the height of the war," insisted campaign spokeswoman Mary Matalin, an acerbic Atwater protégée. Republican operatives whispered a false rumor that Clinton had renounced his American citizenship while overseas.

Nothing came of all this smearing, except an independent counsel investigation of possible criminal violations by an Assistant Secretary of State, who was forced to resign over the passport scandal—and a lingering defamation of the man who was elected the forty-second President of the United States.

The ugly methods adopted by Bush in two consecutive national elections probably would have disgusted his own father. Prescott Bush Sr. was a moderately conservative Republican from Connecticut who had courageously urged the censure of McCarthy on the Senate floor. (George H. W. Bush discreetly omitted that defining moment in his father's career from his 1988 campaign autobiography.) The late historian Stephen Ambrose, hardly a doctrinaire liberal, once told a reporter that "what Bush did [to Clinton in 1992] does smack of McCarthyism."

Unlike the hapless Dukakis, however, Clinton struck back forcefully. Using satellite technology, congressional Democrats turned Bush's smears back on him, flashing videotaped condemnations of his tactics into every electoral battleground. Clinton's victory drove the Republicans into a sustained fury that had not abated even two years after his return to private life. The institutional embodiment of that rage was Newt Gingrich, who spent most of his brief tenure as House Speaker directing his minions to harass the Clinton administration. The vehicle that brought Gingrich to power was the campaign committee known as GOPAC, where he developed the tactics and themes that would lead to the Republican takeover of Congress in 1994.

Gingrich, a former teacher in a small Georgia college, created a campaign syllabus that surpassed the worst of Atwater. His GOPAC handbook for candidates was titled "Language, a Key Mechanism of Control" and included a "directory of words to use in writing literature and mail, in preparing speeches, and in producing electronic medium." Anyone reading that strange document might observe, among other things, that Gingrich, a self-proclaimed enemy of elitism, perceived his eager pupils as inarticulate hicks, more capable of memorizing than thinking.

The lexicon recommended by Gingrich to describe Democrats emphasized such terms as *sick, corrupt, anti-flag, liberal* — and *traitors*. That last slur was officially withdrawn by GOPAC when bad publicity about it embarrassed Gingrich, who realized that he had violated what was then still a powerful taboo. Somehow it had never occurred to

Gingrich—an Army brat who avoided the Vietnam draft with a student deferment—that he should refrain from tarring Democratic veterans as traitors. Gingrich associates such as Trent Lott and Tom DeLay never rose above their impulse to scream "treason" at their adversaries.

The image of disloyal liberals also harked back to the national trauma of Vietnam, when a fragment of the broad antiwar movement drew media attention by burning the American flag, carrying the banner of the National Liberation Front, and indulging in random violence. Profoundly infuriating to most Americans, the revolting conduct of a few privileged students was seized upon by the Nixon administration to discredit the completely loyal dissent of mainstream Democrats, Republicans, and independents from places like South Dakota, Oregon, Idaho, Texas, and New Jersey as well as liberal New York, Massachusetts, and California.

In the Nixon White House, a young conservative named Patrick Buchanan penned many of the harshest attacks on the antiwar liberals. Buchanan's aggressive patriotism didn't extend to wearing his country's uniform, however. He had slipped past the District of Columbia draft board with a "bad knee." But he didn't hesitate to question the loyalty of prominent liberals who had worn that uniform with valor—including heroic veterans and leaders of the liberal opposition to the war such as George McGovern, a bomber pilot who won the Distinguished Service Cross for flying many dangerous missions over Germany, and John Kerry, a decorated Navy captain wounded in Vietnam.

Among prominent conservatives of the Vietnam generation, the kind of hypocritical posturing symbolized by Buchanan and Limbaugh is so widespread that they have acquired a derogatory nickname: "chicken hawks." Right-wing draft evasion first emerged as an embarrassing issue in 1988, when reporters delved into the personal history of the handsome young senator nominated for vice president at the GOP convention. Thanks to the influence of his father, Indiana's most powerful newspaper publisher and an ardent editorial proponent of the war, Dan Quayle had spent the Vietnam years improving his excellent golf swing, while holding down a desk job at Indiana National

Guard headquarters. (Among Quayle's contemporaries in the Senate, incidentally, those who had served in active duty during the Vietnam War included two Republicans—and five Democrats.) The story of Quayle's privileged berth in the National Guard dominated news coverage of his nomination at the New Orleans convention and provoked much commentary in the weeks that followed.

Twelve years later, little attention was paid to the strikingly similar story of George W. Bush's service in the Texas Air National Guard, a sojourn that had likewise protected him from the Vietnam draft. About to graduate from Yale and lose his student deferment in 1968, he obviously felt no overwhelming urge to fight in the bloody jungle conflict that his father—then a Republican congressman—would someday blast Bill Clinton for avoiding.

Ushered into the Texas Air National Guard ahead of hundreds of other young men on the waiting list for a few coveted places, George W. Bush later insisted that he had never received any "special favoritism." Perhaps he only benefited from the ordinary favoritism that the Texas elite enjoyed during the Vietnam War, when the Air National Guard became one of the primary means of escaping the draft. His father was a mere congressman at the time, but that was good enough to get Dubya in despite his low score on the pilot aptitude test. Pushed to the top of the waiting list, he was also awarded a highly unusual promotion to second lieutenant on completing his basic training, despite his lack of qualifications.

Exactly how all this happened remains a matter of dispute. In a civil lawsuit, former Texas Lieutenant Governor Ben Barnes testified that he received a call from Sid Adger, a socially prominent Houston oilman and friend of the elder Bush. According to Barnes, Adger wanted to ensure that the unit at Ellington Air Force Base would take care of young Bush. (Adger had already obtained Guard slots for two of his own sons.) Barnes also testified that one of his aides forwarded the request to a Guard general. During the 2000 campaign, both Bush and his father denied using any such influence on his behalf. Pleading a bad memory, the elder Bush told reporters that he was "almost positive" he had never spoken with Adger, who died in 1996, about the Guard matter.

Having made a six-year commitment to the Guard, Bush successfully completed the challenging course of training in the F-102 fighter. In his 1999 autobiography, *A Charge to Keep*, he offered lyrical memories of his Guard stint. "I continued flying with my unit for the next several years," he wrote. But that simply wasn't true: Lieutenant Bush never flew another jet after being suspended from flight duty in August 1972 for failing to take a mandated annual physical. That was a fact he simply couldn't remember when asked to account for the discrepancy in 2000. (*A Charge to Keep* also omits his stint as head cheerleader at Phillips Andover, his old prep school.)

Among the most questionable assertions in his book is that he sought to volunteer for service in Vietnam "to relieve active-duty pilots." In a more candid mood in 1998, Bush had told a reporter for the *Fort Worth Star-Telegram*: "I don't want to play like I was somebody out there marching [to war] when I wasn't. It was either Canada or the service and I was headed into the service."

Bush also wrote that his military service "gave me respect for the chain of command." Not enough respect, apparently, to report for duty as ordered, since his records show that he ignored two direct orders to do so—and in fact was absent from duty for a year between May 1972 and May 1973.

By the time he applied to Harvard Business School in 1972, Bush claimed, "I was almost finished with my commitment in the Air National Guard, and was no longer flying because the F-102 jet I had trained in was being replaced by a different fighter." That too was false. According to an interview with his commanding officer that appeared in the *Boston Globe*, Bush's Guard unit continued to fly the F-102 until 1974, an assertion confirmed by Air Force records. "If he had come back to Houston, I would have kept him flying the 102 until he got out," said retired Major General Bobby W. Hodges.

In 2000 a few journalists asked the Bush campaign to account for his near-total absence from duty during the final two years of the six-year stint he agreed to serve. The Republican candidate and his spokespersons replied that he made up his missed days in an Alabama National Guard unit, but there is scant evidence to confirm that claim. Bush sought a permanent transfer to a "postal unit" in Alabama that didn't require weekend drills or active duty, which was approved by his Texas superiors. In May 1972, National Guard headquarters denied his request—which would have amounted to a permanent vacation from duty. The following autumn, he was assigned instead to temporary "alternative" training at the 187th Squadron in Montgomery, Alabama.

According to two former officers in that Alabama Guard unit, however, Bush never showed up. Retired General William Turnipseed, the unit's former commander, said he was certain that Bush did not report to him, although the young reserve airman was specifically required to do so. The orders dated September 15, 1972, were clear. "Lieutenant Bush should report to Lt. Col. William Turnipseed, DCO, to perform equivalent training."

Bush has insisted, usually through a spokesman, that he did report for duty in Alabama, although his campaign could offer no proof. In late 2000 a group of Alabama Vietnam veterans offered $3,500 to anyone who could verify Bush's claim that he performed service at a Montgomery, Alabama, National Guard unit in 1972. No one ever claimed that reward. Nor could his campaign produce a single witness who confirmed that Bush had attended any Guard drills in Houston after he returned from Alabama in late 1972.

According to the *Boston Globe*, Bush's discharge papers list his service and duty station for each of his first four years in the Air National Guard. After May 1972, there was no record of training on those forms and "no mention of any service in Alabama." The supervising pilots at Ellington Air Force Base wrongly believed that Bush was serving in Alabama. In a report dated May 2, 1973, they explained that they were unable to rate his efficiency because "Lt. Bush has not been observed at this unit during the period of report. A civilian occupation made it necessary for him to move to Montgomery, Alabama. He cleared this base on 15 May 1972 and has been performing equivalent training in a non-flying status with the 187 Tac Recon Gp, Dannelly ANG Base, Alabama."

As for Bush's curious failure to take his Air Force physical in July 1972, his only excuse is that because he was then in Alabama working on a Republican Senate campaign, he was unable to return to Houston for a checkup by his personal physician. That too was untrue. A pilot physical, required to continue flying, can only be performed by a certified Air Force flight surgeon (as Bush must have known, since he had undergone at least three such exams). An investigation of Bush's military career published in June 2000 by the *Times* of London noted that the Air Force had instituted rigorous drug testing a few months before he failed to show up for the medical exam.

The commander in chief's official National Guard record shows no evidence of service between May 1972 and May 1973. Although he was certainly in Houston during most of that period, he didn't return to duty at Ellington until the spring of 1973. The records show that he spent thirty-six days in drills (though not flying) from May through June 1973, apparently to compensate for all the months he had been absent. By then he was preparing to attend Harvard Business School. His final day in uniform was July 30, 1973, and he was officially released from active duty the following October—eight months before he would have finished his original six-year commitment to the Guard.

The next time Bush strapped himself into a fighter cockpit would be thirty years later, when he was flown to the deck of the USS *Lincoln* for a triumphal speech marking the American victory over Saddam Hussein's dictatorship. Privately, Republican media advisers admitted that they were likely to use the "Top Gun" videotape of the President strutting across the carrier deck in his flightsuit for campaign commercials in 2004.

Despite all the remarkable contradictions between his military record and his self-serving stories, and despite the plentiful evidence that he had shirked a year of his service and then lied about it, the "liberal media" never subjected Bush to the searing interrogations inflicted on Quayle in 1988 and Clinton in 1992. Only the *Boston Globe*, the *Los Angeles Times*, the *Dallas Morning News*, and a Democratic Web site bothered to explore the curious absences and lapses of duty that resulted in Bush's grounding after two years of fighter training. Nobody insisted that he hold press conferences to explain himself. Pundits dismissed the issue when they mentioned it at all. The cultural assumption that Republicans are paragons of flag-saluting martial virtue is rarely challenged, regardless of reality.

Yet the startling fact is that liberal Democratic politicians are at least as likely to have done military service as their Republican opponents and critics. Among the U.S. senators in the 107th Congress, the percentage of veterans was slightly higher among Democrats than among Republicans (if service in the Vietnam-era National Guard is excluded). That sort of statistic wouldn't matter so much if not for the right's continuing indulgence in venomous attacks on the patriotism of liberals and Democrats. Lining up the conservative civilians alongside the liberal veterans is an unpleasant but necessary exercise in an era when right-wingers and Republicans are inclined to exploit patriotism for partisan advantage.

The long, distinguished list of Republican tough guys who never served descends from Vice President Cheney, who has explained that he had "other priorities" during Vietnam, all the way down to Limbaugh, who frequently impugns the patriotism of liberal veterans like Tom Daschle. It includes former Majority Leader Lott; former Speaker Gingrich and his successor, Denny Hastert; the two Texans who actually ran the House after Gingrich's departure, Tom DeLay and Dick Armey; White House political adviser Karl Rove; and Phil Gramm, the senior senator from Texas who retired in 2002.

John Ashcroft would have been subject to the Vietnam draft when he graduated from law school in 1967, but a family friend swiftly set him up in a job teaching business law to undergraduates at a Springfield, Missouri, college. The local draft board deemed this job "essential" and awarded him an occupational deferment, one of eight deferments he received between 1963 and 1969. As Attorney General, Ashcroft has been quick to question the patriotism of anyone who protests his evisceration of basic liberties.

Not everyone excused from service was a chicken hawk, but every chicken hawk has an excuse. Few were ever as creatively comical as Tom DeLay, a belligerent politician who loudly maligns the patriotism of his betters. At the Republican Convention in 1988, he explained to reporters that there had been no space in the Army for "patriotic folks" like himself and Dan Quayle during the Vietnam War—because too many minority youths had joined the service to earn money and escape the ghetto.

His own failure to serve only seems to have made the former exterminator more vociferously obnoxious to those who did. When retired General Brent Scowcroft cautioned against a precipitous invasion of Iraq during the summer of 2002, DeLay denounced such warnings as "a campaign driven by a congenital mistrust of American principles and consistent hostility to American action." Later that year, during an especially shrill appearance on CNN, he insisted that congressional Democrats who dared to raise questions about national security "don't want to protect the American people . . . [T]hey will do anything, spend all the time and resources they can, to avoid confronting evil." DeLay is simply a cowardly thug in a business suit, who abuses patriotic rhetoric to stifle debate.

Of course, there are many honorable Republicans who did serve, and many liberal Democrats who didn't. Among the dozens of veterans on the Democratic side of the aisle are Daschle and Kerry; Hawaii Senators Daniel Akaka and Daniel Inouye, who lost an arm and won the Congressional Medal of Honor when the Allies captured Italy; and Senator Tom Harkin of Iowa, who served as a Navy pilot for five years. Until he was defeated in November 2002, the Senate Democratic vets included Max Cleland of Georgia, another Medal of Honor winner who returned from Vietnam without his legs and his right arm.

Such a sacrifice is no guarantee of respect from a right-wing opportunist, as Cleland discovered during his last campaign. The wheelchair-bound senator had to listen to Representative Saxby Chambliss, his Republican opponent, cast doubt on his dedication to his country, loudly attacking him "for breaking his oath to protect and defend the Constitution."

The blustering Chambliss had avoided service during Vietnam with four student deferments and a "football injury," but he explained that his own lack of service was "absolutely not an issue." He excoriated Cleland as "the most liberal senator Georgia has ever had." And Georgia's voters responded to the vile assault on Cleland's patriotism by throwing a true hero out of office — and replacing him with a double-talking draft avoider.

While Cleland is in truth a moderate southern Democrat, more than a few of the most liberal figures in Congress have also served in uniform. Among the veterans who have joined the left-leaning House Progressive Caucus are Representatives Charlie Rangel (Bronze Star), Peter DeFazio, Maurice Hinchey, David Bonior (since retired), John Conyers, Jose Serrano, Lane Evans, Jim McDermott, Bobby Rush, and Pete Stark.

Max Cleland and John Kerry surely aren't the only decorated Democratic Vietnam vets to serve in elected office. Mike Thompson of California is a liberal who was awarded the Purple Heart for wounds he suffered as a platoon leader with the 173rd Airborne Brigade. Iowa Democrat Leonard Boswell earned two Distinguished Flying Crosses, two Bronze Stars, and the Soldier's Medal as a helicopter pilot. Pete Peterson, the former Democratic congressman from Florida who became the first U.S. Ambassador to Vietnam after Clinton restored diplomatic relations, is a former prisoner of war who received a Purple Heart, a Silver Star, and the Legion of Merit.

The point here is not that anyone who failed to serve should be excluded from decisions about war and peace — an objection raised by conservatives when they want to evade this touchy subject. The point instead is that conservatives should stop pretending they have a monopoly on patriotic virtue and military valor, because the record clearly disproves that myth. Conservatives who didn't serve would be wise to refrain from mocking the patriotism of liberals and Democrats who did.

Beyond the vexed issues of military service and draft avoidance during Vietnam, American liberals have no reason to be defensive about their role in the nation's defense. A powerful argument can be made that over the past two centuries, the liberal left has done better service to the United States and to American ideals than the conservative right.

It isn't merely that liberals fought for justice and liberty where conservatives repeatedly failed to, in causes ranging from the abolition of child labor to the end of Jim Crow oppression. Any debate over patriotism must account for the contrasting roles of liberals and conservatives in America's bloodiest conflicts, from the Revolutionary War to the Civil War to World War II. Political forces identified with the right—Tories, Confederates, isolationists—undermined the Republic and consorted with the nation's foreign enemies.

Republicans can't seem to decide whether Democrats are trembling pacifists or furious militarists (a dilemma Bob Dole resolved to his own discredit when he muttered about all the "Democrat wars" of the twentieth century in a 1976 debate). But liberal internationalism is neither warlike nor pacifist; its aim is to advance American interests and principles within a framework of alliances, treaties, and laws.

Liberals founded NATO and the other multilateral security institutions, against fierce opposition from the conservative Taft Republicans. Liberals proposed to rebuild Europe under the Marshall Plan, creating an economic bulwark against Stalin's expansion to the west and a vital market for American exports. Liberals led the international campaign for human rights that renewed respect for American values around the world.

Although "right" and "left" weren't the categories of political debate when the thirteen colonies broke free from England, there isn't much doubt that the leading instigators of the American Revolution—and in particular the Declaration of Independence—were the "left-wingers" of that extraordinary historic moment. They were the original liberals, and several of them, most notably Thomas Jefferson and James Madison, were also the founders of the Democratic Party.

The nation's founders disagreed about issues ranging from debt to slavery, but among the most active and prolific of them were men who can only be defined as progressive. What other description fits Samuel Adams, populist organizer of the Boston Tea Party, or Thomas Paine, author of the revolutionist pamphlet "Common Sense," who both openly declared their contempt for monarchy and aristocracy? Paine was a self-taught but farsighted thinker whose classic liberal manifesto, *Rights of Man,* proposed such innovations as free public education, child welfare, and income security long before they became reality here or in his native England. The popular republicanism advocated by the patriots Adams, Paine, Jefferson, and Franklin was considered a radical doctrine in the colonial era.

The "right-wingers" of the Revolutionary era were the Tories, of course. They were in thrall to the British crown and feared that change would deprive them of their privileges. After the British retreat, they were widely reviled and punished; a number were hanged; many were beaten, driven from their homes, expelled into Canada, or shipped back to England. In their assistance to the occupying army of George III, the Tories were viewed by most of the new Americans as traitors.

Today, modern conservatives like to talk about their "strict construction" of law based on the Constitution, as if the men who wrote that document still speak directly to Antonin Scalia and Clarence Thomas. They revere the aristocratic, reactionary Edmund Burke and ignore the democratic workingman Tom Paine, and they try to claim the principles of the Revolution as an endorsement of their own doctrines of privilege. But only from the perspective of two centuries of ideological shift can the republican faith of the Founding Fathers be depicted as "conservative"—and even then the fit is poor.

The Civil War, too, was a struggle between left and right. Today's rightists still cherish Dixie, as if the barbarous cruelty and feudal culture of the Old South represented a lost Eden. Academics will argue forever about the Civil War's economic and social origins, but it was undeniably liberals such as William Lloyd Garrison and Horace Greeley who sought to abolish slavery and preserve the Union. The conservatives who sought to dissolve the Union wanted to preserve and extend slavery; not only did they try to ruin the nation before it was a century old, but they turned to the throne of England for assistance. When Lincoln was President, the Union properly indicted the Confederate leaders and their northern supporters as traitors (an epithet now generally avoided out of concern for delicate southern sensibilities).

Amazingly, there remains a strong emotional reverence for the symbols of the Confederacy, not only among the Klan, the Aryan Brotherhood, and skinhead Nazis, but among certain Republican politicians and intellectuals as well. They nurture a political cult of neo-Confederates, diehard defenders of secession and states' rights. Aside from romanticizing the Old South, neo-Confederates tend to advocate a regional brand of conservatism that is chauvinistic, hostile to immigrants, and often blatantly bigoted against blacks, Hispanics, Jews, and Asians.

Like Strom Thurmond and his followers, who abandoned the Democratic Party in 1948 during the early struggle over civil rights, the neo-Confederates are Republicans now. The GOP reciprocates this support by pretending not to notice their Dixie flags, their racial obsessions, and their scurrilous attitude toward Lincoln. The loyalties of the neo-Confederates are uncertain. According to Clyde Wilson, a leading neo-Confederate ideologue and professor at the University of South Carolina, these devotees of Dixie should feel no loyalty to the United States at all.

In a long interview in a neo-Confederate organ called the *Southern Partisan*, Professor Wilson suggested that the South should still be seeking to secede. The professor further complained about the well-known propensity of young men and women from the South to serve in the U.S. military. "It's terrible that Southerners have been so willing to sacrifice their lives for the United States," he said. "We have to stop that kind of knee-jerk American allegiance." The publisher of the

Southern Partisan happens to be Richard Quinn, a former partner of Lee Atwater, and South Carolina's most successful Republican consultant. He has advised Ronald Reagan, Strom Thurmond, John McCain, and Lindsey Graham, but his magazine puffs John Wilkes Booth and David Duke.

At the risk of offending the southern supremacists like Quinn who salute the Stars and Bars, and their conservative friends, it may reasonably be asked what is patriotic about all that.

Another inglorious episode in the annals of conservatism preceded the global victory against fascism that consolidated American power. During the late thirties, powerful elements on the right sponsored the so-called America First movement to prevent U.S. intervention against Nazism in Europe. Though heavily camouflaged behind a phalanx of American flags and loud patriotic speeches, America First was eventually exposed as a haven for German and Japanese agents plotting against the U.S. government. For a time, these admirers and appeasers of Hitler found themselves in a kind of alliance with the Communists, who initially opposed American entry into World War II under orders from Stalin. During the critical years when Britain was resisting the Nazi onslaught, the only reliable opposition to fascism was mounted by the union-based, multiethnic, and quintessentially liberal New Deal coalition.

When the Japanese attacked Pearl Harbor, most conservatives dropped their isolationism and joined the war effort. Yet more than a few on the far right continued to promote defeatism and appeasement. In 1942 the Justice Department convicted twenty-eight American Nazi sympathizers of sedition. The grand jury investigation that led to their indictment revealed that George Sylvester Viereck, the most active German agent in Washington, had been operating out of the office of a respectable Republican congressman from an old New York family.

With all due respect to neoconservatives and other late arrivals, the historical roots of postwar conservatism—the "Old Right" of Joe McCarthy and Pat Buchanan—can be traced back to those domestic instruments of the Axis. (Coddling Nazis was a hallmark of both men's careers.) The Buckleys, founders of the *National Review*, were notorious in Connecticut for their fanatical isolationism. *Human Events*, the weekly chronicle of the far right that first recognized Ann Coulter's literary talent, was founded in 1944 by a group of the most rabid prewar isolationists. They included W. H. Regnery Sr., the patriarch of the nation's premier conservative publishing house and a principal financier, along with assorted right-wing industrialists and bankers, of the America First movement.

As the former Bush speechwriter and author David Frum once noted, "conservatives preferred to forget about America First" in the postwar era, and understandably so. None of the Old Rightists who bear direct responsibility for that organization are still around to answer for its disgrace. But Buchanan, who still celebrates America First and adopted its name as his own slogan, was admired among conservatives until he became a nuisance to the Republican establishment. Intellectual and political pedigrees matter, as the conservatives who supposedly venerate national traditions always insist.

Only the most selective reading of history can support the right-wing claim that they are the sole true patriots. And only Americans' collective amnesia permits the right to tighten its grasp on the flag, the national anthem, and the whole panoply of patriotic expression, while denying liberals and progressives the heritage they have every right to share.

DÉJÀ VOODOO, ALL OVER AGAIN

"Republicans are strict accountants who balance budgets and promote economic growth, while Democrats are tax-and-spenders who bust budgets, stifle the economy, and distrust capitalism."

Among the right's most cherished dogmas is that when it comes to economics, conservatives alone understand "how the world works"— and are thus uniquely qualified to run the world efficiently. Adhering to this simple romantic creed, they are capable of deflecting unwelcome intrusions of reality as blithely as any cult member. And much like a cult, they tend to prescribe the same set of true-believer solutions for almost any human problem: big tax cuts for the top brackets and the abolition of almost all government regulation.

Their rigid creed leads them into complicated rhetorical contortions. Depending on what they're trying to argue at any given moment, they may claim that Ronald Reagan's tax cuts were the engine of economic growth in the eighties but that his deficits had nothing to do with the recession that followed; that those same tax cuts were the engine of growth during the nineties as well, even though Reagan, George H. W. Bush, and Bill Clinton all raised taxes later; that Clinton could claim no credit for the growth that occurred during the nineties but is responsible for the recession that opened the new century; that federal budget deficits are terrible, when Democrats can be blamed; and that deficits are fine, when Republicans can't escape blame.

Ignoring the painful evidence of their repeated screwups, conser-

vatives are convinced that they have been brilliant, faithful stewards of
our finances. They will expound at tedious length on their good works
as strict budgetary accountants, rigorous engineers of growth, and in-
corruptible enemies of fraud and waste. They bill themselves as the
only trustworthy defenders of the free enterprise system. In more than
a few cases (as in the writings and speeches of Dick Armey, Pat Robertson, and George Gilder), these starry-eyed right-wingers will further
explain that the Almighty has blessed their self-serving schemes with
the seal of heavenly approval.

Playing an important but unwholesome role in the cultish fantasies
of conservative ideology, of course, are liberals. Naturally, they're the
bad guys: free-spending wastrels, useless bureaucrats, mindless confis-
cators of wealth, and agents of stagnation. They are the unholy antagonists of Christian capitalism, forever seeking to hinder its wondrous
workings with taxes, regulations, complaints, prosecutions, parking
tickets, and so on.

After a decade of Democratic prosperity, the Republican record of
failure was largely forgotten. For a dozen years under Reagan and
Bush, the U.S. government had experimented with "supply-side" nos-
trums, producing the largest deficits in the history of the world, severe
unemployment, falling family incomes, declining industries, and rising
federal and household indebtedness.

An amazing episode of conservative stupidity at its most costly was
the now-forgotten savings and loan fiasco, which bled the Treasury of
hundreds of billions and imposed unknown costs on the national economy. Young taxpayers who have never heard the S&L scandal mentioned on cable TV don't realize that they're paying for its cleanup,
hidden under the category of interest expenses. Reagan and his advisers believed that in every sector government was the problem, and
that if they simply deregulated the financial industry, a bonanza of
growth and investment would soon follow. (As usual, the worst Republican ideas attracted a number of foolish Democrats as well.)

When he signed the bill to deregulate thrift institutions in October
1982, the Gipper quipped, "All in all, I think we've hit the jackpot."

How big a booby prize America actually won wasn't discovered until after Reagan left office — but with bond interest and disposition costs, the final tab came to over a trillion dollars. The unregulated looting of the thrifts by insiders helped to finance the speculative junk bond mania of the Reagan years, which concluded in Wall Street perp walks and national recession. That wasn't quite the end of the fiasco, however.

A few people really did hit the jackpot in the S&L casino, thanks to George Herbert Walker Bush. The first President Bush's appointees handed over the remaining assets of the busted-out thrift institutions to major financial players such as the Bass family and Ronald Perelman — along with huge tax breaks and guarantees of profit — on sweetheart terms. Perelman and his associates paid $315 million, in return for which they got $7.1 billion in good assets, $5.1 billion in cash to indemnify bad loans, and $900 million in tax breaks. By a funny coincidence, the New York billionaire had also spent $100,000 to join Team 100, the elder Bush's stable of big contributors. In fact, several of the blessed investors who hit the bailout jackpot also happened to be lavish donors to the Bush campaign and the Republican Party.

When an administration official reluctantly confirmed the outline of the Perelman bonanza during congressional hearings on the S&L bailout, he was asked by black Democrat Walter Fauntroy, "Why is it only white folks who get that kind of deal?" Fauntroy was being facetious, of course. He knew that only certain white folks at the top of the heap got such favors, while average taxpayers of all complexions got screwed. The hidden history of the S&L crisis and the Reagan deficits is relevant not only because we are still paying for them, but because the same philosophy has returned to power in Washington: deregulate, spend, cut taxes for the wealthy, and let someone else pay for it all someday.

According to Reagan's former budget director David Stockman, those eighties deficits represented a long-term right-wing strategy for government retrenchment in education, environmental protection, health care, public infrastructure, and community development. The flood of red ink would "give you an argument for cutting back the programs that weren't desired." Stockman admitted there was one problem with this diabolical strategy: "It got out of hand." It got way out of hand, despite later efforts under both Reagan and Bush to undo the worst budgetary excesses of the eighties with substantial tax increases.

To paraphrase George H. W. Bush, the economic legacy of the Republican years from 1981 to 1993 left America in deep voodoo. The combined effects of irresponsible tax cuts, unrestrained spending, and the deregulation disaster were left for Clinton and the Democrats to clean up. The Republicans brushed off their responsibility for the fiscal debacle, briskly insisting that they were the party of balanced budgets when they unveiled the "Contract with America."

When Clinton entered the Oval Office and peered into the bare cupboard left by his "fiscally conservative" predecessors, he toted up the full price of the Reagan binge. In his 1992 campaign, Clinton had promised a vague "middle-class tax cut." Surprised to learn on taking office that the '93 deficit had passed $300 billlion, he felt compelled to raise taxes instead.

His change of direction — necessitated by the reeling financial markets and an insupportable $3 trillion national debt run up during the Reagan years — set off a monumental tantrum on the right. "Largest tax increase in history" became the mantra of conservatives, repeated so often by so many that it may be possible to find that phrase quoted by almost every Republican politician and pundit sometime between 1993 and 1996. Conservative agitator David Horowitz continued to repeat the same accusation as late as March 2001, when he wrote that Clinton "engineered the largest tax increase in history." That charge was a lie the first time anyone said it, and remained a lie eight years later.

The truth about history's largest tax increase was widely available to anyone who could read and use a calculator. In October 1994 the *Wall Street Journal* explained: "Contrary to Republican claims, the 1993 package is not 'the largest tax increase in history.' The 1982 deficit reduction package of President Reagan and Sen. Robert Dole in a GOP-controlled Senate was a bigger tax bill, both in 1993-adjusted dollars and as a percentage of the overall economy." The *New York Times* and the congressional Joint Committee on Taxation

reached the same conclusion, which required no formula more difficult than translating 1982 dollars into their 1993 equivalent. In other
words, a year after passing his tax cuts, Reagan signed the largest tax
increase in history. The Gipper still holds that record today.

The Republican distortion of reality had two distinct purposes.
Conservatives tried to prevent Clinton from passing his first tax-and-
budget package because they hated its progressivity. The tax increases
affected only the very wealthiest Americans, or about 1.2 percent of
the top taxpayers. Certain corporate executives, notably the ultra-
greedy Jack Welch, still haven't forgiven the former President for raising their taxes. Clinton's budget cuts affected a much broader segment
of the population, but he believed that was a fair social contract if the
deficit was to be reduced quickly.

Although the Republicans couldn't block Clinton's historic budget,
they inflicted a severe political price for its passage. As he noted with
great regret in later years, his tax increase was at least partly responsible
for the heavy Democratic congressional losses in the 1994 midterm
election. Few voters understood that their taxes had not been raised.
In political campaigns, a lie backed by enough money effectively becomes truth.

At the time, conservatives warned gravely of the disaster that Clinton's deficit-reduction plan would bring. History has not been kind to
their predictions. In August 1993 Newt Gingrich, then the leading
Republican spokesman in the House, said that "the tax increase will
kill jobs and lead to a recession, and the recession will force people
off of work and onto unemployment and will actually increase the
deficit." Soon every conservative in Washington was sounding alarms.
"We are buying a one-way ticket to a recession," cried Phil Gramm,
chairman of the Senate Banking Committee and a former economics
professor. "I want to predict here tonight that if we adopt this bill, the
American economy is going to get weaker and not stronger, the deficit
four years from today will be higher than it is today and not lower."

By imposing a substantial share of deficit reduction on the rich
rather than placing the entire burden on the poor and the middle class,

Clinton enraged the corporate conservatives and their political partners. They ended up looking foolish and never forgave him, even when
their own wealth grew exponentially during the ensuing boom. Nor did
they acknowledge how wrong their gloomy forecasts had been, as the national economy achieved unprecedented growth and began to erase
their party's legacy of useless debt and deficits. To credit the Democratic
President would have been to discredit conservative ideology.

Clinton's achievements weren't so easily ignored. While many factors beyond the President's control contributed to the boom, the numbers were, nevertheless, quite impressive. He had presided over 115
straight months of economic expansion, the longest period of uninter-
rupted growth in American history, at an average rate of 4 percent
annually. In less than eight years, he had seen the creation of 22
million new jobs, more than any other President and more than Reagan and Bush combined.

The unemployment rate dipped to 4 percent, renewing the progressive dream of full employment—without the traditional downside
of serious inflation. It was the lowest unemployment figure since 1970.
Unemployment for blacks, Hispanics, and women also fell to historic
lows. The broad availability of jobs made possible the smallest welfare
rolls since the sixties, following the welfare reform legislation Clinton
signed in 1996.

Although the greatest share of the nation's increasing wealth went
to those who were already rich, income rose significantly at all levels—
after years of economic stagnation for middle- and lower-income families. Adjusted for inflation, the median family's income rose by nearly
$6,500. The bottom quintile, aided by two increases in the minimum
wage, achieved more than 16 percent income growth. The poverty
rate began to decrease, descending to the lowest percentage of the
population since 1980, with record numbers of single mothers, blacks,
and Hispanics moving above the poverty line.

Between 1998 and 2000, Clinton's Treasury paid off more than
$360 billion of the national debt, saving taxpayers billions annually in
interest payments. The deficits left by Reagan and Bush had been

converted into surpluses, in part because government spending as a share of gross domestic product was reduced to sixties levels.

Deficit reduction and fiscal stringency had helped keep interest rates low, which in turn helped a larger percentage of Americans buy homes than ever before. Many more American families owned stock as well by the end of the nineties. And by the time Clinton left office, federal income taxes as a percentage of income for the typical American family were lower than they had been at any time since 1966.

Unable to cope with the success of Clinton's economic plan, conservatives had no program except a return to the Reaganite past—déjà voodoo—with predictable consequences. Enter George W. Bush, who squandered the nation's largest surplus ever in a single euphoric season, to wild applause from his right-wing claque (and, it must be noted, with the assistance of too many intimidated Democrats). When his first budget passed in the spring of 2001, the Republican predictions of miraculous economic improvement were as loud and strident as their cries of doom eight years earlier. As soon as they got their hands on the surplus left by Clinton, they promised everything to everyone. Tax relief! New and better jobs! Growing the economy and paying down the debt! Funding Social Security and Medicare! With balanced budgets, too!

Is it necessary to point out that those happy results didn't materialize? Instead, long before Bush marked his second anniversary in the White House, 2 million jobs had disappeared, along with trillions of dollars in market capitalization. Family income declined, poverty began to rise again, and the government itself took a nearly $400 billion turn into the red, from a surplus of $236 billion to a deficit of $159 billion. Before his first term ends, Bush could become the first president since Herbert Hoover to manage an absolute decline in employment.

The recession had commenced before Bush took office, although he and Dick Cheney may have made it worse with pessimistic political talk. The terrorist attacks in September 2001 inflicted terrible damage on the economy. But Bush's floundering domestic policy team did little to improve the situation. As for the stark contrast between budgetary promises and results: either the President and his budget director were unable to comprehend the math that foretold gaping deficits when they proposed their tax cuts — or, as Princeton economist Paul Krugman explained on several occasions in his *New York Times* op-ed column, they consciously lied.

It isn't necessary to believe Krugman, a moderate, market-oriented liberal who has been vindicated repeatedly. Believe Andrew Sullivan, a Bush-worshiping conservative who admits that his hero lied about taxes and the budget: "The fact that Bush has to obfuscate his real goals of reducing spending with the smoke screen of 'compassionate conservatism' shows how uphill the struggle is. Yes, some of the time he is full of it on his economic policies. But a certain amount of [bullshit] is necessary for any vaguely successful retrenchment of government power in an insatiable entitlement state. . . . Bush and Karl Rove are no dummies. They have rightly judged that, in a culture of ineluctable government expansion, where every new plateau of public spending is simply the baseline for the next expansion, a rhetorical smoke screen is sometimes necessary." (Translation into plain English: Lying is fine, as long as it's about something trivial like a trillion-dollar deficit and not the oral endearments of an intern.)

By the summer of 2002, the White House Office of Management and Budget admitted that its sunny fiscal projections of a few months earlier were completely wrong. Every other expert in the country, including the Republican-controlled Congressional Budget Office, had figured this out already. Bush's repeated pledges not to fund the tax cuts from Social Security revenues were officially defunct. So were his campaign promises to pay down the federal debt, with the annual prospect of deficits in the hundreds of millions for at least five years to come. The possibility of a $5 trillion surplus, bequeathed to Bush by Clinton, was gone.

Independent analysts believe that deficits will continue for the remainder of the decade. They don't buy Bush's excuse that the reversal from surplus to deficit was caused mainly by the war in Afghanistan or even the recession. (Actually, neither do the analysts in his own budget office.) While both war and recession were factors, the politically dangerous truth is that the bulk of the deficit—and of future deficit forecasts—resulted from the Bush tax cuts.

On June 11, 2002, for the first time in five years, the White House was forced to ask Congress to raise the ceiling on the national debt. Reluctant to admit what their tax-cutting had wrought in an election year, the House Republicans resisted. The air of economic unreality in Republican circles could be measured by another event on June 11. That also happened to be the day Texas Senator Phil Gramm (since retired) proposed to permanently repeal the federal estate tax— another tax break for a fraction of the nation's wealthiest heirs, at an estimated cost of at least $100 billion over ten years.

Facing a state of war and a stagnant world economy, the nation lacked sufficient resources to ensure its own security, let alone fund its future commitments, but that didn't change the habits of the conservatives in the White House and Congress. They were still obsessed with tax cuts, no matter how irresponsible. The first cuts failed to stimulate the economy, as Bush aides have acknowledged—so they proposed a second round, again skewed heavily to the wealthy. The central feature of the second tax package was the elimination of dividend taxation, which would blow an enormous hole in budgets over the next decade without necessarily sparking any new investment. It could also have the additional damaging impact of raising interest rates on the bonds issued by states and cities—whose budgets and economies are in the grimmest condition in decades.

As for cutting spending, anyone who closely scrutinizes the House Republican Study Committee, a seventy-member caucus that includes the most conservative members, will immediately discover that rightwing posturing about budgetary restraint is a sham. These characters stand in front of the cameras and drone on about protecting the taxpayers—and then go into a closed meeting minutes later to demand millions in costly, often ridiculous projects in their districts.

During negotiations over the 2003 budget—after years of listening to spokesmen for the Republican Study Committee complain about wasteful spending items while the group's members privately clamored for pork—their Republican colleagues finally had enough. Breaking with institutional traditions of silence, they started talking to the press about the secrets of the budgetary process.

By then, the budget-busting propensities of the Republican leadership had become a serious worry in the White House. As if they were spoiled children, the House Republicans wanted to spend without taxing, just like their idol Reagan. This has become their habit in power. Discretionary spending—the portion of the federal budget that Congress dispenses through legislation, as differentiated from Social Security, bond interest, and other fixed expenses—has grown by more than 50 percent since the Gingrich "revolutionaries" took control of the House. From that day in January 1995 to the present, the number of *earmarks*, meaning pork projects attached to spending bills for the benefit of individual districts, has grown by several thousands. Nobody seems to know the exact number, but by 2002 it was around 8,300. Compared with these Republicans, the "spendthrift Democrats" resemble diligent Swiss bankers.

When the chicanery of House conservatives became intolerable in the summer of 2002, their harshest critics were fellow Republicans, trying to manage a budget that was again headed into sustained deficits. These legislators were sick of conservatives who held up passage of crucial budget bills, supposedly because of concerns about excess spending, while those very same conservatives approached them privately asking for special multimillion-dollar earmarks.

Harold Rogers, the Kentucky Republican who chairs a subcommittee overseeing transportation appropriations, told a reporter for *The Hill*, a Capitol Hill weekly, that he was offended by the hypocrisy of hard-core right-wingers who publicly complained about federal spending—and then asked him for extra money to build roads and bridges in their districts. "It's the age-old adage of do as I say and not as I do," complained Mike Castle, a respected moderate Republican from Delaware, referring to the behavior of his party's ideologues.

This charade became so ridiculous that Jim Dyer, staff director of the House Appropriations Committee, went on the record with the kind of withering comments that are usually uttered only on background. "Everything Chairman Rogers says is true, it's a very high number," Dyer said of the flood of projects demanded by conservatives. "There are hundreds and hundreds. . . . We've had the policy of protecting members and not exposing them, but we've taken a lot of abuse. There are members on the bandwagon of anti-spending, but they come and get their share."

In other words, those great conservative friends of the taxpayer have been rifling the Treasury with both hands. They still talk about frugality, whenever they take a breather from gorging at the pork barrel. Many examples of right-wing waste cited by watchdog groups are relatively small; others, such as former Senate Republican leader Trent Lott's subsidies to shipbuilders in his hometown of Pascagoula, Mississippi, consume hundreds of millions of dollars. Democrats and liberals glom porky projects for their districts, too, of course. But few Democrats or liberals win bogus awards from conservative front groups proclaiming them to be "heroes of the taxpayer" while they line up at the public trough.

The case of Robert Aderholt, an ultraconservative Republican from Alabama, illustrates this amusing facet of right-wing fakery. During 2002, as he prepared to run for reelection, Aderholt sent out press releases boasting of more than forty-two special projects in his district, at a cost to taxpayers of more than $25 million. The federal government was even paying to repair the sidewalk outside a local school, normally a local function paid for by local taxpayers. But as *The Hill* reported, with deadpan irony, Aderholt had also received a "Hero of the Taxpayer" award in April 2002 from Americans for Tax Reform, a "nonpartisan" organization headed by Grover Norquist, one of the leading Republican operatives in the capital.

What Aderholt did in his district, the Republican leadership does all over the country. An exhaustive Associated Press study of federal spending published in 2002 showed that since the Republicans took over Congress, they had moved "tens of billions of dollars from Democratic to GOP districts." This was accomplished by a Robin-Hoodin-reverse agenda that transferred funds from food stamps and housing programs to business loans and farm subsidies. The Republicans take from the poor, give to the rich, and get themselves reelected.

In the average district, the additional bounty for having a Republican congressman comes to about $612 million. The Democrats were never so bold. When they still controlled the House in 1994, the average Democratic district received only $35 million more than the average Republican district. And now the difference is financed by spending more rather than just moving money around. Spending went up in all districts, the AP found; it just went up a lot more in the Republican districts, from $3.9 billion in 1995 to $5.8 billion in 2001.

Asked by an AP reporter why such boodling had come to pass under the conservative House leadership, then Majority Leader Dick Armey, another former economics teacher, was blunt if ungrammatical. "There is an old adage," he said. "To the victor goes the spoils."

How Republicans achieved their reputation for knowing how to manage the economy is a mystery. For a group of politicians who like to tout their hardheaded management of the nation's money, their record is consistently poor. They babble incessantly about running the government like a business, but a business run by them would have failed long ago—and as businessmen they might well be looking at the wrong end of a fraud indictment. Lucky for them, it's only politics.

The available data show consistently that Democrats are more capable, productive economic stewards than Republicans. (That's why they always play "Happy Days Are Here Again" at those donkey conventions.) Consider the history of the stock market, where plummeting values since 2001 have caused wider distress than ever—ironically thanks to the vastly expanded ownership of equities, either directly or indirectly, during the Clinton era.

When *Slate* magazine analyzed the average returns on the Standard & Poor's 500 in October 2002, its researchers found that Democratic Presidents posted vastly better numbers than Republicans. Over the past century, in fact, Democratic presidencies produced annual returns of 12.3 percent, while the Republicans produced 8 percent.

Moreover, stock valuations during Democratic control of Congress also beat the Republican record in both the Senate and the House by considerable margins, averaging 10.7 percent returns for the donkeys against 8.7 percent for the elephants. The Democrats should perhaps consider adopting the bull as their party animal, while the Republicans deserve to be stuck with the bear.

Not long ago, Northwestern Mutual, the insurance and financial services giant, published a survey of presidential administrations and S&P 500 performance between 1929 and 1999 that showed the Democratic advantage quite starkly. Even when the company's analysts massaged those numbers to remove two of the worst Republican periods — the Hoover administration and Nixon's second term — the outcome still favored Democrats by 16.9 percent to 14.2. The largest gains occurred under FDR, Truman, Johnson, and Clinton.

The editors of the *Stock Trader's Almanac* — an authoritative source of Wall Street statistics — drew very similar conclusions in 2000 when they looked at the prices of Dow Jones stocks, although their analysis was even more favorable to the Democrats, who posted gains of 13.4 percent versus 8.1 percent for Republicans. Jeffrey Hirsch, who edits and publishes the almanac, told *Slate* that the correlation between presidential party and stock appreciation was among the most significant statistical relationships he has found.

Market historian Hirsch's verdict? "I don't know why people are convinced Republicans are good for the stock market."

Rising stock indexes are not necessarily the best means, however, to measure national economic progress from a liberal perspective. What about gross domestic product, job creation, unemployment, disposable income, deficit reduction, federal spending, and inflation? By every one of those yardsticks, Democratic Presidents achieved a superior record: on average, their administrations fostered more growth, higher wages, lower deficits, lower government spending, and lower inflation than Republican regimes. If voters understood how poorly the GOP has operated the nation's business — and the gaping difference between promises and results—they would file the electoral equivalent of a shareholder lawsuit.

In recent years, conservative ideologues have been humiliated by reality on every important economic issue—from the macroeconomic effects of the minimum wage and progressive taxation to the necessity for stricter financial market supervision and the future prospects of the stock market. The minimum wage was increased twice during the Clinton years, and contrary to right-wing dogma, a record number of jobs was created. The top tax rate was increased in 1993, and the economy boomed. Deregulation of banking and lax regulation of accounting and financial markets in recent years encouraged the corporate scandals that destroyed trillions of dollars in shareholder value. As for the price of stocks, it is only necessary to recall *Dow 36,000*, the title of a 1999 book co-authored by conservative pundit James Glassman.

Glassman was hardly alone on the right in his ultraexuberance. Before the crash, such faith in the eternal power of the "new economy" was usually accompanied by libertarian speculation about the withering away of the welfare state. (With everyone a millionaire, why would anyone need government?) And if the state didn't wither away, the conservatives intended to tear it down anyway with a series of policy schemes, from Social Security and Medicare privatization to private school vouchers. Although Republicans waffle and flip-flop on these issues for political expedience, such plans remain at the top of their domestic agenda for the coming decade.

The problem isn't that conservatives are wrong about the efficiency of markets or the creativity of enterprise. It's that they have made false idols of both, usually without acknowledging that markets work best when well regulated, that private enterprise cannot meet every human need, that government has always played a critical role in our economy, and that the profit motive can be socially and environmentally destructive as well as dynamic.

While liberals are often mocked as naïve idealists, they are in fact the true realists. Instead of turning capitalism into a pseudoreligion, they see it as it is: a powerful system that requires government intervention to temper the business cycle, to protect individuals and communities from abuse by corporate behemoths, and to provide the complex physical, educational, and scientific infrastructure that encourages growth.

Yet there are still deeper contradictions that separate conservative Republicans from their professed ideology. They claim to believe in "free enterprise," and many of them sincerely do. But the system that is practiced at the top—by politicians, their families, friends, and corporate benefactors—would be more aptly described as "crony capitalism."

That term is an import from the Philippines, a former American colony where the systematic looting of public resources and private property by the late Ferdinand Marcos, along with his friends and cronies, parodied free enterprise. With the enthusiastic support of conservative Republicans in this country, Marcos handed out monopolies in agricultural exports and other major industries to his friends, always secretly taking a stock position for himself. (He did the same with the country's offshore petroleum fields, in a secret partnership with Robert Mosbacher, the Houston oil millionaire who later became George H. W. Bush's chief presidential campaign fund-raiser and then his Secretary of Commerce.)

The quasi-communist leaders of China do business much the same crooked way, as does the ferociously anticommunist family that has ruled Singapore for decades; and similar practices distort the economies of countries as distant as Nigeria and as close as Mexico.

We don't have a rotten system like that in the United States—not yet, anyway. But we do suffer from an increasingly venal political economy, rife with scams and payoffs that reward the connected few, often at the expense of the deceived many. The pandemic of corporate scandal has exposed an American style of crony capitalism that infects boardrooms, accounting firms, congressional offices, Governor's mansions, and all sorts of important institutions, all the way up to the Oval Office.

5 WHY DICK ARMEY JOINED THE ACLU

> **"Conservatives are the only reliable defenders of individual liberty, because liberals worship political correctness and suppress freedom."**

One of the greatest public-relations triumphs in contemporary American politics is the transformation of the dreary image of conservatism. Not so long ago, Republican politicians were regarded as stodgy, authoritarian figures, concerned mainly with maintaining law and order (and commerce). Sometime during the past two decades, however, Republicans and conservatives escaped their repressive reputation — and, more important, rebranded themselves as the world's foremost advocates of "freedom."

To understand just what brand of freedom they are advertising, it is necessary to examine the fine print of Republican Party platforms and various other conservative manifestos. Their definition clearly includes freedom from taxation on certain kinds of income, such as capital gains and multimillion-dollar inheritances, as well as freedom from regulations on pollution and safety for corporations. It also means freedom to purchase an unlimited number of automatic weapons.

In the conservative lexicon, "freedom" usually does not include women's sexual and reproductive rights or civil rights for gays and lesbians. It doesn't mean freedom to obtain information from the federal government, freedom to travel to Cuba, or freedom to read certain banned books in public school libraries. Since the advent of the war on terrorism, it no longer means freedom from omniscient surveillance by agents of the state.

As the careers of Richard Nixon, Joe McCarthy, J. Edgar Hoover, and Edwin Meese proved, the right has traditionally preferred order to liberty. Like those worthies, many conservatives are at best equivocal in their attitude toward the Bill of Rights. They waffle on the First Amendment, revere the Second, and aren't very keen on the Fourth. Liberals, not conservatives, advanced the rights of free speech and association during the twentieth century, and created the American Civil Liberties Union to ensure their protection. The right has kept its distance from the ACLU—and from time to time, conservative politicians have engaged in cheap, shameful, McCarthyite attacks on that venerable organization—except when seeking its assistance for opportunistic reasons, as in recent litigation over campaign finance reform.

Yet despite their rather dismal legacy in safeguarding civil liberties, conservatives have awarded themselves a franchise on the idea of freedom.

How did that happen? Appearance matters more than substance in contemporary politics—and since the Reagan era, appearances on the right have changed dramatically. The stuffed suits of yesteryear have retired or receded into the background, while into the limelight has stepped a fresher and more freewheeling cast of characters. Frumpy, beehived Phyllis Schafly gave way to swinging Laura Ingraham, in her leopard-print miniskirt; the cornball voice of Paul Harvey was replaced by the aggressive baritone of Rush Limbaugh, dominating the airwaves to the thumping beat of the Pretenders; and the GOP's gray-suited lobbyists and officials are now fronted by a virtual zoo of Republican party animals, from P. J. O'Rourke, Matt Drudge, and Bob Tyrrell to Ted Nugent, Dennis Miller, and Andrew Sullivan.

As any advertising executive could have predicted, these wisecracking entertainers and pundits have radically altered the perception of conservatism without changing the reality at all. It's the same principle used to sell soft drinks, sanitary napkins, and cigarettes. What has changed, and much for the worse, is the level of conservative discourse. When Ann Coulter compared Hillary Clinton to a "prostitute" on national TV, it was only one of many signs of a steep descent from the standard of literacy and wit once set by William F. Buckley Jr. But the quasi-pornographic banter and racially tinged humor indulged in by right-wing TV and radio personalities only enhances conservatism's aura of rebellion.

This slick repackaging of the same old ideology couldn't succeed without the simultaneous discrediting of liberals. If conservatives represented the new counterculture, then liberals had to become the stifling establishment. Liberals are incessantly depicted as drab and overbearing "nanny statists," conspiring to outlaw ethnic jokes, junk food, nude centerfolds, gas-guzzling cars, workplace flirting, and almost anything that's fun. Paradoxically, those same boring, uptight, PC liberals are also held responsible for adultery, divorce, premarital sex, abortion, narcotics abuse, teenage pregnancy, movie sex and violence, rap music, and other lurid indicators of American society's hastening decline. (Or maybe those are just the "Hollywood liberals.")

Neal Boortz, a nationally syndicated conservative radio talk show host, warned his listeners about the enemy's objectives: "Liberals are not lovers of freedom. Liberals believe that the average person is simply too ignorant to be free. They believe that the average person can only live a fulfilling life with the help and guidance of those who are more qualified, capable, and intelligent—and that, of course, would be the leftist intelligentsia."

According to this vision, liberals would eventually herd everyone into their grim vision of a progressive utopia unless stopped by heroic conservatives. America could be on the verge of turning into the old Soviet Russia, only worse: there would be no vodka and no cigarettes. All the negatives once used to describe conservatism—narrow-minded, intolerant, rigid—were attached to liberalism with a buzz phrase that also evoked Communist regimentation. The epithet that stuck was *politically correct.*

Nobody is certain who first used that term. Its American roots can be traced to the Communist Party in the thirties; at some point it seems to have migrated to Maoist China. Lifted from left-wing jargon, "PC" began to be used ironically during the seventies by liberal and progressive students to mock the solemnly rigid cadres of the campus ultraleft. Before it was turned into an unbearable cliché by the right, "politically correct" was the kind of phrase that could have been used by Orwell to deride the "smelly little orthodoxies" of authoritarianism.

At the dawn of the Reagan era, conservatives seized upon *PC* to describe the most outlandish excesses of multiculturalism, feminism, and racial sensitivity, including irksome solutions such as speech codes. Growing diversity on college campuses created tensions that weren't always easy to resolve. Administrators were sometimes caught between preventing hate speech and protecting free speech. In that dilemma, conservatives saw an opportunity to expand their "culture war" against the legacy of the sixties, wreaking plenty of collateral damage in their zeal to discredit liberalism, put down restive minorities, and restore patriarchy.

Hysteria over the threat to freedom posed by political correctness reached its peak in 1993, after a minor incident at the University of Pennsylvania, when a white male student shouted an epithet at three black female students walking outside his dormitory. He said he called them "water buffalo"; they said he called them "black water buffalo."

Whether or not to discipline the white student when the three women brought charges against him under the university's speech code became a nightmarish problem for university president Sheldon Hackney, a distinguished historian who had been nominated to chair the National Council on the Humanities by President Clinton. He eventually settled the case without grave harm to anyone—but not before Clinton's antagonists in the media and Congress had seized on the "water buffalo" case as an example of political correctness run amok.

In *The Politics of Presidential Appointment*, Hackney's concisely brilliant memoir of those events and his subsequent struggle to win Senate confirmation, he explains why the issues surrounding "political correctness" were always more complex than the right cared to acknowledge. Balancing diversity, civility and freedom in society posed a problem that conservatives sought to exploit rather than resolve.

Condoleezza Rice, a figure of reverence among Republicans, echoed Hackney when a British journalist asked her about the term *political correctness*: "I think it's one of those phrases that oversimplifies what is a very complicated problem," replied Rice, then the provost at Stanford. "The complicated problem is that this is an increasingly diversifying society, and people are coming into much closer contact with each other than they ever did. I find that a problem for a university, because bumping up against people who disagree with you is fundamental to the creation of new knowledge. And so universities can't go silent. You can't have a place where it's not permitted to make a certain kind of argument. But you can have a place which forbids epithets to be thrown at people."

In the end, Hackney was confirmed by the Senate with bipartisan support, despite a concerted, highly dishonest effort to ruin him by the editorial writers at the *Wall Street Journal* as well as by Rush Limbaugh and other right-wing extremists. A thoughtful liberal with a profound commitment to critical inquiry and the First Amendment, Hackney finally concluded that speech codes were the wrong means of dealing with problems of incivility and harassment. But the inquisition conducted against the former Penn president was ludicrously overblown, like so much of the PC mania inflamed by the national media. There was never a wave of censorship by liberal academics, although there were a few provocative cases of left-wing idiocy. (At Penn State, for instance, an English professor charged a colleague with sexual harassment for displaying a reproduction of a Goya nude.) Well publicized and often exaggerated by the right, "political correctness" was seen as a threat by millions of white males who became convinced that liberal "thought police" would soon be looking over their shoulders.

Although political correctness is now mostly a dead issue, conservatives still appeal to those same fears and resentments. They can play both sides of any PC issue, depending on convenience. The niche marketing of "political incorrectness" persists even while national Republican leaders promote very different ideas and images (notably "compassionate conservatism"). The most recent example occurred during the 2002 midterm election, when Republican campaigns in the South fought to restore Confederate symbols on state flags. Flying the banner of secession and slavery is probably the most "politically incorrect" stance championed by any mainstream candidate, and the offense thus inflicted on black citizens apparently troubled nobody in the party of Abraham Lincoln.

One of the masterminds of the Dixie flag crusade in the 2002 election was Georgia's Republican state chairman, Ralph Reed. Only a few years earlier, as director of the Christian Coalition, Reed had brought together black ministers to offer a tearful public apology for white evangelism's failure to support the civil rights movement. The revival of the Confederate flag in places like Georgia, of course, had symbolized angry resistance to federal civil rights enforcement.

Reed's gross personal hypocrisy revealed the two faces of contemporary conservatism. Conservatives like him had never sincerely atoned for their equivocal attitude toward black civil rights, nor had they wholly abandoned the racial appeals that helped them win political power across the South. Hiding the most unattractive elements of the Republican coalition was essential if "compassionate conservatism" was to attract moderate whites and ethnic minorities to the GOP. When Trent Lott showed up to celebrate Strom Thurmond's birthday centennial a month after the midterm election, he clumsily exposed what Rove and Bush are so determined to conceal.

"I want to say something about my state," chirped the Mississippi Republican in a toast to his ancient colleague, with video cameras rolling. "We voted for Strom Thurmond in 1948. We're proud of it. And if he had won, we wouldn't have a lot of these problems we've been having ever since." Lott sounded slightly pugnacious as he spoke, but he didn't tell an ethnic joke or make a racial slur. His implied endorsement of the antiblack, prolynching presidential candidacy of the doddering former Dixiecrat almost escaped notice at first.

A brief item noting Lott's remarks on the ABC News political Web site incited a blast of angry commentary on Internet Web logs—notably Joshua Micah Marshall's superb Talking Points Memo—which in turn attracted newspaper and television coverage. Criticism erupted from outraged liberals and embarrassed conservatives as Lott began his round of futile apologies.

The reflexive answer of many on the right, however, was to defend Lott as an innocent target of political correctness. Those speaking up on his behalf included Sean Hannity, who provided a radio forum for one of the Mississippian's multiple apologies, and Ann Coulter, who accused liberals of showing greater indignation about Lott's remarks than about the September 11 terror attack.

"I think anyone who was pretending that Trent Lott was saying anything about segregation is not telling the truth," she declared on Hannity's Fox News Channel show. "No one thinks that's true. It was an old man's birthday party."

The most unvarnished reaction came from Paul Weyrich, long an influential figure among Washington conservatives. "We should defend Trent Lott to the end of the earth when he is being unfairly attacked as he is now," wrote Weyrich in a personal commentary. "If Lott goes down, this will only encourage more expeditions by the left to bag conservatives for making statements deemed to be politically incorrect, no matter if they are just off-the-cuff, ill-considered remarks." Weyrich may not have been sensitive, but he was certainly consistent. Freedom-loving conservatives weren't supposed to be stampeded by "the left" into fratricidal panic over "statements deemed to be politically incorrect." Weren't conservatives still opposed to "political correctness"?

Not necessarily, as the *Washington Times* pointed out in a frank editorial that joined the *National Review*, Andrew Sullivan, Peggy Noonan, and the editorial boards of the *New York Post* and the *Wall Street Journal* in a chorus of demands that Senate Republicans demote Lott immediately. "The harsh political fact facing the Republican senators is that they have a choice between advancing or diminishing the Republican Party's ability to reach out to voters beyond white males," warned the editorial. "Unfair though it may be, if they keep Mr. Lott as leader, millions of voters will be susceptible to the argument that the Republican Party is not welcoming to people of all races and ethnicities." With similar messages emanating from the White House, the Republican leader abruptly resigned.

Within days of his sudden political demise, the clueless Lott was quoted as saying he had stumbled into a trap set by all the usual enemies of "a Christian conservative" from Mississippi. He didn't seem to understand that although liberals had enjoyed his undignified flameout, it was the terrified conservatives who finally snuffed him. Lott wasn't alone in failing to grasp the bitter ironies of his misfortune. The smooth politician from Pascagoula had indeed been sacrificed on the altar of "political correctness."

Worse still, his eager executioners were the same crowd who constantly mocked liberals for being so insufferably PC. They would never be able to use that term again without emitting a flatulent whiff of hypocrisy. The conservatives dumped Lott to prove their racial sensitivity, though nearly all of them insisted that he wasn't really a racist at all. The few who had at first defended him swiftly went silent. It should be a while before a prominent conservative is again heard boasting about "political incorrectness" as a badge of courage.

The indictment of liberalism for political correctness was a diversion as well as a deception. While conservatives generated fright about PC, the most potent threat to American freedom existed not among a few addled college professors but in an ambitious mass movement that is openly hostile to the nation's traditional ideals of liberty: the religious right.

Over many years of speaking, writing, and broadcasting, leaders of the religious right have repeatedly expressed contempt for First Amendment guarantees of free speech and the separation of church and state. (Several of them, such as Jerry Falwell, were opponents of civil rights during the sixties struggle to desegregate the South.) Pat Robertson, Jerry Falwell, and their colleagues are certain that God has instructed them to "Christianize" America, and their literal interpretation of the

Bible leaves little space for constitutional protections of freedom, privacy, and individual conscience. Abrogating the reproductive freedom of women and curtailing the civil rights of gays and lesbians would merely be their starting points. They have made no secret of their desire to require prayer in public schools and to institute censorship of any film, television program, book, or magazine they deem to be pornographic or blasphemous.

In their own publications and in private meetings, leaders like Robertson have talked about their goal of replacing "secular humanist" democracy with a theocratic regime. Robertson once explained that he had named his institution of higher education Regent University because "a regent is one who governs in the absence of a sovereign," meaning that someday "we will rule and reign along with our sovereign, Jesus Christ." That purpose hasn't changed since the televangelist told a revival meeting in 1983 that he foresaw a time when "there is a Spirit-filled President in the White House, and the men in the Senate and the House of Representatives are Spirit-filled and worship Jesus Christ, and the judges do the same thing."

At the Christian Coalition's annual Washington gathering in October 2002, Robertson boasted about his movement's fulfillment of the plan it had conceived in 1990, when the coalition was founded. He cited the electoral victories that brought conservatives to power in Congress and the election that brought a "born-again man" to the White House in 2000. He pointed to the "born-again" politicians serving as House Speaker, House Majority Leader, Senate Majority Leader, and President.

"And that ain't too bad for a little organization," he gloated, reminding his followers that the nation's courts "would be next." Among the speakers at the coalition's conference were Senator Orrin Hatch, chairman of the Senate Judiciary Committee, and House Majority Leader Tom DeLay.

In recent years the Christian Coalition has suffered some difficulties and defections. As Robertson suggested, however, the influence of the broader religious right is far greater than it was a decade ago, and many of its initial goals have been achieved. Much of the responsibility for its success, strangely, lies with libertarians in the conservative movement and the Republican Party. Tempted by power, the secular conservatives not only failed to resist the likes of Robertson and Falwell, but encouraged their political and partisan ambitions.

It was preposterous for the self-styled libertarians in the conservative movement and the Republican Party to form an alliance with Christian fundamentalists. (H. L. Mencken, literary idol of the libertarian right and scourge of fundamentalist superstition, would have considered this liaison craven and contemptible.) Yet while conservatives invited the authoritarian religious right to establish itself within the Republican framework, they simultaneously and cynically accused liberals of abandoning freedom for the sake of political correctness.

The price of that betrayal came due after the inauguration of George W. Bush. Almost immediately, he awarded the nation's highest law enforcement office to the religious right by naming John Ashcroft as Attorney General. Ashcroft is more disdainful of civil liberties than any Attorney General since John Mitchell left office on his way to prison—and he embodies the most serious threat to the Constitution since the Nixon era.

Ashcroft's hostility to secular liberties was predictable, even if the circumstances that allowed him to exercise his authoritarian impulses were not. His peculiar approach to public service was revealed in a book he wrote in 1998, when he was preparing to run for President as the preferred candidate of the religious right. Ashcroft dropped out before the first primaries to endorse Bush, who quickly garnered the support of Robertson, Falwell, and other fundamentalist politicos.

Ashcroft's book contains an extraordinary account of the ancient biblical ritual that his father performed on him every time he took an oath of office, first as Governor of Missouri and then for his single term as U.S. Senator. (As the son and grandson of prominent Pentecostal ministers, he was raised according to a harsh biblical code that proscribes alcohol, tobacco, gambling, dancing, and movies as unwholesome temptations to "worldliness." He still adheres to those rules.)

Like the Old Testament kings of Israel, whose God-given mandate was marked by anointing their heads with holy oil, Ashcroft would kneel down to receive a similar blessing from his aging dad. Lacking holy oil on the evening before Ashcroft was to be sworn in as a senator in 1994, his father instead rubbed the politician's forehead with a few dabs of Crisco while praying aloud.

Perhaps that tableau would have pleased Antonin Scalia, a conservative Catholic and Bush's favorite Supreme Court justice, who declared in 2002 that "government . . . derives its moral authority from God" and acts as the "minister of God." Acknowledging that such theories of divine dispensation conflict with democratic ideals, Scalia added rather ominously: "The reaction of people of faith to this tendency of democracy to obscure the divine authority behind government should not be resignation to it, but the resolution to combat it as effectively as possible." Scalia's medieval view of government as divinely ordained, rather than as the expression of popular sovereignty, is utterly foreign to the founding concept of the United States.

With his mimicry of an ancient theocratic rite, Ashcroft seems all too susceptible to such pious justifications for tyranny. Of course, he had every right to engage in whatever religious practice he might choose. But why would a man who swears to uphold the Constitution of the United States prepare himself by imitating the behavior of ancient Hebrew kings? Does the Attorney General believe that the Lord Almighty chose him? How would that affect his oath to uphold secular freedoms that conflict with his religious convictions?

As for Bush, his decision to appoint Ashcroft amounted to a confession of his servility to the religious right. During the earliest days of his shaky presidential mandate, he intended to name someone else as Attorney General. Bush's first choice was Mark Racicot, then Governor of Montana and later named the Republican National Committee chairman, who had spoken out forcefully on behalf of the Republicans in Florida. Despite Racicot's strong conservative credentials, however, influential figures on the religious right quickly moved against him, suspecting that he was insufficiently antiabortion and antigay.

The danger perceived by Racicot's critics was that he might prove too independent of Bush's allies on the far right. Quietly and effectively, those same forces swept him aside, circulating a report on his alleged ideological shortcomings written by Robert George, a conservative Catholic law professor at Princeton University. Karl Rove briefly attempted to save the nomination in conversations with Catholic and Protestant conservative leaders. When Rove failed to persuade them, Racicot withdrew from consideration. Within a few days, Bush announced that he had chosen Ashcroft, reliable favorite of the Falwell crowd. Little was ever said about why Racicot had withdrawn, while Bush aides pretended that Ashcroft had always been their leader's first choice. Several weeks passed before anyone in the press found out what had really happened.

When Ashcroft's name was sent up to the evenly divided Senate for confirmation, there was cloakroom talk of a filibuster to stop him. Many of his former colleagues were well aware of the Missourian's extremism. They worried that his religious views would distort policy on abortion rights, gay rights, and other aspects of the ceaseless culture war. Less attention was given to his unseemly desire to deface the document he was sworn to uphold, in ways that would undermine individual liberty—and that now seem all too relevant in hindsight.

During six years in the Senate, Ashcroft introduced or sponsored at least seven constitutional amendments. Among the many "improvements" he proposed was an amendment that would allow future amendments to be passed more easily. And, of course, he was always a leading advocate of the so-called flag-burning amendment, which would make desecration of the American flag a federal offense.

Realizing that his nomination might be in serious jeopardy, he took great care to emphasize his commitment to uphold the law regardless of his own political opinions and religious beliefs. "I well understand that the role of the Attorney General is to enforce the law as it is, not as I would have it," he said in his opening statement before the Senate Judiciary Committee. "I also know from my service that a successful attorney general must be able to listen and find common ground with leaders of diversely held viewpoints." His doubting ex-colleagues nevertheless cast a stunning forty-two nay votes when his name reached the Senate floor.

Since then, Ashcroft has provided ample and disturbing evidence that he understands little about the Constitution and feels no need to consult anyone with a different opinion about its meaning. With Bush's approval and without strong congressional opposition, the Attorney General has systematically undermined American liberties in the name of the war against terrorism. Unlike other wars, this one may have no finite duration—which could mean that the freedoms abrogated under the USA Patriot Act and various orders from Ashcroft will not be restored while this administration is in office. Depending on public fear of terrorism to intimidate the opposition, he regularly perpetrates fresh outrages against the Bill of Rights.

His current viewpoint is that the government may, at its discretion, detain any citizen indefinitely, without access to an attorney, without preferring any charges or producing any evidence, and without justifying its actions in a court of law. Since the virtually instantaneous passage of the USA Patriot Act in the fall of 2001, which greatly expanded his authority, Ashcroft has only become more contemptuous of the elected representatives who jumped at his command.

For weeks he ignored letters from Senator Patrick Leahy, then chairman of the Judiciary Committee, about the critical civil liberties issues raised by the war on terror. He brushed aside bipartisan requests that he appear on Capitol Hill to explain himself. When he finally did show up, Ashcroft ominously suggested that anyone who dared to dispute his methods was serving the cause of the terrorists.

The Bush administration's semimilitarized justice system has already detained hundreds and perhaps thousands of people without charging them with any crime. It has closed immigration hearings that were formerly public. It has detained at least two American citizens — Jose Padilla and Yaser Hamdi—without trial and without access to attorneys, on the grounds that they are both "enemy combatants." Ashcroft has suggested that in wartime, he has the authority to charge and convict American citizens in military courts. Indeed, he believes that he can hold any American without bail in a detention camp for as long as he sees fit—without charging the unfortunate citizen with any crime and without revealing to a lawyer or a court what evidentiary basis, if any, exists for that action.

According to a *Wall Street Journal* report, the Attorney General has approved procedures for overseeing and operating such camps. Jonathan Turley, a constitutional law professor at George Washington University who endorsed Ashcroft's controversial nomination, regards his plan for detention camps as an outrage. In an article demanding Ashcroft's resignation or removal, Turley said he had transformed himself "from merely being a political embarrassment to being a constitutional menace."

Questioned about his extra-constitutional conduct in Senate hearings, Ashcroft replied, "To those who scare peace-loving people with phantoms of lost liberty, my message is this: Your tactics only aid terrorists, for they erode our national unity and resolve. They give ammunition to America's enemies, and pause to America's friends." In other words, dissent is treason—the perennial answer of the authoritarian ruler, who quite often believes he was chosen by God.

Quietly but effectively, the USA Patriot Act and the other powers usurped by the executive branch have encouraged a nascent military regime. Among the collaborators with Bush and Ashcroft in this project is, unsurprisingly, Chief Justice William Rehnquist, whose court is supposed to uphold the Bill of Rights and restrain the executive branch's excesses. Selected by Nixon for his right-wing partisanship and his indifference to civil liberties, Rehnquist has abdicated his constitutional responsibilities because, quoting Cicero, he says that "in time of war, the laws are silent."

Instead of restraining Ashcroft's excesses, Rehnquist appointed a secret "special court," set up outside the federal judicial system, to oversee the administration's expanded national security apparatus. With three judges hand-selected by the Chief Justice from among veterans of the Reagan and Bush administrations, this "star chamber" has already overruled a circuit court decision that held the government had abused its power to spy on ordinary citizens. As a result, that power was expanded so that, in essence, the FBI will no longer be required to meet any significant standard of proof before invading the privacy of citizens via wiretaps or by seizing documents, computers, or other property. Those agencies will be able to spy on any citizen without permission from a judge.

Nat Hentoff, the left-libertarian commentator often celebrated by conservatives for his hatred of the Clintons and his opposition to abortion, says that Ashcroft "has subverted more elements of the Bill of Rights than any Attorney General in American history." Both he and Turley have called for congressional hearings aimed toward Ashcroft's immediate removal from office. Liberal Harvard law professor Laurence Tribe has also spoken out against the Ashcroft-Bush trashing of constitutional protections. "It bothers me that the executive branch is taking the amazing position that just on the president's say-so, any American citizen can be picked up, not just in Afghanistan, but at O'Hare Airport or on the streets of any city in this country, and locked up without access to a lawyer or court just because the government says he's connected somehow with the Taliban or al-Qaeda," Tribe said on ABC's *Nightline* in 2002. "That's not the American way."

So far, however, no conservative law professors of Tribe's stature have raised their voices in defense of constitutional liberty.

The loudest protests against Ashcroft's abuses are heard from ordinary citizens, in reliably liberal cities and towns such as Madison, Wisconsin; Santa Fe, New Mexico; Takoma Park, Maryland; and Northampton, Massachusetts, where a national Bill of Rights Defense Committee first sprang up in the winter of 2002. Town and city councils in those municipalities and dozens more passed resolutions that urge their congressional representatives to seek the repeal of unconstitutional portions of the Patriot Act—and that instruct local police and district attorneys to avoid violating the constitutional rights of local citizens. The ACLU has been advising municipal officials on steps they can take to redress Ashcroft's constitutional vandalism.

These grassroots patriots should be careful what they say and whom they speak to. Americans are still free to join political and religious groups of their choice, but the government may now continuously monitor the activities of such organizations in its domestic investigations of alleged terrorism, whether or not there is probable cause to suspect any criminal activity. In practice, this means a free hand for spying on citizen groups in what Bush calls "the homeland."

Only a tiny band of conservatives, led by *New York Times* columnist William Safire and former Representatives Bob Barr and Dick Armey, have expressed dissent over Ashcroft's constitutional depredations. All of them had enthusiastically endorsed the former Missouri senator's controversial nomination to head the Justice Department—and all of them apparently continue to support Bush despite their misgivings about Ashcroft's actions. Armey and Barr have joined the ACLU as consultants on First and Fourth Amendment issues (which shows how tolerant liberals can be of even the most obnoxious conservatives when freedom is endangered).

Conservative organizations and right-wing legal foundations have been conspicuously absent from the defense of the Bill of Rights. Instead, leaders of the Federalist Society—the powerful conservative lawyers' organization that boasts support from Scalia, Solicitor General Theodore Olson, former independent counsel Kenneth Starr, and dozens of other right-wing luminaries—have been gloating over Republican electoral victories and justifying the administration's draconian curtailment of traditional rights.

Although the government claims the right to spy on its citizens, those subjugated citizens are able to learn less and less about their government. Access to substantial information about federal agencies and actions is being shut off on orders from the top, with typical authoritarian logic. Both Bush and Ashcroft have encouraged federal bureaucracies to withhold documents and resist requests for data in the name of national security. Vice President Dick Cheney insists that neither citizens nor Congress has the right to know which corporate leaders (and Bush-Cheney donors) met with him to influence the administration's national energy policy. That master of bland effrontery, White House press secretary Ari Fleischer, justified Cheney's cover-up with a suitably insulting argument: "The very document that protects our liberties more than anything else, the Constitution, was, of course, drafted in total secrecy," said Fleischer. "The founders . . . recognized that in order to make careful decisions, they wanted to set forth a deliberative and thoughtful process and they concluded to do so quietly."

From Fleischer's robotic demeanor, it isn't always possible to tell whether he understands how spurious his pronouncements are. Someone should inform him that although the original Constitutional Convention met behind closed doors, the founders immediately published every document associated with the drafting of the Constitution, revealed the names of everyone who had been involved in its creation, and kept nothing secret, including the minutes of the debate over its provisions. Many of the participants published their diaries as well.

In contrast to that democratic spirit, the White House is seeking to shut down the Government Printing Office, the agency that has provided a central source of information from the executive and legislative branches since the earliest days of the Republic. This is billed as a cost-cutting measure, but its effect will be to curtail yet another means for citizens to secure their freedoms.

Even senators are no longer permitted to know what they are voting on when the White House claims that national security is at stake. The Senate approved the President's enormous Homeland Security Act in 2002 only two days after the draft was delivered to its offices, without a single committee hearing and with just thirty hours of debate.

"Never have I seen such a monstrous piece of legislation sent to this body," said Senator Robert Byrd of West Virginia as he prepared to cast his nay vote. "And we are being asked to vote on that 484 pages tomorrow. Our poor staffs were up most of the night studying it. They know some of the things that are in there, but they don't know all of them. It is a sham and it is a shame. We are all complicit in going along with it. I read in the paper that nobody will have the courage to vote against it. Well, Robert Byrd is going to vote against it because I don't know what I am voting for."

"Freedom" is not ramming through a monumental piece of legislation that no representative has had an opportunity to read. The American system requires checks and balances, not a rubber stamp. The rubber stamp is how business gets done in banana republics and dictator's parliaments. Business wasn't done that way in the United States Congress—until the advent of Bush and Ashcroft.

At least one of Ashcroft's nightmarish operations has been frustrated, for the time being. That was "Operation TIPS," a plan that would have encouraged average citizens—plumbers, cable repair workers, and others—to spy on their fellow Americans and report their suspicions to the government. After furious protest from liberals and honorable conservatives such as Barr and Armey, that lunatic program was removed from the Homeland Security bill.

More of the same and far worse is to be expected from the Bush administration, however. In late 2002, reports emerged from the Defense Department of an ambitious new project known as "Total Information Awareness." Funded by the Defense Advanced Research Projects Agency, which created the earliest version of the Internet, the TIA project is seeking to build a surveillance system that would be literally universal. Its working theory is that if intelligence agencies know everything, and can organize hundreds of billions of bits of information according to certain patterns, they will be able to predict and prevent future acts of terrorism.

Does that sound sufficiently megalomaniacal? Whether its scheme is feasible or not, the TIA is moving ahead with a multibillion-dollar "prototype" database technology. The scope of this scheme can only be described as Orwellian, in the sense that Orwell's fictional citizens in 1984 were under total observation by the state at all times. TIA's original logo, appropriately, was the all-seeing mystical eye atop a pyramid that adorns the Great Seal of the United States (and the U.S. dollar).

The TIA's omniscient gaze makes libertarians like William Safire nervous, for good reason. "Every purchase you make with a credit card, every magazine subscription you buy and medical prescription you fill, every Web site you visit and e-mail you send or receive, every academic grade you receive, every bank deposit you make, every trip you book and every event you attend—all these transactions and communications will go into what the Defense Department describes as 'a virtual, centralized grand database,'" he wrote after learning about the project. The TIA bureaucrats would seize all of those documents electronically, not bothering with such archaic formalities as a search warrant.

There were reassurances from the TIA project's director that it would ensure citizen privacy while scouring public and private databases. Nobody felt very reassured, however, in part because the director is John Poindexter, retired Admiral and former National Security Adviser in the Reagan White House. Poindexter left government service under a thunderous black cloud, having narrowly avoided a prison sentence for lying to Congress and destroying documents in the Iran-Contra scandal. He is now rewarded by the son of the President who did so much to cover up the inner secrets of Iran-Contra. George W. Bush expects the public to trust this liar and felon—whose conviction was overturned on a technicality—with the most powerful surveillance technology ever built. If it weren't true it would be unbelievable.

Several years ago, a member of the U.S. Senate stood up to denounce controversial demands by Clinton administration officials for new invasive powers of surveillance over the Internet. While conceding that some additional measures to curtail crime and terror might be necessary, the senator insisted that fundamental freedoms could not be compromised: "These needs must be addressed, but the provisions must not destroy our constitutional liberties, including the First, Fourth, and Fifth Amendments," said the senator. "But frankly, no amendment to the Constitution needs more protection than any other. They all must be respected and protected at the highest levels."

The senator went on to describe the Clinton administration's awful plans, which sound almost quaint in comparison with John Poindexter's godlike surveillance machine. The federal government would "have the capability to read any international or domestic computer communications. The FBI wants access to decode, digest, and discuss financial transactions, personal e-mail, and proprietary information sent abroad—all in the name of national security. To accomplish this, President Clinton would like government agencies to have the keys for decoding all exported U.S. software and Internet communications."

In this scheme, the senator discerned the frightening face of Big Brother looming over the Internet: "The protections of the Fourth Amendment are clear. The right to protection from unlawful searches is an indivisible American value. Two hundred years of court decisions have stood in defense of this fundamental right. The state's interest in effective crime-fighting should never vitiate the citizens' Bill of Rights."

That impassioned spokesman for civil liberties was Senator John Ashcroft of Missouri. His lofty encomium to liberty may have been inspired by practical concerns beyond his sheer dedication to the Constitution. In addition to unaccustomed praise from civil libertarians, Ashcroft received generous contributions from the computer industry and the top Republican lobbyists hired by the industry to protect its technology from government intrusions.

Now that he and his fellow ideologues are in power, the Missouri conservative seems unconcerned about those two centuries of court decisions against unlawful searches. He no longer worries much about federal intrusions upon the Bill of Rights.

If Ashcroft is corrupted by power, what happened to all the other conservatives who claim to love liberty? Where are all the right-wing alarmists who heard the thump of the jackboot in every campus speech code? Where are those great libertarians who warned us against the encroachments of "political correctness," now that a Republican administration is creating an omniscient surveillance agency and a system of detention without trial? At least Bob Barr and Dick Armey are speaking up. They have joined all those often-mocked liberals at the American Civil Liberties Union—the nation's first, last, and best friends of freedom.

6 PRIVATE LIVES AND PUBLIC LIES

"Conservatives protect family values and moral virtue, while liberals promote immorality and vice."

That so many right-wingers can still preach about "family values" and "declining American morality" without dissolving in laughter is a testament to their mental discipline. No matter how many of the right's virtuecrats are caught committing the sins they claim to condemn, they continue to pretend that they're lecturing the rest of us from the moral high ground.

Are these bogus moralizers trying to deceive themselves as well as the rest of us? Or are they simply relying on the willingness of millions of Americans to be duped? It is remarkable indeed that those trusting herds remain convinced of the moral superiority of conservatism, giving their money to ranting televangelists and their votes to ostentatiously pious politicians. Such credulous folk must be unaware of the evidence that traditional morals are declining more rapidly and more precipitously on the right—and in the so-called red states—than anywhere else.

As *New York Times* columnist Paul Krugman noted not long ago, "the red states do a bit worse than the blue states when you look at indicators of individual responsibility and commitment to family. Children in red states are more likely to be born to teenagers or unmarried mothers; in 1999, 33.7 percent of babies in red states were born out of wedlock, versus 32.5 percent in blue states. National divorce statistics are spotty, but per capita there were 60 percent more divorces in Montana than in New Jersey."

Actually, the available divorce data show that marital breakdown is now considerably more common in the Bible Belt than in the secular Northeast. During the "decadent" Clinton years, that trend was somewhat mitigated by nationwide improvements in social indicators, including teenage pregnancy and drug abuse as well as divorce. While those changes provided a respite from two decades of increasing social trouble, they were more attributable to better economic opportunities and higher family incomes than to sermons by fundamentalist clergymen. The percentages of broken families and unwed mothers remained higher in places like Arkansas and Oklahoma than in New York and Massachusetts.

Yet the myth of conservative moral superiority persists, in part because a lucrative ideological industry depends on the perpetuation of that comforting fiction. The annual revenues of politicized ministries such as the Family Research Council and the Christian Broadcasting Network, for example, are in the hundreds of millions annually; similar amounts finance Republican political committees, conservative lobbies, foundations, and assorted righteous causes, all in the name of morality.

All but the most naïve conservatives understand that sinners are evenly distributed across the political spectrum. But the business of politics requires them to pretend that they are purer than the rest of us—especially those libertine liberals. That was why Dinesh D'Souza so smarmily advised Democrats in November 2002 to be true to themselves in future campaigns—by confessing that they are "the party of moral degeneracy," and forthrightly advocating "divorce, illegitimacy, adultery, homosexuality, bestiality, and pornography."

The right derives psychic profit as well as money from its moral mythology. Imagery of licentious liberals and depraved Democrats provides a convenient scapegoat for every guilty conservative's spiritual angst. The more profoundly immoral a conservative sinner feels, the more loudly he or she will bleat about the immorality of liberals. (Among the prime examples of this syndrome were those raunchy televangelists Jim Bakker and Jimmy Swaggart; another is former House Speaker and serial adulterer Newt Gingrich, whose case is examined more closely below.) An epidemic of neurotic projection in right-wing circles has also fostered a virulent strain of paranoia about immoral conspiracies by "antifamily" liberals.

Paranoids on the right imagine a progressive plot against the heterosexual family. Reproductive rights, women's rights, and gay rights (all of which help real families to remain cohesive and strong) are cited constantly in right-wing literature as evidence of this satanic scheme. The conservatives mesmerized by this ideological construct don't seem to notice that, year after year, liberal Democrats grow up in traditional families, get married, and raise children, who then do the same. These perfectly ordinary citizens, according to the "antifamily" dogma, are in fact sinister social termites gnawing away at the foundations of human civilization.

For some reason female commentators on the right—particularly those ubiquitous miniskirted blondes—seem particularly excited by this overwrought theory. Yet there is plenty of reason to doubt that these women conform to any strictly conservative code of conduct in their personal lives. Ann Coulter and Laura Ingraham may idolize Phyllis Schlafly, but they aren't known to be models for her "abstinence education" campaign. Why should they be? The unmarried pundits know that sexual abstinence (like strict sobriety and profound piety) is for the poor rubes who stay home watching the *700 Club*, not for urbane young Republicans hanging out in saloons on Capitol Hill and the Upper East Side.

For these high-minded conservatives, morality represents a political bludgeon rather than a religious inspiration. So they and their friends delight in bilious gossip about the private lives of liberal Democrats.

Laura Ingraham first embraced the politics of personal destruction when she edited the *Dartmouth Review*, a scabrous periodical published by conservative students at her alma mater. Among the *Review*'s most tempting targets—aside from gay students its editors "outed" without their permission—was a young minister then serving as the college's associate chaplain. In a series of mocking articles, the paper raised questions about the liberal minister's marital status and his possible involvement with another woman. At the time, Ingraham defended this witless smear as an acceptable form of "satire." After the minister filed a libel lawsuit claiming $3 million in damages, however, the *Review* settled the case by publishing an abject apology. In 1999, after establishing herself as a television commentator on the subject of President Clinton's sex life, Ingraham wrote a book-length diatribe about the Clintons' troubled marriage, whose publication was timed to damage Hillary Rodham Clinton's 2000 Senate campaign. It did more harm to author than subject.

The junior senator from New York likewise enrages Ann Coulter, who compared her with a "prostitute" on cable television when Clinton was still First Lady. Debasing political discourse and promoting pornographic images comes naturally to conservatives of Coulter's stripe. Vulgarity serves their political agenda, even as they pretend to fret about the sexual coarseness of American culture. Coulter once told an interviewer on Fox News Channel that "Clinton is in love with the erect penis." (The *Starr Report*, replete with inserted cigars and other raunchy imagery that the prudish independent counsel insisted on publishing, is the indelible classic of conservative public pornography.) The fact that the Clintons have kept their family together for more than twenty years, and raised a smart, thriving daughter, somehow eludes these carping harpies.

The perennially single, career-obsessed Coulter insists that Hillary Clinton and other feminists are advancing a left-wing conspiracy to abolish the family. "Liberals seek to destroy sexual differentiation in order to destroy morality," she writes. The proof of their immorality is that "liberals refuse to condemn what societies have condemned for thousands of years—e.g., promiscuity, divorce, illegitimacy, homosexuality."

Coulter only poses as a "Christian" scourge to fleece her gullible fans—who might be distressed to learn that in sinful Manhattan, where she chose to live, she dated the son of *Penthouse* publisher Bob Guccione, and many of her closest friends are gay men. (Occasionally the party girl peeks out from behind the moralistic mask, as on the evening when she told the viewers of *Rivera Live*: "Let's say I go out every night, I meet a guy and have sex with him. Good for me. I'm not married.")

It's certainly true that liberals don't reflexively condemn gays and lesbians, unmarried parents, the promiscuous, or the divorced. It's true that conservatives do condemn such people, vigorously and often. And it is nevertheless also true that conservatives indulge in promiscuous sex, both straight and gay; that conservatives get divorced, sometimes repeatedly; and that conservatives—or at least a few high-profile conservative politicians—have been known to produce babies unblessed by wedlock.

If the right can't quite adhere to its professed purity, the left doesn't quite live up to its rakish reputation, either. There are plenty of boringly (and happily) married Democrats, even in New York and Hollywood. But liberals usually aren't as judgmental as conservatives about human weakness, and tend to accept if not admire the libidinal foibles of their leaders, from FDR to JFK to Martin Luther King Jr. With their tolerant humanism—or their tolerant religious faith—liberals tend to be more realistic than conservatives who profess a phony Puritanism.

After seeing so many of these reactionary clowns caught with their pants around their ankles (and on fire), it should be obvious that the public figures who most ardently denounce sin are often the most abandoned sinners. They only exceed their private shame with their public shamelessness. What America lacks today is a modern Molière or Mark Twain capable of doing literary justice to these moral impostors.

A striking example of their brazenness came to light a few weeks before Election Day 2002. On a Monday morning in October, a press release announcing the latest emergency mobilization of Christian voters buzzed over the wires. (The term *Christian* in such releases invariably denotes far-right Republican fundamentalism, as if the Gospel were in fact a political doctrine that the Lord revealed exclusively to conservatives.) The sponsor of this preelection crusade, an organization known as America 21, was calling upon pastors around the country to join its "Margin of Victory" project and to take up the mission of bringing stray fundamentalists to the polls on Election Day.

Operating under Section 527 the federal election code—a legal loophole that allows large, anonymous donations to be funneled into advocacy campaigns—America 21 looked like a front for the House Republican leadership. In fact, it bore a suspicious resemblance to the Republican Majority Issues Committee, an outfit created for the 2000 election under the auspices of House Whip Tom DeLay. America 21 and the Republican Majority Issues Committee shared the same GOP attorney, and the RMIC's secretary-treasurer became America 21's president.

By far the most interesting person involved with America 21, however, was its chairwoman. In an open letter to the pastors, deacons, and elders of America's churches on the group's Web site, she warned that "we're losing the moral high ground in this country." At stake in the upcoming election was nothing less than "whether godly leaders will control the agenda and the policy in the U.S. Congress." The name at the bottom of the letter was Helen Chenoweth-Hage.

The former member of Congress from Idaho should be familiar to anyone who still recalls the seamier sideshows of the impeachment drama. It was back then that Helen Chenoweth (minus the added surname of her second husband) briefly became notorious for the sort of uninhibited misbehavior that made Republicans smirk and scowl about Bill Clinton. Like several other right-wing politicians who were most determined to humiliate and destroy the President, Chenoweth had concealed a history of adultery that emerged at a very inconvenient moment.

The startling details of Chenoweth's naughty past received little coverage in the national media—perhaps because, like her, so many of her upright colleagues suddenly found themselves facing the sharp end of their own supposed outrage. First, an angry husband told Salon.com about his ex-wife's eight-year adulterous affair with Illinois Representative Henry Hyde, who brushed off the admittedly truthful story as a "youthful indiscretion." Rapidly following the Salon exposé of Hyde came revelations about the private peccadilloes of Indiana's Dan Burton, Georgia's Bob Barr, Idaho's Chenoweth, and then, finally and most spectacularly, the new Speaker of the House, Robert Livingston of Louisiana—whose multiple infidelities were about to be unveiled by pornographer Larry Flynt when Livingston abruptly resigned on the floor of Congress.

The characteristics that all these worthies had in common, apart from party and ideology, were the bad habits of trumpeting their own virtue and questioning the morality of their opponents. All enjoyed the fervent support of the Christian Coalition, Concerned Women for America, and kindred entities of the religious right. (Livingston liked to boast that his Christian Coalition rating was 100 percent.) All had spoken out fervently and frequently on behalf of family values.

And all of them had taken a long walk on the wild side.

A pert brunette grandmother in her fifties, Helen Chenoweth hardly looked the part of a sexual buccaneer. She was the feisty, gun-loving heroine of the militia movement who had helped to launch the hard-line Idaho Family Forum. After toiling many years for other candidates in her home state, she was elected to Congress in the "revolutionary" class of 1994 because of a sex scandal involving the Democratic incumbent. Also helpful to her campaign had been the distribution of 300,000 religious-right "voter guides" in evangelical, Catholic, and Mormon churches, which portrayed Chenoweth as the embodiment of resistance to abortion, homosexuality, pornography, and feminism. She was family values personified.

But the insiders who had observed the state's most outspoken pro-family politicians after hours weren't surprised by the revelation of Chenoweth's extramarital frolics. In her first big political job, she had served as chief of staff to Steve Symms (the senator who falsely accused Kitty Dukakis in 1988 of having burned the American flag). Like

Chenoweth, he took hard-right positions on all the social and environmental issues. What distinguished Symms in Washington, however,
was his hyperactive social life.

In the Senate cloakroom, as one Idaho columnist put it, "Symms
had a better reputation for drafting attractive female companions than
for drafting legislation." He blew his chances for reelection in 1992
by divorcing his very ill wife after thirty years of marriage. His political
obituary was an editorial in the *Idaho Statesman*, which recalled how
Symms had "posed as somebody morally superior to people whose
families come apart at a time when he was pulling his own family
apart. . . . That puts him in the same league with the evangelist who
preaches faithful marriage while prowling seedy motels."

Six years later, Chenoweth surpassed her old boss in hypocrisy. During the midterm campaign in the fall of 1998, she posed in her own
television commercial as the righteous scourge of the philandering
President she had voted to impeach. "Our founding fathers knew that
political leaders' personal conduct must be held to the highest standards," she intoned gravely. "President Clinton's behavior has severely
damaged his ability to lead our nation, and the free world. To restore
honor in public office, and the trust of the American people, we must
affirm that personal conduct does count, and integrity matters."

That stirring advertisement provoked a reporter in Idaho, who had
long heard whispers about Chenoweth's many affairs with married and
unmarried men. He asked her directly about an alleged liaison with
her former business partner, another right-wing extremist and family-
values poseur named Vern Ravenscroft.

According to the *Spokane Spokesman-Review*, she had "blatantly
lied" when she denied the same rumor to one of its reporters in 1995.
Three years later, faced with confirmations by Ravenscroft and his
wife, she admitted that her affair with him had begun in 1978, after
Chenoweth's divorce, and continued until 1984. "Fourteen years ago,
when I was a private citizen and a single woman, I was involved in a
relationship that I came to regret, that I'm not proud of," said the
congresswoman in a very short statement. "I've asked for God's for-

giveness, and I've received it." (God was not available for comment.)

Whatever reassurances Chenoweth may have received from the Almighty, *godly* was not the term used to describe the congresswoman by the wronged wife who squealed to a local newspaper. "I don't know how Helen can live with herself," said Mrs. Ravenscroft of the Clinton-bashing ad.

When journalist David Neiwert later interviewed veteran journalists in her home state, he discovered that Chenoweth's wantonness almost certainly exceeded her one acknowledged lapse. A political reporter told Neiwert, on the day she made her curt confession, that "there were a lot of nervous legislators down at the Statehouse." Neiwert also quoted a quip by an Idaho GOP political operative who apparently shared the insider opinion of her intelligence and virtue: "Helen is living proof that you can fuck your brains out."

The smutty tales about Republicans infuriated Washington conservatives and their allies in the national press corps, who by then had spent six years completely engrossed in filth about Bill and Hillary Clinton. They could dish it out but—when the spotlight suddenly turned to Chenoweth's promiscuity, and Henry Hyde's breaking up of someone else's marriage, and Dan Burton's illegitimate son, and Bob Livingston's baroque sex life—they couldn't take it. Tom DeLay demanded that the journalists who dared to write about Republican peccadilloes be investigated for "obstructing justice." Cable TV hosts, talk radio jocks, and print columnists bemoaned the eruption of "sexual McCarthyism" and worried that prominent media figures might be next.

Eventually, calm was restored in the nation's capital. With the end of the press's brief, frenzied feeding on conservative moral lapses came the postponement, for a while, of the unveiling of that king of hypocrites, Newt Gingrich. The former Speaker's rise and fall is a modern epic of spurious moralizing.

Gingrich defined his own fraudulence in the methods he used to achieve power. A central theme of his propaganda lexicon was the "breakdown in public manners and morals" he blamed on liberalism. He recommended that when Republicans discussed themselves and their party's values, they should use words such as *moral, crusade,* and *family.* When they talked about Democrats, he urged them to emphasize terms like *decay, sick, liberal, permissive attitude, antifamily,* and *bizarre.*

As he drove the Republicans toward their takeover of Congress, the portly firebrand plugged his movement's morality with evangelistic fervor. "You have absolutely, in the abstract, a cultural civil war going on," he told *US News & World Report* in 1992. "A nihilistic hedonism and secular belief pattern is by definition involved in a religious war with a spiritual system."

While he blathered on about the culture war, Gingrich's close associates waged a private jihad on Bill Clinton. In the closing months of the 1992 election, Chicago financier Peter Smith, a top contributor to Gingrich's GOPAC fund, hired the Georgian's consultant and confidant Eddie Mahe and two Gingrich lawyers to dredge up dirt about the Democratic nominee's sex life. They focused on a far-fetched tale about an affair with a black prostitute in Little Rock that had produced a male "love child." Their objective was an old-fashioned sexual smear, tinted with race.

Gingrich kept a safe distance from his friends' dirtiest tricks, but he didn't hesitate to launch broad smears of the Democrats. Just days before the 1994 election that made him House Speaker, he spoke up about the drowning of her two children by a young South Carolina woman named Susan Smith. "I think that the mother killing the two children in South Carolina vividly reminds every American how sick the society is getting and how much we need to change things," he said. "The only way you get change is to vote Republican. That's the message for the last three days." In other words, liberal Democrats were somehow responsible for the Smith children's terrible death.

Sensational facts about the incident soon emerged that suggested quite the opposite. Smith was neither a feminist nor a welfare mother; she wasn't even a Democrat. She was the stepdaughter of an affluent local stockbroker named Beverly Russell, who also happened to be the county chairman of the Christian Coalition and a member of the

South Carolina Republican Party's executive committee. The nephew of a former governor and senator, he was just the kind of wealthy, well-connected gentleman cultivated by politicians like Gingrich. He even sang in the local Methodist Church choir.

At home, however, Bev Russell wasn't quite the ideal dad. Court records revealed that he had sexually molested his stepdaughter regularly after she turned fifteen. He had continued having sex with her for the following eight years—despite her two suicide attempts—until the weeks preceding her crime. While Russell's personal ideology had nothing to do with his monstrous behavior, he certainly shared the flair for sanctimony that is common among leaders of the political and religious right. "Of course, had I known at that time what the result of my sin would be, I would have mustered the strength to behave according to my responsibility," he said after the press exposed his relationship with his stepdaughter. If this grotesque tale left any impression on Gingrich, he never mentioned it. He was still exploiting family tragedy as propaganda a year later, when he blamed "the left" and "the welfare state" for the slashing murder of a mother and her children in Illinois.

Meanwhile, Gingrich himself was indulging in a reckless extramarital affair with a much younger woman. She was a House Republican staff member named Callista Bisek. When their romance began in 1993, she was twenty-seven years old and he was fifty. While the new Speaker trysted with the nubile staffer, conservative analysts like Bill Kristol were describing the Republican takeover as an almost biblical renovation of Congress. "You could make a case that they came to the majority," Kristol said, "because they tapped into a deep sense that the country was morally and culturally in trouble."

It would be interesting to know whether Kristol was aware of Gingrich's mistress back then. Many leading conservatives in Washington surely knew about Bisek—including her name and her job—virtually from the beginning. By early 1995, whispers about Bisek and Gingrich had reached the offices of the *Nation* magazine and a syndicated tabloid television program, both of which sought to obtain proof of the relationship. Although those efforts were unsuccessful, it is clear that people quite distant from the Speaker's immediate orbit were aware of his debauchery.

In the permissive atmosphere of the House Republican Conference, Gingrich pursued his illicit affair while an epidemic of ruined marriages swept through the freshman class of 1994. These Republicans weren't quite the Puritan paragons that Gingrich had sold to a gullible electorate. A month after the first anniversary of their "revolution," in December 1995, the *Los Angeles Times* assessed the moral damage: "Four freshman marriages have fallen apart. At least two more are on the rocks. And the House cloakroom is rampant with reports of more impending separations and tales of infidelity."

Again the most scandalous behavior could be found not among the supposedly decadent Democrats, but in the very proper precincts of the pious Republicans. Despite the growing popularity of the House Bible study caucus, there seemed to be no end to the sad burlesque of "family values" in the 104th Congress.

Jim Bunn, an Oregon freshman boosted into office by the Christian Coalition, dumped his wife of seventeen years before the end of his first year in Washington. The announcement came amid rumors of Bunn's infidelity in the Portland press. The following August, he married his chief of staff. Before his plans to divorce became public, Bunn had briefly considered running for the Senate seat vacated by sexual harasser Bob Packwood. To win the race against a liberal Democratic divorcee in 1994, he had relied on his image as a "deeply rooted family man." That wouldn't work again.

Jim Nussle of Iowa, a Gingrich protégé who had managed the transition during the Republican takeover of the House, left his wife and two children in July 1996. His office issued a brief statement that asked family and friends to keep the congressman in "their continued thoughts and prayers." (Several years later, Nussle married an attractive lobbyist.)

Other freshmen soon joined the list of broken vows, including Jim Longley of Maine, Enid Waldholtz Green of Utah, and, a year or so later, Joe Scarborough of Florida. The most startling split involved Jon and Meredith Christensen, a former insurance salesman from Nebraska and the wealthy Texas beauty queen he had married.

The Christensens were the golden couple of Gingrich's "revolution." With no political experience, Christensen had risen full-blown from an influential Omaha church, winning over the Republican and fundamentalist voters with his good looks and sincere recitation of profamily clichés. He vanquished the Democratic incumbent, who labeled him a "radical right extremist," with eager assistance from GOPAC and the Christian Coalition. For her part, Meredith did more than look pretty at Jon's side; she also raised a lot of money.

Their tumble into disrepute was dizzying. Christensen was soon being derided as one of the "dimmest bulbs" in the House. More humiliating, however, were the rumors of forbidden intimacies between Meredith and one or more of her husband's colleagues.

When their divorce went public in September 1995, she admitted in court papers that she had been unfaithful, although she didn't reveal with whom. It was widely believed that her confession was part of a deal to help her ex-husband keep his congressional seat in exchange for surrendering any claims to her money. He was defeated in 1996 anyway.

Not many members of the class of '94 were willing to talk about this plague of domestic misery. Rather than take responsibility, they tried to blame the divorce rate on a heavy congressional workload— as if nobody else in America coped with a demanding schedule. They complained about gossip spread by the Democrats, who tried to keep the irresistible gloating quiet. And despite all the emotional turmoil on Capitol Hill, none of Gingrich's cronies snitched on the swaggering, caddish Speaker. Although *Vanity Fair* published an account of his past infidelities that hinted at the Bisek liaison, the story quickly faded.

Only after a Republican leadership coup forced his resignation in late 1998 did Gingrich finally abandon the fiction of his marriage. He had dedicated his memoir, *Lessons Learned the Hard Way*, to his wife, Marianne, along with his daughters, his mother, and his mother-in-law. It featured eight photos of Newt with Marianne, including a classic pose of the couple cutting their wedding cake in 1981 and a candid shot of them holding hands in the Washington Metro. One of the captions called her "the woman I love . . . my best friend and closest advisor."

In May 1999, exactly a year after *Lessons* appeared on the *New York Times* best-seller list, Gingrich called his wife at her mother's home. He wished his mother-in-law a happy birthday, and then asked to speak to Marianne. Over the telephone, he informed her that he wanted a divorce. She later said she was shocked — but what did she expect from a man who had dropped the divorce papers on his first wife while she lay in a hospital bed recovering from ovarian cancer?

Even then, Newt Gingrich had not yet reached the nadir of his swinishness. When the divorce proceedings began, he accused his wife of abandoning him and taking a lover, in order to justify his own adultery. That still wasn't the bottom, though. After his wedding to Callista Bisek, Gingrich asked the Catholic diocese of Atlanta to annul his nineteen-year marriage to Marianne.

The former Speaker never released his reply to the question put to him by his second wife's attorney, before their divorce was settled and the documents sealed: "Do you believe that you have conducted your private life in this marriage in accordance with the concept of 'family values' you have espoused politically and professionally?"

Considering the grossness of his misconduct, Gingrich escaped almost unscathed. No less than Clinton, he had let down his supporters — and considering what he always claimed to represent, his offenses were arguably far worse. Yet nobody held him accountable, because his indifference to the moral absolutes he preached was so pervasive among his conservative peers.

The same could be said of the upper reaches of the conservative media. Right-wing broadcasters and pundits were always eager to pour scorn on the adulterous Clinton and to mock his wronged wife, but they didn't pillory Gingrich for his iniquities. And if they had wanted to, who among them could cast the first stone? Gingrich's pal Rush Limbaugh has been divorced twice himself, and his third wife is an aerobics instructor from Florida he met on the Internet. John Mc-Laughlin, a former Jesuit priest, is on his second marriage and has settled at least one sexual harassment lawsuit brought by a former employee. The columnist and television commentator George Will's first wife reportedly put his office furniture and other baggage out of their suburban Maryland home when she discovered his affair with another conservative journalist.

Conservatism's prominent philanderers—obviously a powerful contingent—feel answerable to no one. They rarely condescend to discuss their own personal affairs in public, and when they do, what they invariably emphasize is the enormous difference between their secret lives and the impeachable misbehavior of that scoundrel Bill Clinton. As Gingrich angrily told a reporter for the *New York Times Magazine*, "I wasn't lying under oath. I've been through two divorce depositions in my life and I told the truth both times, because you swear to tell the truth." That may not be the opinion held by his former wives. The truly salient difference from Clinton is that Gingrich and his fellow right-wing swingers weren't subjected to a phony political sex lawsuit and a partisan prosecution.

The former Speaker is a discarded hero, but the politicians he left behind on Capitol Hill had similar faults. Tim Hutchinson, for example, offered the Gingrich argument when discussing his vote to impeach Clinton. Hutchinson is the brother of former House impeachment manager (and current Undersecretary for Homeland Security) Asa Hutchinson. He is a graduate of fundamentalist Bob Jones University, a past winner of the Christian Coalition's Friend of the Family award, and the cofounder of a Christian educational academy. He is also the ex-husband of a wife to whom he was married for twenty-nine years, having left her to marry a much younger aide in his Washington office.

Trying to convince his Arkansas constituents to return him to the Senate in 2002—against an upstanding moderate Democrat—Hutchinson explained that he had been "more judgmental and more sanctimonious" before his scandalous divorce. But there is no evidence that he or any of his conservative colleagues have learned much from their humbling experiences except that it's better not to get caught. Hutchinson was caught and lost his seat.

An encyclopedia of raunchy fables could be based on the hidden lives of American conservatives. Excavating their secrets is an unpleasant, mentally exhausting task. But be assured that the incidents mentioned in this chapter don't begin to exhaust this tragicomic genre, which also encompasses: the sex-crazed evangelists Jim Bakker and Jimmy Swaggart; the sex-crazed, messianic, and dangerous Korean evangelist Sun Myung Moon, whose extramarital affairs, illegitimate son, personal violence, and routinely bizarre behavior have been revealed by his former daughter-in-law; the very public infidelity of former New York Mayor Rudy Giuliani; the bizarre mother-daughter love affairs of *Wall Street Journal* polemicist John Fund; the awful secret of George Roche III, president of right-wing Hillsdale College and long-time lover of his son's wife, who ended their affair by killing herself; the criminal perversion of Earl "Butch" Kimmerling, midwestern crusader against gay adoption, who sexually abused his foster children; the extramarital affair that forced the resignation of Mike Trout, cohost of Focus on the Family's radio program; the disgrace of Jon Grunseth, conservative Republican candidate for Minnesota governor, whose political career ended after he allegedly swam nude with his teenage daughter's friends; the old-fashioned lechery of rising Georgia Republican Mike Bowers, whose "profamily" campaign for governor crashed when his ten-year affair with his secretary was exposed; the nude Internet pictures and estranged family of Dr. Laura Schlessinger, ultra-judgmental radio personality; the drunken hot-tub prom party enlivened by Packers tight end Mark Chmura, an outspoken social conservative once groomed for elected office by Wisconsin Republicans; the curiously "intense relationship" between married Republican Representative Bill Thomas of California and pharmaceutical lobbyist Deborah Steelman (who once testified that she had left her first husband, GOP consultant Don Sipple, because he beat her up); the comeuppance of right-wing fundraiser Richard Delgaudio, the man who introduced Paula Jones to America, and more recently pled guilty to child pornography charges; and the amazing survival of Representative Ken Calvert, another California Republican, who was arrested with a prostitute in 1994 but continues to serve in Congress, with perfect scores from the Christian Coalition and other conservative groups. ("We can't forgive what occurred between the President and Lewinsky," Calvert barked during the impeachment crisis.)

The above isn't even an exhaustive list of the heterosexual cases. And then there are the gays.

No matter how vehemently right-wingers claim to loathe homosexuality, the history of modern conservatism in America begins in the crowded closet of fifties anti-Communism, with J. Edgar Hoover, Whittaker Chambers, and Roy Cohn, the right-wing attorney and Reagan confidant who condemned gays until the day he died of AIDS. Nobody has come up with a satisfactory explanation for the prevalence of gay men in the conservative movement, but it is a reality as undeniable as the movement's hostility to homosexual rights.

Senator Orrin Hatch, the Utah Republican, once called Democrats "the party of homosexuals." Hatch should take an inventory of the Republican closet before he says that again. Quite a few of conservatism's leading figures have been gay, including the late Marvin Liebman, a direct-mail innovator; Congressman Robert Bauman, the founder of Young Americans for Freedom and chairman of the American Conservative Union; the late Terry Dolan, who chaired the National Conservative Political Action Committee; Arthur Finkelstein, the legendary Republican political consultant and scourge of liberalism whose clients included Jesse Helms, Alfonse D'Amato, and dozens of other "profamily" legislators (who now lives in suburban Boston with his male lover and adopted son); and of course David Brock, the celebrated journalistic "hit man" whose moral reversal led him to write *Blinded by the Right*, an exposé of himself and his former associates.

Brock describes an extensive underground network of gays in the Republican Party, on Capitol Hill, and in Washington's conservative organizations, including a number of still-closeted congressmen. A hint of that network emerged several years ago, when Gingrich's lieutenants launched a campaign of homosexual innuendo against then Speaker Tom Foley. When openly gay Representative Barney Frank of

Massachusetts warned that he would begin outing gay Republicans if the attacks on Foley continued, they ended overnight.

A handful of openly gay Republicans are active in the party, but most elected officials still shun them. Meanwhile, the same hypocrisy that plagues the straight conservatives is prevalent among the gays. Two recent episodes illustrate this pathetic paradox.

John Paulk was the most famous "ex-gay" man in the world. As the director of the largest religious right ministry that seeks to "convert" lesbians and gays to heterosexuality (and Christian fundamentalism), Paulk had appeared on *Oprah* and *60 Minutes*. But on September 19, 2000, he was photographed inside one of Washington's most notorious gay bars. Suspended but ultimately forgiven by Focus on the Family boss James Dobson, who blamed Paulk's downfall on "Satan," Paulk claimed that he had stepped into the bar because "I felt comfortable there." But nobody in the gay community believed that Paulk, married to an "ex-lesbian," had just stopped in for a glass of lemonade.

Not so easily forgiven was Matt Glavin of the Southeastern Legal Foundation, a protégé of former Representative Bob Barr whose tax-exempt group pursued the Clinton scandals relentlessly, even after the impeachment failed. Among the other causes adopted by Glavin were keeping the Boy Scouts strictly straight and denying full employment benefits to gay couples.

"I also was a Boy Scout and an Explorer," he said primly on Fox News to explain why he had filed a "friend of the court" brief backing the youth organization's homosexual ban. "The Boy Scouts have a very clear message of high moral character." But in October 2000 — several months after Glavin urged the Supreme Court to uphold the Scouts' moral purity — a federal officer charged him with public indecency. The undercover park ranger said that during an encounter on a trail known for gay cruising in Chattahoochee National Park, Glavin had masturbated in his presence and "fondled" the ranger's crotch. The court documents revealed that Glavin was a two-time loser. He had been arrested on similar charges in 1996, fined $1,000, and ordered by a judge to stay out of the park while he was on six months probation.

While denying the charges, Glavin resigned, as he put it, "to protect my family."

No self-respecting liberal would argue that the left has any monopoly on morality. Any such claim would not survive mention of Ted Kennedy, Jesse Jackson, and Bill Clinton. What liberals do claim is that they care about families and children just as much as conservatives do — and that their more tolerant, humane policies do more to help families than the selfish and self-righteous approach of the Republican right.

The repressive attitudes endorsed by conservatism don't change human behavior. Forcing gays into the closet and forbidding them to marry only harms them and their families, while doing nothing to preserve anyone else's family. Depriving teenagers of sex education and contraception doesn't keep them from having sex, but merely exposes them to risks of unwanted pregnancy and disease. Creating legal barriers to divorce won't save marriages, but will foster adultery, misery, and domestic violence.

What can we do to "save the family?" Liberal Democrats assist families — and "the family" — by relieving the economic and social pressures that tear apart so many poor and middle-class households. The Social Security Act and Medicare allow younger generations to care for elderly parents without depriving their own children. Student loans give parents hope for the next generation. Family and medical leave legislation lets working people care for children and spouses without losing their employment. The earned income tax credit provides sufficient income for the working poor to form decent households and feed their kids.

There are, in fact, dozens of ways that the liberal welfare state helps families to maintain stability, take care of each other, keep themselves adequately housed, and advance the next generation. More broadly, liberal policies that spread the benefits of economic growth across society help families to form and grow, and forestall the social decay that always worsens in hard times. The real enemies of the family are conservatives who seek to polarize income upward, to rip away the social safety net, and to impose an antiquated moral code that they only pretend to honor themselves.

7

TOKENS OF
THEIR ESTEEM

"Conservatives believe in color-
blind equality, while liberals cynically exploit the victimization of
blacks and other minorities."

Nowhere have Republicans failed quite so spectacularly in recent years as in their strange, fitful, sometimes duplicitous attempts to win over black Americans to their party and its conservative ideology. They have enjoyed slightly more success among Latinos and Asian-Americans, but the results of Republican outreach in those communities have hardly been impressive. Conservative publicists blather on enthusiastically about the churchgoing, upwardly mobile, moralistic minorities who will or should be trending rightward—but elections come and go without any substantial Republican gains in any of those communities.

When minority voter turnout increases, it is always the Democrats who win. Before Election Day 2000, some polls suggested that George W. Bush might win 17 percent of the black vote. The black vote went up from previous elections, but Bush won less than 10 percent—the worst showing by any presidential candidate in almost four decades.

Why do ethnic minorities, especially blacks, so emphatically repudiate the right? Why do those same groups perennially prefer liberal Democrats? For conservatives these are painful questions, to which there can be easy answers or honest answers. Honesty demands a degree of introspection and accountability about race that most conservatives prefer to avoid. The easy, morally convenient, self-flattering, and strongly preferred explanation is that it's all the liberals' fault.

According to conservative demonology, liberals maintain the allegiance of more than nine out of ten black Americans by exploiting their fears, pandering to their grievances, and discriminating against whites. Conservatives cannot compete in the black community because they uphold color-blind principle, civil equality, and the Constitution — or some such self-serving pap.

The first misconception that must be discarded is that Republicans abhor racial preferences and affirmative action in favor of "merit." Some do, perhaps; many don't. Consider the country-club Republicans, whose leisure haunts prefer white Protestants to Jews and blacks. Consider the Ivy League and prep-school Republicans, whose educational institutions confer preferences on alumni offspring, an overwhelmingly white and not necessarily highly qualified category of applicants. Or better still, consider the case of Clarence Thomas.

The Thomas case revealed how Republicans practice their own cynical versions of racial preference, mostly for public relations. Every recent Republican President has felt obligated to name at least one black appointee to his cabinet. (Ronald Reagan once greeted his own black Secretary of Housing and Urban Development as "Mr. Mayor," because he didn't have any idea who the man was.) While such tokenism comes more naturally to conservatives than real efforts to eliminate discrimination, George W. Bush has improved on the record of his GOP predecessors, partly because real diversity became normal and necessary during the Clinton era.

These days, the Republicans always like to make sure there are black and brown faces in the picture with them, while insisting that they would never impose a quota. Conservatives appoint a few minorities so that they can "look like America" while they continue to implement policies of exclusion. And the second black man to sit on the United States Supreme Court presents a classic example of Republican racial preference in all its Machiavellian irony.

No one, except conceivably Clarence Thomas himself, believed that he was the most qualified nominee available — whether black, white, brown, yellow, red, or blue. There were better potential justices of every race. As columnist George Will noted in the aftermath of Thomas's hideous confirmation hearings: "Trashing the truth is now so natural in Washington that there were only worldly smirks and shrugs when George Bush began the Thomas saga by saying two things he and everyone else knows are untrue—that Thomas is the person best qualified for the Supreme Court, and that his race was irrelevant to his selection."

The Thomas fiasco was one of very few occasions when Will, a harsh critic of affirmative action, agreed with liberal Anthony Lewis, then writing for the *New York Times* op-ed page. "In saying that he picked Thomas because he was the best-qualified person in the country," wrote Lewis, "Bush only shamed himself. . . . Several of the Democrats had gone into the hearings expecting to give the president leeway and vote for Thomas. But they were put off by his obvious unfamiliarity with the Supreme Court's work, his lack of demonstrated interest in it, and the paucity of his legal experience."

All of Washington knew that conservatives in the White House had picked Thomas for reasons extraneous to his merits. He was a hard-line conservative who would provide a needed vote for the Court's right wing; and, as a black man, he would be far harder for the Senate to reject than a white conservative like Robert Bork. So Thomas was, in essence, an affirmative action hire of an especially cynical kind. He was selected to simulate diversity, when his real purpose was to sabotage diversity. Chosen because of his opposition to affirmative action, Thomas symbolizes the conservatives' racial paradox. To escape their reputation for exclusion, without actually abandoning exclusionary policies, means elevating symbolism over substance. The results have been predictably disappointing and unintentionally comical.

More recently, George W. Bush nominated Honduran-born conservative Miguel Estrada to the U.S. Court of Appeals for the District of Columbia, the second most powerful appellate bench in the nation. Estrada was widely known in Washington legal and media circles for his extremely right-wing views (he is thanked by Ann Coulter in the acknowledgments for *Slander*), but there was virtually no paper trail that revealed his philosophy. He also happened to be a former partner of Solicitor General Theodore Olson, the conservative eminence who represented the Bush-Cheney camp in the 2000 election case, *Bush v. Gore*. It was Estrada's first judicial appointment, and Senate Democrats balked at confirming him because he declined to answer questions about his views on such controversial topics as abortion rights.

At his confirmation hearings, Estrada insisted that he had never really considered the legal ramifications of those issues — a rather unlikely claim for a former Supreme Court clerk. Republican supporters of Estrada stridently accused the Democrats of anti-Hispanic prejudice, a ludicrous claim considering their own record of stalling Clinton's appointments of Hispanic judges.

The Bush family is particularly prone to embarrassing racial episodes, due to their own strange ambivalence toward minorities. They can't decide whether they're pugnacious Texas rednecks or guilt-ridden Connecticut preppies. When he ran for the Senate in the Lone Star State, George Herbert Walker Bush opposed the 1964 Civil Rights Act. (He forgot to mention that inglorious moment in his 1987 autobiography, *Looking Forward*, although he remembered chairing the United Negro College Fund appeal at Yale.) He supported Barry Goldwater, whose appeal in Texas and throughout the South was based on racial antagonism. Four years later, following the April 1968 assassination of Martin Luther King, the elder Bush voted for a fair housing bill as a member of Congress. His reputation suffered permanent damage in 1988, however, after his supporters aired one of the most racially inflammatory political commercials in postwar history — the notorious Willie Horton ad.

The former President's sons are much more comfortable with blacks and Latinos, although the Bush name remains none too popular in communities of color. Perhaps the ultimate Bush moment was the Republican Convention that nominated George W., which featured more black singers and dancers than a gospel reunion. The Bushes thought the show was swell, but black and white journalists alike derided it as a distasteful "minstrel show." All too many blacks regard that form of entertainment as the best metaphor for Republican displays of racial tolerance.

Conservative foundations try to solve the Republican race problem by throwing millions of dollars at experiments to synthesize a "black conservatism." What their money has fostered is a smallish clique of black conservative intellectuals and pundits, who spend much of their well-compensated time lamenting the undeniable fact that other black people don't listen to them. Just how little all the expensive "outreach" accomplishes must have become dismayingly clear to the right during the impeachment crisis of 1999, when the black community rose to defend Bill Clinton as if he were its natural-born son.

From the New Deal through the Clinton presidency and beyond, the African-American affinity for liberalism and the Democratic Party has steadily increased. This strong political current—which influences the growing Latino and Asian-American voting blocs as well—represents more than a typical ethnic attraction to a party or an ideology. Although black Americans have been deprived of many things, their suffering has endowed them with a degree of moral authority; in their expression of an almost monolithic political preference, they rebuke the party and ideology they have rejected. Whether conservatives concern themselves with racial justice or not—and some certainly do—the moral and political damage inflicted by black alienation is a source of continuing frustration on the right.

As David Horowitz, a conservative writer and Bush adviser, has noted bitterly: "Without their captive black constituency—the most powerful symbol of their concern for the victimized—liberals would be electorally dead. They would lose every major urban center and become a permanent political minority."

Based strictly on the numbers, Horowitz's argument is indisputable. Without their near monopoly on black and other minority voters, Democrats would not only face electoral difficulties in the North but insurmountable odds throughout the South. (The reverse would be equally true, of course, if Republicans were to lose their overwhelming advantage among white males.) Horowitz, a former far-left stooge of the Black Panther Party, also understands the symbolic value of the black endorsement. What he doesn't understand, however, is why the black endorsement of liberalism is indelible.

Theorists on the right have labored over many an exhaustive, redundant dissection of the black alliance with white liberals. The standard conservative breakdown depicts black Democrats as benighted, immoral, easily bribed, and even more easily frightened. It is hard not to wonder why conservatives so glibly insult the people they supposedly wish to attract and persuade, but they can't seem to help themselves.

Rather than take responsibility for their own racial isolation, Republicans tend to deflect the blame. With some justice, they complain that Democrats "play the race card," using scurrilous advertising to scare black voters. They whine that civil rights leaders—memorably denounced by former Representative J. C. Watts as "race-hustling poverty pimps"—have sold out to the liberals.

Conservatives assign all blame to the Democrats for the culture of welfare that allegedly fostered black dependency on government. (These critics usually forget the other once-downtrodden ethnic groups, like the Irish, the Italians, and the Jews, whose upward striving relied heavily on public assistance, government employment, and patronage.) "It was only when [blacks] vested their beliefs in the Democratic Party, and allowed government to control their lives," Watts declared, "that they encountered deepening poverty, decaying families, and a sick welfare system that penalizes women for wanting to marry the father of their children and mothers for saving money."

Until Watts quit Congress in 2002—clearly frustrated by his own party's obstinate neglect of black concerns—the Republican Party's sole black representative often wondered aloud why black voters were too prejudiced to trust his party. Yet before he resigned, the former football player expressed his own desperate dissatisfaction with the party leadership that treated him as a powerless token. He even told friends that he had considered running against Tom DeLay for a party leadership post in protest. Watts got tired of being called in for the photo ops and ignored on questions of policy.

Blaming liberals only postpones the day when conservatives will deal with black alienation from them and their party. This is a topic of the greatest sensitivity, because acknowledging the truth would require a harsh reassessment of right-wing icons and the abandonment of self-deluding myths. Many conservatives prefer to believe that they are being victimized by a cynical conspiracy of blacks and liberal Democrats.

"They have 90 percent of the black vote," as Horowitz once told a conservative audience. "And the way they keep the black vote is by scaring black people that white people are racist. Liberals exploit their image as the party of blacks to stigmatize conservatives as the party of racists." This right-wing victim mentality ironically echoes the mindset of black victimization that right-wingers love to lampoon. Change is always possible, however. If they want to understand why all but a handful of black Americans are so hostile to conservatism, they should heed their own tough advice: quit whining and take a long, hard look in the mirror.

Glaring back would be the faces of Barry Goldwater, Ronald Reagan, Richard Nixon, Jesse Helms, Pat Buchanan, Rush Limbaugh, William F. Buckley Jr., and a host of lesser-known but equally virulent opponents of civil rights and black advancement. Lurking somewhere in the background would be the terrifying visage of Willie Horton, the black rapist and murderer who was transformed into a racial icon of crime by conservatives during the 1988 presidential campaign.

The problem is not necessarily that all those renowned conservatives are racists, although that judgment can be applied quite fairly to Nixon, Helms, and Buchanan, and might well have applied to Buckley years ago. The problem is that so many prominent right-wing politicians and pundits have countenanced and used racism to further their own ends—and that they have done so without the least concern for how their conduct affects the fate of black people.

Contemporary black alienation from the Republican Party is all the more striking because the GOP once held a virtual monopoly on the allegiance of black voters as the party of Lincoln and emancipation. Well after Eleanor Roosevelt's crusade to integrate the New Deal co-alition, the Republicans were still capable of competing effectively for black electoral support. In the presidential elections of 1956 and 1960, Republicans Dwight Eisenhower and Richard Nixon drew well over a third of the black vote. That changed drastically in 1964, when modern conservatives commenced their gradual takeover of the GOP with the nomination of Barry Goldwater, their doomed Arizona ideologue. One of only six Republican senators who had voted against the 1964 Civil Rights Act, Goldwater attracted a meager 6 percent of black voters, a record low that still stands, on his way to a landslide defeat.

That trend-setting debacle can be traced to the founding of modern conservatism and the ascendancy of William F. Buckley Jr.'s *National Review* in the late fifties. Buckley's struggle to revive conservatism co-incided and clashed with the rise of the civil rights movement. The brash young editor parroted the code phrases of the segregationists, justifying black oppression as the price of preserving "states' rights" and the "civilized standards" of southern white society. A *National Review* editorial in 1957, opposing that year's landmark voting rights bill, appeared under the headline "Why the South Must Prevail." Buckley was even willing to promote rules that disenfranchised most whites in order to ensure that few, if any, blacks could vote.

"I am not ready to abandon the ideal of local government in order to kill Jim Crow," he declared in 1961. (Stunningly, he reaffirmed that sentiment without shame nearly four decades later.)

Still more appalling were the genteel Buckley's expressions of con-tempt for the non-violent civil rights movement, which now sound barbaric. He blamed the civil rights marchers in Selma for the beatings inflicted on them by racist police. He dismissed the murder of civil rights worker Viola Liuzzo by Klansmen as an event unworthy of na-tional attention. He attributed the 1965 Watts rioting to the "anarchic teachings" of Martin Luther King Jr., and three years later, unforgiv-ably, asserted that King's assassin was influenced by the nonviolent leader's own rhetoric "about the supremacy of the individual conscience."

Like Buckley, Goldwater attracted the support of white supremacists, though he framed his opposition to the 1964 Civil Rights Act as libertarian rather than racist or traditionalist. (So did George H. W. Bush, then a candidate for the Senate from Texas.) Goldwater compared Nixon's acceptance of a civil rights plank in the 1960 Republican platform to Chamberlain's capitulation to the Nazis at Munich, and he expunged the offending plank four years later. The only states he carried aside from his native Arizona were Alabama, Georgia, Louisiana, Mississippi, and South Carolina.

Compared with Buckley and Goldwater, Nixon was a racial moderate, although his remarks about blacks in private were filled with gutter bigotry. His record as President was contradictory. He reached out to black Republicans but gathered around him unreformed Old South nostalgists like Buchanan and Thurmond. He briefly embraced affirmative action in the construction industry and took some halting steps to comply with school desegregation ordered by the federal courts. But he simultaneously pursued the successful "southern strategy" of welcoming segregationist Dixiecrats into the GOP—a decision of far greater political consequence.

Nixon's southern strategy was emblematic of the racial opportunism that has disfigured conservatism and the Republican Party ever since. Among the fledgling politicians who switched parties and won elective office in the first wave of defecting Dixiecrats were both Jesse Helms of North Carolina and Trent Lott of Mississippi.

The racial demagoguery of Helms, who mercifully departed the Senate in 2002, is so well documented that it scarcely requires much repetition here. He built a powerful campaign and fund-raising organization with close ties to white supremacist groups, while gradually cloaking his animosity toward blacks as opposition to racial quotas. (Defending an inflammatory Helms TV ad designed to arouse white resentment, a spokesman for the Heritage Foundation blandly described the North Carolina senator as "ahead of his time.") What remains most significant about his racism is less what Helms did or said than the adulation of him by mainstream conservatives.

It was not Helms but his adversaries in the Washington establishment who had always "played the race card" against him, insisted commentator Robert Novak. Among the many unsavory incidents Novak forgot to mention in his defense of Helms was the senator's lonely yet determined filibuster against making Martin Luther King's birthday a national holiday.

Another prominent conservative pundit, Fred Barnes of the *Weekly Standard* and Fox News, brushed aside the issue of race when he admiringly profiled Helms as "the most important conservative of the last 25 years," next to Ronald Reagan himself. According to Barnes, the North Carolinian is an outstanding hero who "brought his relentless, unswerving application of conservative principles to practically every issue." While Reagan comported himself more genially, he agreed with Helms about "nearly everything, including the social issues."

After Helms ended his King filibuster—during which he insisted that the civil rights martyr was a Communist agent—Reagan reluctantly signed the King holiday bill, but his administration's hostility to the civil rights leadership and black empowerment was unwavering. Even Newt Gingrich and Bob Dole worried openly about the growing social polarization exacerbated by the President's actions.

Expressions of shock greeted Reagan's opposition to strengthening the Voting Rights Act, and his administration's attempt to grant tax-exempt status to Bob Jones University, an old-fashioned fundamentalist and segregationist institution—but in fact those policies were unsurprising. Reagan had commenced his 1980 presidential campaign with a press conference touting "states' rights" in Neshoba, Mississippi, where three civil rights workers were murdered in 1963. The former governor had always consistently opposed civil rights legislation, dating back to his attempts to repeal a California law that outlawed housing discrimination based on race or religion. As far as race is concerned, the mildest description of either Reagan or Helms would be that their principles most assuredly did not include defending blacks and other minorities from discrimination. Much worse can fairly be said of both.

Looking back on all this unpleasant history, what most black Americans may remember is that conservative Republicans placed the freedom to discriminate above freedom from discrimination. If the conservatives weren't racist themselves, they were squishy soft on racism in their own ranks. And rather than abandon the appeals to bigotry that had consolidated Republican power across the South, they devised sophisticated arguments to rescind the gains of the civil rights era.

There was a handful of conservative dissenters, notably Jack Kemp, the former congressman from Buffalo who tried to fashion a more generous, caring Republican approach to urban problems. But the former Bills quarterback was shoved aside by conservatives for admitting that those problems were too big to be solved without federal intervention. His hopeful voice was soon lost in a dismal chorus that stigmatized blacks as inferior and derided their quest for equality as morally suspect, socially destructive, and scientifically naïve.

The mainstream conservative position on race emerged in two important books that still remain authoritative on the right. Heavily subsidized by conservative foundations and ubiquitously promoted in both right-wing and mainstream media, those companion volumes summarized the argument against equality in pages buttressed with footnotes, charts, and page upon page of statistical tables. If the authors didn't agree on every point, their basic message was nevertheless plain. Speaking from the commanding heights of the American right, they informed the nation that blacks are destined to fail, that racial discrimination is logically and morally defensible as well as natural, and that the government should stop trying to enforce civil rights and help the black underclass.

In 1994 Charles Murray and Richard Herrnstein published *The Bell Curve*, a work purporting to prove that inherited levels of intelligence essentially predetermine the fate of every person in society at birth. Government cannot ameliorate economic and social inequality, they argued; indeed, government assistance to the disadvantaged only injures the nation by wasting resources and discouraging enterprise. Their book represented a radical departure from American ideals.

The most highly publicized and controversial chapters of *The Bell Curve* drew conclusions about groups rather than individuals. Racial differences in standardized IQ tests, the authors claimed, demonstrate that blacks and Latinos are less intelligent than whites — and that those differences are almost certainly genetic.

From there, Herrnstein and Murray postulated that affirmative action inevitably rewards blacks far more than their talents merit in education and employment opportunities. "Reverse discrimination" is damaging to economic efficiency. They came up with a historical estimate that was pure politics in scientific drag: true fairness to blacks in jobs and schools had been achieved in the period just prior to enactment of the 1964 civil rights statute. That date hardly seemed coincidental.

The following year, Dinesh D'Souza went further in *The End of Racism.* An Indian immigrant and former *enfant terrible* who had edited the racially provocative *Dartmouth Review* (with Laura Ingraham), D'Souza sought not to end racism but to endorse it. He tried to prove that slavery had not been a racist institution, and insisted that discrimination by landlords, taxi drivers, and employers is rational because of "statistical" proof that blacks are violent, shiftless, and stupid. He described such discrimination as natural and even admirable. "What we need is a long-term strategy that holds the government to a rigorous standard of race neutrality," he wrote, "while allowing private actors to be free to discriminate as they wish." In his ideal society, "individuals and companies would be allowed to discriminate in private transactions such as renting an apartment or hiring for a job."

Even more explicitly than Herrnstein and Murray — also a subsidized fellow in residence at the august American Enterprise Institute — D'Souza urged the repeal of civil rights legislation as the first step toward a color-blind society. In constructing that argument, he discussed blacks in the most stereotypical and ugly terms, referring to such persistent personality types as the "playful Sambo," the "sullen 'field nigger,'" and the "dependable Mammy," and describing urban streets "irrigated with alcohol, urine and blood."

Both books received wide and mostly favorable attention in the mainstream media as well as the conservative press. Andrew Sullivan, then editor of the *New Republic*, featured *The Bell Curve* on the magazine's cover. In the end, scholars who closely scrutinized Murray and Herrnstein's "science" debunked their data and conclusions; other critics discovered that the authors had relied in part on research financed by a crackpot eugenics foundation.

As a "landmark" work of social science, *The Bell Curve* flamed out quickly despite enormous sales of more than 400,000 copies in hardcover. Few took D'Souza's outlandish prescriptions seriously, either (and far fewer bought his book), except as additional propaganda in the right's ongoing offensive against affirmative action. The new Speaker of the House, a former college professor, regarded such volumes as intellectual ammunition in his war on the welfare state and "racial entitlements."

But at the American Enterprise Institute, there was an embarrassing coda: Two of the nation's most prominent black conservatives decided that too much was finally enough, and publicly resigned their AEI fellowships. Robert L. Woodson Sr. and Glenn Loury called a press conference to announce that they were no longer willing to lend their names to the project of demeaning black Americans and returning them to a degraded past. Woodson was a well-known advocate of neighborhood enterprise and minority self-reliance; Loury had won considerable notoriety for his willingness to criticize affirmative action and endorse Republican candidates, including Reagan. But for both of them, the D'Souza book was an unpardonable insult.

Loury launched an attack on D'Souza's ideas that continued in print for nearly a year. "This book is a defense of bigotry and prejudice," he told an interviewer when the paperback edition was published. "[It] is written in the language of blame and in the language of stereotypes. It treats black America as 'the other,' as an undifferentiated statistical mass, as a social 'dysfunction,' as a problem."

Several years later, Loury revealed that he had developed an addiction to cocaine during his fat years as a Reaganite "poster boy," providing an ironic counterpoint to conservative criticism of the underclass. In 2002 he reemerged as a "recovering reactionary," with his own new book examining the persistence of white racism. Woodson remained a Republican but never returned to AEI, which in 2002–2003 had no black or Latino fellows. Charles Murray, however, remains a senior fellow there. Dinesh D'Souza, a fervent advocate of free enterprise whose livelihood has depended heavily on right-wing foundation grants almost from the moment he set foot on these shores, moved on from AEI to an equally comfortable berth at the Hoover Institution.

The Loury and Woodson protests revealed more about race and politics than anything written by Murray or D'Souza. The willingness of black conservatives to fight against affirmative action clearly wasn't enough for their white comrades. Three decades after Barry Goldwater and William F. Buckley Jr. established modern conservatism's hostility to civil rights, virtually nothing had changed on the right. The only sign of progress was the cosmetic presence of a few well-rewarded blacks, who were expected to open their mouths mainly when smiling. The persistence of right-wing racism could be measured in many ways, some of them quite bizarre.

In 1998 reporters discovered that Trent Lott, then the Senate Republican leader, had for many years promoted an outfit known as the Council of Conservative Citizens—the blatantly bigoted successor of the old White Citizens Councils that had functioned in Dixie as the respectable, white-collar counterpart of the Ku Klux Klan. Lott had given speeches identifying the Republican platform with the "ideals" of Confederate President Jefferson Davis, whatever those might be. Four years later, Lott's clumsy endorsement of Strom Thurmond's 1948 segregationist presidential candidacy was shocking only in its candor.

The brief exposure of Lott's connection with the CCC opened a window into a much wider scandal: the affinity of many Republicans and conservatives with the cult of the neo-Confederates, who worship the antebellum South, revile Lincoln, and abominate such modern innovations as civil rights. A number of them still think the South should rise again.

The Attorney General of the United States, John Ashcroft, evidently shares some of those peculiar values—or so he suggested in his interview a few years ago with the editors of *Southern Partisan*, the nation's leading neo-Confederate journal. Like Lott, Ashcroft maintained ties with the Council of Conservative Citizens, whose Missouri-based leaders described his appointment by Bush as "our ship coming in." During the closely fought battle over his confirmation in February 2001, Ashcroft's former colleagues in the Senate exonerated him from accusations of personal racism. But like many Republicans and conservatives, he was soft on white bigotry.

For the extremist heirs of conservatism, only the political humiliation of blacks could provide a satisfactory solution to the nation's racial problems. Like Goldwater and Buckley in 1964, they tend to consider blacks and Latinos inferior to whites, and oppose the most basic guarantees of equality. It would be untrue to say that every conservative shares in this disgrace. There have been some, like Jack Kemp, who tried to lead their party in a different direction. Occasionally a figure like Jerry Falwell or former Christian Coalition leader Ralph Reed will acknowledge the "mistakes" of the past. But those rare exceptions only highlight conservatism's awful racial record. To anyone familiar with this shabby history, the inescapable question is not why more minorities don't flock to conservatism and vote Republican. The wonder is why any would at all.

Liberals can point to a prouder history that begins with abolitionism, the progressives' most compelling cause from the end of the colonial era through the Civil War, and continues to the present, when Democrats have taken on the politically difficult task of defending affirmative action. Without the determination of liberals—including liberal Republicans who no longer have a place in their own party—there would have been no civil rights legislation: no Civil Rights Act, no Voting Rights Act, no Title IX, no affirmative action, and no steadily expanding black and Latino middle class.

The honorable path has brought rewards, but it certainly hasn't been free of risk. When northern liberal Democrats took the first tentative steps toward breaking with their segregationist colleagues at the 1948 party convention, they set in motion a process that forfeited the southern states almost entirely to the Republicans over a period of four decades. When Lyndon Johnson signed the 1964 Civil Rights Act, he told his aides that he had just lost the South for the Democrats for at least a generation. The more firmly liberals pressed toward full equality for blacks and other minorities, the more trouble Democratic politicians experienced in the urban and suburban North as well, especially among blue-collar and middle-class ethnic whites. The defection of the "angry white man," which began with the George Wallace campaigns in 1968 and 1972 and culminated in the Republican takeover of Congress in 1994, was yet another consequence of the Democratic devotion to civil rights.

By the time Bill Clinton ran for a second term in 1996, pressure to abandon affirmative action was swelling not only among the Republicans but within his own party and, indeed, from Dick Morris, then the chief pollster in the Clinton White House. After a thorough review of the effects of affirmative action, Clinton decided that the proper course was to "mend it, not end it," so that black and white America could continue on the "rocky but fundamentally righteous journey" toward equality.

Despite the D'Souzas and Murrays, there are no significant political figures in either party today who would seek to repeal the basic civil rights legislation. Republican politicians are acutely aware that a racist image repels moderate white voters, which is why they dumped Trent Lott so abruptly from the Senate leadership. Yet even subtle preferences for diversity that fall well short of quotas remain controversial.

The arguments for and against affirmative action are as complex as the dozens of programs known by that rubric. Recent academic studies indicate that the number of whites who lose educational or job opportunities is small, despite the hysterical bleating of a few reactionary columnists. Examples of affirmative action working to benefit the nation may be found everywhere, from the career of Secretary of State Colin Powell to the successful integration of the armed forces' officer corps, which leads the greatest military organization the world has ever seen. Among the anomalies of the Bush administration is the President's opposition to affirmative action, when Powell and the National Security Advisor, Condoleezza Rice, are the most celebrated examples of its success.

Whatever anyone may think of affirmative action—and my view is that it has done far more good than harm, although such programs require careful regulation to prevent injury to innocent whites and to avoid unconstitutional quotas—the point is that Democrats and liberals haven't acted from opportunism. Whatever they gained among black and Latino voters, they have lost among unreconciled whites. In a constitutional system that disproportionately represents small southern and western states in the Senate and that depends on winning electoral votes in presidential elections, the loss of those votes is a lasting political handicap.

None of this is meant to suggest that liberals and Democrats are exempt from the contradictions of what social critic Stanley Crouch once called the "all-American skin game." For more than a century— from the debate that led to the Civil War until the split with Strom Thurmond's Dixiecrats in 1948—the Democratic Party served the interests of southern slaveholders and their descendants. In the antebellum era, Democrats who opposed slavery, like the great New York newspaper editor William Cullen Bryant, were forced to defect to the radical new Republican Party.

Senator Robert Byrd of West Virginia, a former member of the Ku Klux Klan, is a living reminder of that legacy. (Byrd also happens to be the last Democrat remaining in the Senate who voted against the 1964 Civil Rights Act, although he, like Strom Thurmond, has publicly repented his racism.) As late as August 1964, Democratic power brokers were still seeking to mollify the party's segregationist wing by rejecting the Mississippi Freedom Democratic delegation led by activist Fannie Lou Hamer at their Atlantic City convention. The Civil Rights Act of 1964 would not have passed without the votes of liberal and moderate Republicans, and even the Kennedy brothers initially hesitated in their embrace of the great cause.

White progressives are as capable as conservatives of abrading the sensibilities of black America. Liberal whites have sometimes patronized and humiliated people whom they profess to regard as equals. And in recent decades, liberals have sometimes erred by overemphasizing political correctness and identity politics to the detriment of higher ideals of citizenship, solidarity, and integration.

Ethnic relations within the highly diverse "party of the people" inevitably reflect American society, which means that they range from amiable to angry. Racial friction flares from time to time among the Democrats because they belong to an integrated party that contrasts nicely with the pale monochrome of the Republicans. And despite the paradoxes, prejudices, and paranoia that persist within the liberal coalition, blacks and other minorities generally support the Democrats and shun the Republicans for one overriding reason.

They prefer liberals to conservatives because they know from experience and with great certainty that racism is unacceptable among progressive Democrats. No matter how many black children are recruited to appear onstage with George W. Bush, they can still feel no such confidence about conservatives.

CRONY CAPITALISM, INFECTIOUS GREED, AND THE WAY THE WORLD REALLY WORKS

"Conservatives are the only true
champions of free enterprise."

In the recent annals of the Republican right, few moments have been as startling as Alan Greenspan's appearance before the Senate Banking Committee on July 16, 2002. The Federal Reserve chairman's visit to Capitol Hill that day wasn't the usual opportunity for traders to divine the direction of nominal interest rates from body language or opaque testimony. Demoralized by continuing revelations of corporate criminality, the nation was listening even more attentively than usual for reassurance from the lionized economist.

But the great Greenspan himself no longer felt quite so confident and perspicacious. At the very late age of seventy-six, he was questioning ideas he had accepted for half a century.

For much of his adult life, Greenspan has been an important official symbol of market idolatry in the tradition of the late Ayn Rand, author of *Atlas Shrugged*, *The Fountainhead*, and *The Virtue of Selfishness*. As a young graduate of New York University during the early fifties, Greenspan joined her cultish band of followers, whose dogma rejected all economic regulation and government intervention as evil assaults on human freedom.

In essence, Rand's philosophy reveres unfettered avarice and rejects social constraints on individual selfishness. (Note the similarity between this infantile attitude and what currently passes for conservatism.) Greenspan has edged away from Rand's absolutism during the decades since his initiation at her Manhattan apartment; still, the Fed chairman remains the most prominent libertarian fellow traveler ever to hold high office in the United States. And in his own discreet way, he has advanced the laissez-faire faith.

By the summer of 2002, however, Greenspan had witnessed events that shook his deep faith in capitalism unbound. He had felt the sickening shudder of the financial implosions that destroyed Enron, WorldCom, Global Crossing, Adelphia, and, perhaps worst of all, Arthur Andersen. He had watched the market that made his reputation finally crash. His intelligence undimmed by his advancing years, Greenspan had been forced to question the simple creed that guides the editorial board of the *Wall Street Journal*, innumerable right-wing pundits, talk-show hosts, publications, and Web sites, as well as the House Republican leadership (and two or three generations of lonely, troubled college students).

On that July morning, after expressing his newfound dismay over the expansion of "avenues to express greed," Greenspan made a surprising admission. Until very recently, he explained, he had assumed that market forces alone would discipline the major accounting firms and corporate management. He had believed that "regulation by government was utterly unnecessary and, indeed, most inappropriate."

Then he said: "I was wrong."

Those three words were more than a concession of personal error, more than an endorsement of legislation to reform corporate accounting. Coming from Greenspan, they were an epitaph for the arrogant conservatism that had advertised exclusive knowledge of "how the world works." Another god had failed. As the next day's bitter denunciation of him on the *Wall Street Journal*'s editorial page unintentionally revealed, Greenspan's public confession of error and criticism of greed were, for his old comrades on the right, their own troubling "darkness at noon."

Whether the limited reforms supported by Greenspan will actually hinder cheating, fraud, and self-dealing by managers and accountants wasn't the point, as the furious *Journal* editorial board realized. Accounting tricks are the symptom, not the disease. Cascading corporate scandals have stripped away the pretenses of institutional conservatism and exposed the utopian masquerade of right-wing ideology. It is no longer plausible to claim that markets and businesses can police themselves, that investors need no protection from predatory executives, or that regulation is always the enemy of efficiency.

What Americans have forgotten was how crooked businessmen operating under the banner of laissez-faire drove the nation into depression repeatedly during the nineteenth and early twentieth centuries. They have forgotten, too, the lesson their parents and grandparents learned during the New Deal, when Franklin Roosevelt fashioned modern democratic capitalism: the economy functions most efficiently and fairly when business is well regulated and workers are well compensated. Every time corporations have accumulated excessive wealth and power, the inevitable result has been abuse of citizens, investors, consumers, employees, and the environment.

Democratic governance—as Alan Greenspan acknowledged at long last—is the only force powerful enough to restrain the computer-assisted robber barons ensconced in corporations such as Enron and WorldCom. More bluntly than the Fed chairman, many business journalists have observed that the most serious threat to free enterprise arises not from government regulation but from the destructive effects of "crony capitalism."

That term, which originated under the kleptocratic regime of Philippine dictator Ferdinand Marcos, was once reserved for corrupt economic systems in developing or formerly Communist countries. Those systems develop under governments where friends and relatives of the ruling elite enjoy special economic privileges and sweetheart deals; where financial markets and business relationships are manipulated for the benefit of that same elite; where self-serving abuses, frauds, law-breaking, and regulatory violations by the elite go unpunished; where the savings and investments of ordinary citizens are vulnerable to legalized plunder; where public treasuries serve as private piggybanks; and where the best possible business partners are the President's offspring or siblings. Crony capitalism flourishes in very different cultures all over the world, from China, Russia, Nigeria, and Argentina to Singapore and Saudi Arabia.

In America's democratic capitalism, by contrast, merit, hard work, innovation, fair dealing, and honest return on investment are supposed to prevail. Very often they do. Too often, they don't. Until Americans suddenly realized that the market's "invisible hand" was actually picking their pockets, many accepted a propagandistic, public-relations portrait of the nation's corporate sector.

The ethos of privilege, power, and entitlement that pervades Republican rule is the reality that underlies the conservative fantasy about free markets. What Americans learned when corporate scandals tore away the facade of companies like Enron is the way the world really works. Capitalism's underside is what the late Lars-Erik Nelson once described as abuse of "the government's coercive powers of taxation and legislation to funnel public wealth to the private sector."

The rise and fall of Enron is a lengthy, convoluted saga with an enormous cast of characters—and with implications for the ways that Americans compensate executives and employees, power homes and industries, finance and regulate businesses. It is and will be for years to come the subject of papers, books, lawsuits, and criminal prosecutions. Its relevance here concerns the Houston company's ascension into the dizzying heights of political influence, in tandem with its political partners in the Republican Party and, most important, the Bush family.

When Enron chairman Kenneth Lay was sinking into the hole created by his company's bankruptcy, George W. Bush tried to pretend he hardly knew the man he had nicknamed "Kenny Boy." On January 11, 2002, he described Lay as "a supporter of Ann Richards in my run [for Texas Governor] in 1994." This attempt to mislead the public about their connection only emphasized its importance. Although accurate in the narrowest sense, Bush's statement was as ridiculous and transparent a falsehood as any of Bill Clinton's utterances about his relationship with Monica Lewinsky.

(As self-serving deception, Bush's alibi also ranked with Dick Cheney's riposte to a joke about his private-sector wealth that Joe Lieberman cracked during their October 2000 debate. "And I can tell you, Joe," Cheney replied, "that the government had nothing to do with it." Snappy, but untrue: aside from the fact that Halliburton hired Cheney solely because of his contacts with U.S. and foreign governments, the firm benefited from billions in government contracts at the Pentagon and around the world, all of which made his supersized salary and stock options possible.)

The quick, easy way to measure Bush's deception is to glance at the record of Ken Lay and Enron's donations during that 1994 campaign: $12,500 to Ann Richards versus $146,500 to George W. Bush. In fact, Enron and Lay were George W.'s most generous lifetime patrons, having donated at least a half-million dollars to his three political campaigns.

Those numbers offer a rough sense of Enron's partisan preference — but they don't begin to define or encompass the alliance of Lay and the Bush family, which dates back at least as far as George H. W. Bush's 1988 presidential campaign. Lay raised a minimum of $100,000 for that race and established himself as both a Republican player and personal friend of the Bushes. Since then he has given hundreds of thousands of dollars to their favorite causes and charities. Lay is still listed, for instance, as a trustee and patron of the elder Bush's presidential library, to which he donated $50,000.

During the first Bush presidency, Ken Lay was among the major donors invited to spend a night at the White House. That was forgotten years later during the tornado of Republican spin around Enron's demise, when George W. was trying to minimize his own and his family's relationship with Lay. In fact, the Lay sleepover was wrongly blamed on Bill Clinton, as phony "proof" of a bipartisan Enron taint. That canard flew from the Drudge Report to Fox News Channel, the *Chicago Tribune*, CNN's *Crossfire*, and *ABC News This Week*, among other outlets. (Other than the *Tribune*, none saw fit to correct the record after the tale was debunked.)

The attempt to tie Lay to Clinton was comical, considering how many Bush political associates have been employed by Enron over the years: Secretary of State James Baker, former Commerce Secretary Robert Mosbacher, White House political adviser Karl Rove, former White House economic guru Lawrence Lindsey, campaign advisers Ralph Reed and Ed Gillespie, U.S. Trade Representative Robert B. Zoellick, Commerce Department general counsel Theodore W. Kassinger, Maritime Administrator William G. Schubert, former Secretary of the Army Thomas E. White (a former Enron vice president), and Republican National Committee Chairman Marc F. Racicot—to name a handful.

As both Governor and President, George W. appointed Patrick Wood III, Lay's handpicked advocate, to oversee the electric power industry that was Enron's principal business. So confident was Lay of his influence over Bush that he had threatened the chairman of the Federal Energy Regulatory Commission with the loss of his job—and then saw his threat realized when Wood was appointed to replace the disfavored chairman. And Wood was only one of many Bush appointees well positioned to assist Enron in its ventures and deregulation initiatives.

Topping the list was Cheney himself, who met personally with Lay to discuss the administration's national energy policy. The Vice President's secretive Energy Task Force met at least six times with Enron executives to seek their advice. Aspects of the resulting policy document were clearly designed to enrich the Houston company.

After Enron went under, the White House announced proudly that Bush appointees at Treasury and Commerce had done nothing to save the company. By the time the firm was going bankrupt, of course, it was too late to do much, and too many eyes were watching. Anyway, by then the Bush administration had already done Enron many favors, the first of which occurred within forty-eight hours of George W's inaugural.

On January 23, 2001, the White House announced the new administration's response to weeks of rolling electrical blackouts in California, which had led even conservative Republicans in the state to demand price controls. With that announcement Bush rescinded Clinton's emergency order, issued five weeks earlier, that required out-of-state electricity wholesalers like Enron to stop withholding power from California to drive prices up. Enron's stock price, having reached a high of about $83 a share in the early days of 2001, was beginning a rapid descent under pressure from investors who feared the return of energy regulation in the wake of Clinton's action.

In the months that followed, the White House killed congressional efforts to cap rates. Among the new President's pronouncements on energy matters was a stern vow to fight price controls and a firm promise to create a national electricity grid, which would enable Enron to trade in a greatly expanded market.

On April 17, 2001, Enron reported a first-quarter net income of $425 million, an increase of $87 million over the previous year. The Enron division that sold gas and electricity enjoyed an operating profit of $755 million in those first few months of the Bush regime—up from $429 million during the same period in 2000. (Since then, several former Enron executives have pled guilty to charges of illegally manipulating California's power supply.)

On the very same day that Enron announced its happy 2001 first-quarter results, Lay met with Cheney to discuss his company's recommendations for the Energy Task Force. The Enron boss gave the Vice President a detailed memo that highlighted his most urgent request: do nothing to hold down power prices. Specifically, the memo urged that "the administration should reject any attempt to re-regulate wholesale power markets by adopting price caps or returning to archaic methods of determining the cost-base of wholesale power." Those "archaic" practices were established to suppress an earlier gang of predators known as the utility trust, with support from Bush's supposed idol Theodore Roosevelt. But that was another era and a very different kind of Republican.

Democrats and Republicans alike took money from Enron, although the GOP got much more; and both partake of the hundreds of millions of dollars that flow through the capital annually from corporate special interests, although in recent years the GOP has received up to twice as much as its rival. Both major parties and politicians of varying ideologies are implicated in cronyism, too; even if some benefit far more than others.

During the corporate scandals of 2002, the most prominent liberal target was Democratic National Committee Chairman Terry McAuliffe. Republicans made great sport of his association with Global Crossing, the giant telecom firm whose shady bankruptcy was the fourth largest in American history. They pointed with suspicion at the $17 million profit McAuliffe had realized on an investment of $100,000 in Global Crossing shares. But as the Republican National Committee chairman admitted, McAuliffe did nothing illegal. He had sold off nearly all his Global Crossing holdings three years before anyone could have anticipated the company's precipitous dive.

What raised questions about McAuliffe's good fortune was that he had originally acquired his stock through personal connections with Global Crossing chairman Gary Winnick—and that Winnick used McAuliffe, then a leading Democratic fund-raiser, to gain access to President Clinton. McAuliffe later arranged a golf date for Clinton with Gary Winnick, who promised to give $1 million to the Clinton presidential library. Whatever Winnick may have gained from his golf outing with the President, no one has cited any quid pro quo from the Clinton administration. In any case, McAuliffe's peccadillo is reduced to insignificance in the shadow of Bush, Inc.

For the Bush dynasty, crony capitalism is rite of passage, way of life, and family business. The President, his father, his three brothers, and sundry other relatives all have joined (and sometimes hastily abandoned) enterprises where their chief contribution was the perception of political influence at home and abroad. It would be possible—although grim and morally exhausting—to write an entire book about nothing but ethically dingy Bush business deals.

The Bush clan's investments and directorships have ranged across nearly every sector of the modern economy: oil exploration, banking, equities, venture capital, computer software, life insurance, major-league baseball, high-tech security, real estate, cable television, shoe wholesaling, fruit and vegetable imports, irrigation pumps, and airline catering, among others.

Family partners, investors, and benefactors have included former government appointees, present and former campaign contributors, foreign potentates and favor-seekers—and numerous business executives who benefited from decisions by government overseen by members of the Bush family. Time after time, Bush family members or their business associates have sidled up to the very edge of legality, and perhaps over it—without being held accountable.

Until the ascendancy of George W. Bush, the most notorious example of that syndrome was his younger brother Neil. He too ran a failed oil company, like those once operated by George W.—and his oil company, too, was awarded exploration rights from a foreign government while their father was in the White House. Neil's best-known venture, however, was in the savings-and-loan business.

For the benefit of those who don't remember the name Silverado, that was the romantic moniker of the Denver savings-and-loan whose board Neil graced during the eighties. In the gigantic federal bailout overseen by Neil's father's administration, Silverado's failure eventually cost taxpayers about a billion dollars. (The cleanup of the much-investigated Madison Guaranty, run by the late James McDougal of Whitewater infamy, cost about $65 million, or about $10 million less than the Starr investigation.)

Neil Bush was invited to join the Silverado board of directors by its president, an ambitious Republican fund-raiser seeking connections to the White House. Before the thrift sank, like so many others, under its burden of unsecured speculative loans, director Neil winked at a variety of questionable deals with his own business partners. For instance, he endorsed a loan of more than $100 million to business partners who were simultaneously investing in his oil ventures.

He also allowed Silverado to forgive $11.5 million in debt from another real estate developer who had agreed to invest $3 million in his company. Meanwhile, the deadbeats who got loans from Silverado did other nice things for Neil, such as loaning him $100,000. Like them, he never repaid the money.

That kind of conflicted deal, typical at Silverado, helped to bring the thrift down. Although federal regulators who investigated the case could have banned Neil Bush from the banking industry for conflict of interest, they slapped his wrist instead with the "mildest penalty available." A prominent Washington banking lobbyist (and old friend of his father) thoughtfully set up a fund to help defray Neil's legal fees.

Before his oil company tanked, Neil Bush managed to ingratiate himself with the ruling figures in Argentina, including its crooked president, Carlos Menem. Neil's company, JNB International, had actually done no international oil exploration, but won a contract from the Argentine government anyway. Neil also invested $3,000 in Apex, another oil firm backed by a longtime Bush political supporter, which paid him $160,000 in annual salary — and received more than $2 million in federally guaranteed small-business loans. He resigned after the dubious arrangement surfaced in press reports.

Neil Bush's checkered career overshadowed the business activities of brother Jeb, which took him from the Florida swamps to the capital of Nigeria in the years before he first ran for governor in 1994. Jeb earned much of his fortune in partnership with Armando Codina, a Miami real estate baron and politically active Cuban exile. They eventually got in trouble with a savings-and-loan, Broward Federal, which had loaned them $4.5 million via a third party to purchase an office building. Like so many other thrifts, Broward failed. When the loan went into default, federal regulators reduced the liability of Bush and Codina to $500,000 (and considerately allowed them to keep their building).

Around this time, Jeb also got involved in a deal with Miguel Recarey, the strange character who ran International Medical Centers, a Miami-based health maintenance organization. IMC and Recarey were eventually indicted for the largest Medicare fraud in history, costing the U.S. government hundreds of millions of dollars.

According to journalist and author Ann Louise Bardach, Recarey lived in a bulletproofed mansion and "had long been associated with Tampa's mob boss Santos Trafficante, Jr." Recarey paid the then Vice President's son a "commission" of $75,000 after Jeb made a few phone calls on his behalf to the highest officials of the Department of Health and Human Services. Jeb's entreaties won a waiver of Medicare regulations that was worth tens of millions of dollars to IMC. The subsequent scandal and his indictment for multiple offenses drove Recarey to skip bail in 1987 and flee to Madrid, where the fugitive has lived ever since.

Four years later, when his father was President, Jeb visited Nigeria as chief salesman and partner of Bush-El, a firm marketing water pumps to the notoriously corrupt African dictatorship. On the corporate jet that carried him around Nigeria, according to the pilot, was a local associate carrying Hartmann suitcases stuffed with Nigerian currency for bribes. The water-pump sale went through, conveniently financed by a $74.3 million loan from the U.S. government. The main beneficiary was Bush's business partner David Eller, who also owned the firm that manufactured the pumps.

Bush denied the pilot's story and told the *Miami Herald* that he did nothing to secure the U.S. government loan. He also said that he turned down a million-dollar commission after he learned about the taxpayer financing of the pump sale. He did, however, earn $650,000 from Bush-El, and "declined to specify the source of that money, other than to say it came from sales in countries other than Nigeria and from selling his half-share of the company to Eller." In a 1998 letter to the *Herald*, Jeb responded with the smirking insouciance of the typical crony capitalist: "Is favorable name recognition helpful in business, as it is in almost every other aspect of life? Perhaps. Is it an 'unfair advantage'? No. It is just a fact of life."

Brother Marvin has rarely caused any negative publicity for his family, with one notable exception. Three months after he left the

White House, the first President Bush flew to Kuwait on the emir's private plane to be decorated with the monarchy's highest honors for commanding the Gulf War. Accompanying the former President were his two youngest sons and his former Secretary of State James Baker III. Several months later, the *New Yorker* magazine revealed that Baker went to Kuwait as a consultant to Enron, which was seeking contracts to rebuild the sheikdom's damaged power plants. Neil Bush was also seeking a share of the fees to operate Enron's power plants. And Marvin Bush was working for a Washington firm that wanted to build an electronic security system for the Kuwaitis. In the eyes of many people there and at home, the grasping conduct of Baker and the Bush sons soiled American honor.

George W. Bush's business career wasn't quite as colorful as those of Neil or Jeb, but the eldest son has also been the most successful in acquiring both power and money. The national media occasionally examined his activities for evidence of influence peddling when his father was still in the White House, but there was no searching scrutiny during his presidential campaign in 2000. Only when the Enron scandal broke did reporters again consider his sojourn in the oil business, especially at Harken Energy, and the baseball deal that made his fortune.

From the outset, the opportunities that eventually led to his baseball bonanza intertwined politics and business, crony capitalist style. The limited partnership that financed Arbusto, his first oil firm, included George W.'s grandmother Dorothy Bush; Rite Aid drugstores chairman Lewis Lehrman, then a rising force in New York Republican politics; William Draper III, a corporate executive and family friend who was later appointed by his father to head the Export-Import Bank; and James Bath, a mysterious Houston aircraft broker who served as a front man for several Saudi Arabian sheiks. About $3 million poured into Arbusto, producing little oil and no profits but expansive tax shelters.

In 1982 George W. changed the infelicitous name Arbusto to Bush Exploration Oil Company. His father by then was Vice President of the United States, but the new company name didn't improve matters.

More than once, George W.'s venture was near ruin when wealthy benefactors suddenly appeared with fresh cash. The most generous was Philip Uzielli, an old Princeton buddy of James Baker III, the family friend then serving as Chief of Staff in the Reagan White House. For the sum of $1 million, Uzielli bought 10 percent of the company at a time in 1982 when the entire enterprise was valued at less than $400,000.

Soon Uzielli's million was gone, too. But just as Bush Exploration was heading toward failure, George W. met William DeWitt and Mercer Reynolds, a pair of Ohio investors with their own small oil firm, called Spectrum 7. After a quick courtship, the Spectrum 7 partners agreed to merge with Bush Exploration, naming George W. as chairman and CEO and awarding him a substantial share of stock. Although the Vice President's son helped Spectrum 7 to raise additional money, catastrophic losses continued. Then George W. attracted yet another financial savior.

That September, Harken Energy Corporation, a midsized firm, stepped in to acquire Spectrum 7. For his worthless company, Harken gave Bush $600,000 worth of its publicly traded stock, plus a seat on its board of directors and a consultancy that paid him up to $120,000 a year. His partners understood perfectly what had happened. As Spectrum 7's former President Paul Rea later recalled, the Harken management "believed having George's name there would be a big help to them."

In 1987 Bush moved his family from Texas to Washington, where he served as "senior adviser" in his father's presidential campaign. Not long before Election Day, he heard from his former Spectrum 7 partner Bill DeWitt that the Texas Rangers were on the market. To make a successful bid, DeWitt would need Texas backers, and the son of the incoming President was perfectly situated to find them. George W. also had a powerful advantage in dealing with the team's owner, an aging oil millionaire named Eddie Chiles, who had been a Bush family friend in Midland, Texas, for more than thirty years.

Baseball commissioner Peter Ueberroth was eager to help the son of the new President, but wasn't happy that Bush's two biggest investors were the New York film financiers Roland Betts and Tom Bernstein. The indispensable local money came from Richard Rainwater, formerly the chief financial adviser to the Bass brothers of Fort Worth. Little known to the general public, Rainwater was famous on Wall Street for growing the Bass inheritance from around $50 million in 1970 to more than $4 billion by the time he left in 1986 to manage his own investments.

After Bush and Ueberroth met with him in early 1989, Rainwater took effective control of the deal, bringing along Edward "Rusty" Rose, a well-known Dallas investor, to oversee the franchise. Under an agreement worked out by Betts and Rainwater, the President's son would serve as the new ownership's public face while Rose ran the business.

Bush's stake in the team, just under 2 percent, was among the smallest. He purchased his shares with a $500,000 loan from a Midland bank of which he had been a director and eventually scraped together $106,000 more to buy out two other limited partners. Two months after his father's inauguration, George W. Bush called a press conference in Arlington to announce that the Rangers sale had been successfully completed for a price that was later reported to be $86 million. While Rainwater, Rose, Betts, and all the other partners remained in the background, George W. greeted the public as if he were "the owner" of the Rangers. He attended every home game and even printed baseball cards bearing his own picture to hand out from his box.

Meanwhile, he maintained a financial interest in Harken Energy. He had been granted enough additional stock options, at a generous discount, to increase his holdings by more than half. By 1989, however, those shares were falling in value. A series of questionable decisions by Chairman Alan Quasha had jeopardized the company's future, and its losses reached $40 million in 1990. Even the company's CEO admitted that its financial statements were "a mess."

Once more, however, the Bush name provided sudden deliverance — in the form of a contract with the emirate of Bahrain. Until

1989 the Bahraini oil minister had been negotiating an agreement for offshore drilling with Amoco, a huge energy conglomerate with decades of worldwide experience. Those talks were abruptly broken off. Then, through a former Mobil executive working on retainer for the State Department, Bahraini officials were put in touch with Harken.

Industry analysts were astonished by the announcement in January 1990 that Bahrain had awarded exclusive offshore exploration rights to Harken, a debt-ridden company that had never drilled a well anywhere but Texas, Louisiana, and Oklahoma, and had never drilled undersea at all. Harken had to bring in the more experienced and solvent Bass brothers, old friends and political supporters of the Bush family, to begin construction on the $25 million project.

Only the presence of President Bush's oldest son could explain the Bahraini ministers' extraordinary decision. "They were clearly aware he was the President's son," said Monte Swetnam, a former Harken executive who conducted the talks with the emirate's oil ministry. George W. denied any part in Harken's bid. "Ask the Bahrainis," he replied flippantly when journalists asked whether the emirate had been enticed by his name.

Among the other major Harken investors around that time was billionaire financier George Soros, who discussed the company and Bush a decade later with the *Nation* magazine. "I didn't know him," Soros said. "He was supposed to bring in the Gulf connection. But it didn't come to anything. We were buying political influence. That was it. He was not much of a businessman." Soros apparently lost patience while waiting for the President's son to arrange matters in the Persian Gulf and unloaded all his stock on July 12, 1989 — six months before Harken signed its deal with Bahrain.

Billionaires are often lucky as well as smart. Years later, those wells off the coast of Bahrain turned out to be dry holes. By then Bush had long since dumped Harken, too.

On June 22, 1990, six months *after* the Bahrain contract was announced, George W. quietly sold off 212,140 Harken shares, which grossed $848,560. He used most of the proceeds to pay off the bank loan he had taken a year earlier to finance his portion of the Texas Rangers deal. In early August, Iraqi dictator Saddam Hussein sent his troops and tanks across the southern border into Kuwait. Saddam's aggression drove down the stock price of every oil company doing business in the Gulf, including Harken, whose shares fell to $3.12.

Although there is no evidence that the President's son was tipped off about the impending Gulf crisis, he certainly had reason to know about Harken's other troubles. He served on the company's three-member audit committee and also on a special "fairness committee" appointed that spring to consider how a corporate restructuring would affect share value.

When Bush's stock dumping was first reported by the *Houston Post* in October 1990, there were no accusations of insider trading. Then in April 1991, the *Wall Street Journal* revealed that the Securities and Exchange Commission had not been notified of his timely trade until eight months after the legal deadline. The regulatory agency commenced an investigation that concluded in 1991 with no action against George W.

That outcome was hardly a surprise. The SEC chairman at the time, Richard Breeden, was an especially ardent Bush loyalist, and the agency's general counsel, James Doty, was the same Texas attorney who had handled the sale of the Rangers baseball team for George W. and his partners in 1989. During the SEC investigation, Bush was represented by Robert Jordan, who had been a law partner of Doty at the Baker Botts firm in Texas. (In 2001, Bush named Jordan as U.S. Ambassador to Saudi Arabia.) Bush has insisted that he didn't know about the firm's mounting losses and that Harken's general counsel approved his stock sell-off.

What he didn't say — and what his lawyers didn't tell the SEC until the day after its investigation officially closed — was that Harken's lawyers had explicitly warned Bush and other directors against insider trading in a memo issued just before he sold his shares. The memo explained that if directors had any unfavorable information about the company's outlook, their sale of Harken stock would be viewed critically if the price dropped soon after. "Unless the favorable facts clearly are more important than the unfavorable, the insider should be advised not to sell," it said.

All the information Bush had about Harken's prospects at that point was negative. The firm was near bankruptcy. A year earlier, the Harken management had created a phony profit of $10 million by selling some of the company's assets, at an inflated price, to Aloha Petroleum, a front company owned by company insiders. That maneuver, similar to what Enron did on a much larger scale a decade later, had preserved the Harken stock price for a while by concealing most of the company's losses.

Two months after Bush sold the bulk of his Harken holdings, the company posted losses for the second quarter of well over $20 million and its shares fell another 24 percent; by year's end, Harken was trading at $1.25. (The current price of Harken shares is around 20 cents — equivalent to 2 cents a share in 1990, before a reverse stock split that later gave investors one new share for every ten held previously.)

Suspicions surrounding Harken and other dubious enterprises associated with the President's sons — particularly Neil's Silverado fiasco — caused the family severe embarrassment during the doomed 1992 reelection campaign. But that unhappy interlude scarcely stalled George W.'s own quest for success. The Rangers partnership needed a new stadium or they would never make any money.

Backed by Rainwater's billions they could have built a new stadium themselves, of course, but that would have violated the crony capitalist methods of the major leagues. In the sports business it's the taxpayers, not the club owners, who pay the construction costs of new facilities. So Rangers management began to hint unsubtly that unless the city government of Arlington, Texas, provided land and financing on concessionary terms, they would be obliged to move the team to nearby Dallas or Fort Worth.

Even by baseball monopoly standards, the capitulation of Arlington mayor Richard Greene was abject. In October 1990, Mayor Greene signed a contract that guaranteed $135 million toward the stadium's estimated price of $190 million. The city would earn a maximum of $5 million annually in rent, no matter how much the Rangers reaped from ticket sales and television (a sum that eventually rose to $100 million a year). Amazingly, the Rangers could buy the stadium after the accumulated rental payments reached a mere $60 million—and the property acquired so cheaply would include not just a fancy new stadium with a seating capacity of 49,000, but an additional 270 acres of valuable land.

When Mayor Greene signed on to this giveaway deal, he was simultaneously negotiating with federal authorities to settle a massive lawsuit against him, in yet another savings-and-loan bust. Greene had formerly been president of the Arlington branch of Sunbelt Savings Association, described by the *Fort Worth Star-Telegram* as "one of the most notorious failures of the S&L scandal."

Sunbelt had lost an estimated $2 billion, and cleaning up the mess there cost the feds about $297 million. Around the same time that Greene signed the deal enriching the Rangers syndicate, federal officials agreed to let him pay $40,000 to settle the Sunbelt case—scarcely enough to cover the costs of the negotiation—and walk away. "George had no knowledge of my problems; there is no connection," he assured the *New York Times* in September 2000.

The stadium scheme predictably generated local opposition to "corporate welfare." But together with Mayor Greene, George W. convinced an overwhelming majority of Arlington voters to approve a sales tax hike that would back the stadium bonds in January 1991. The referendum must have impressed Democratic Governor Ann Richards, who quickly signed legislation creating the Arlington Sports Facilities Development Authority—with power to issue bonds and exercise eminent domain over any obstinate landowners.

That legislation represented crony capitalism at its worst. Never before had a municipal authority in Texas been given license to seize the property of a private citizen for the benefit of other private citizens. When a recalcitrant family refused to sell a 13-acre parcel near the stadium site for half its appraised value, their land was condemned and handed over to Bush and his partners. The ensuing lawsuit revealed that prior to passage of the enabling legislation, the Rangers management had planned to wield condemnation as a weapon to drive down the property's price. In a judgment against the city, an outraged jury awarded more than $4 million to the Arlington family whose land had been expropriated.

Long before that verdict came down, however, the shiny new structure George W. had christened The Ballpark in Arlington was finished. With the stadium being readied to open the following spring, Bush announced in November 1993 that he would be running for governor. He didn't blush when he proclaimed that his campaign theme would promote self-reliance and personal responsibility rather than dependence on government. As governor, Bush would find that his personal financial interests meshed with those of his partners and supporters — and those mutual interests were advanced by his actions in office. In Austin, crony capitalism became a way of life.

On December 6, 1994, George W. received a belated $25,000 campaign contribution from Thomas O. Hicks, whose support Bush had unsuccessfully solicited at the beginning of his campaign. Hicks was easily one of the wealthiest men in Texas, and, more specifically, he was the chief executive of Hicks, Muse, Tate & Furst, a highly diversified investment partnership.

Bush took his donation and supported the investor's ambitious plan to take control of the financial assets of the University of Texas, then worth about $13 billion. As a UT grad, Tom Hicks frankly believed that his alma mater's investment strategy had been far too cautious. He wanted to move billions out of equities and into "alternative" investments of the kind managed by his firm.

From Hicks's point of view, the chief obstacle in tapping such repositories of public treasure was that their activities were subject to scrutiny from a variety of interested parties, including legislators, newspaper reporters, and public interest organizations. So in 1995 Hicks brought a radical innovation to the UT endowment: privatization. He even paid for his own lobbyist to ensure that the legislature passed his plan to transfer all the university's diverse holdings into a new non-profit corporation known as the University of Texas Investment Management Company, or UTIMCO.

It was one of the most significant changes in Texas government during Bush's tenure in the statehouse and among the first important bills that he signed. With Bush's support and the sponsorship of legislators associated with the Governor, the UTIMCO bill flew through the capitol in 1995 with very few questions asked. The new outfit would not be subject to state laws that mandate open meetings and public records. After UTIMCO officially took over from the regents' investment committees in early 1996, with Hicks as its first chairman, all its business was done behind closed doors. The directors often gathered for their monthly board meetings at the lavish offices of Hicks, Muse, Tate & Furst in downtown Dallas.

Largely freed from public accountability, UTIMCO embarked on a series of deals that raised serious questions about conflict of interest and political favoritism. Friends and longtime associates of Thomas Hicks, and his firm's past and future business partners — as well as major Republican contributors and political supporters of the Bush family — received hundreds of millions of dollars from the University of Texas investment funds. There was nothing unlawful about these decisions, all of which were vetted by the powerhouse law firm of Vinson & Elkins, another of Bush's largest lifetime donors.

Named by the Governor to oversee the entire UTIMCO operation, as chairman of the university regents, was oilman Donald Evans. He has raised money for all George W.'s political campaigns, beginning with an unsuccessful congressional race in 1978. For the presidential campaign in 2000, Evans ran the Bush "Pioneers," the team of heavy funders who raised more than $100,000 each. (He is currently serving as Secretary of Commerce.)

Following that first $25,000 contribution to George W. in December 1994, Tom Hicks and his brother Steven eventually gave another $146,000 to the Governor's election war chests. His partners have donated tens of thousands more. Together they are among the biggest donors to George W. Bush since 1995. Total contributions to Republican candidates and causes from Hicks, his family members, and his firm are well over half a million dollars.

In 1996, UTIMCO directors made an investment of $50 million with Kohlberg Kravis Roberts. Among that firm's founding partners is Henry Kravis, the corporate raider who has consistently been among the country's largest contributors to Republican causes during the past decade. Kravis was a financial cochairman of Bush-Quayle 1992, and he boasted to reporters that he was a personal friend and confidant of George Herbert Walker Bush. Two years later, UTIMCO invested $20 million in a deal with Bass Brothers Enterprises. As Republican donors, the Bass clan in Fort Worth rivals Kravis and his partners in generosity. Lee Bass raised $78,000 as a Bush Pioneer in 2000.

UTIMCO also placed $96 million with Maverick Capital, a relatively new partnership in Dallas. Among Maverick's main investors and general partners are members of the Wyly family, the principal stockholders in Sterling Software—and, again, longtime friends of the Bushes. Between 1993 and 1998, various Wyly family members gave well over $300,000 to Republican candidates and committees. But investor Sam Wyly is best known for funding a series of harsh attack ads against John McCain during the 2000 Republican primaries. (As the Republican Party's leading critic of crony capitalism—a term he has often uttered on the Senate floor—McCain made himself into a dangerous enemy of the party insiders. They would have spent much more to defeat him.)

Did George W. Bush understand what his appointee Tom Hicks was doing? "I swear I didn't get into politics to feather my nest or feather my friends' nests," Bush told the *Houston Chronicle* in August 1998. "Any insinuation that I have used my office to help my friends is simply not true."

On completion of the Rangers deal in 1998, Hicks paid about $250 million for the team—or three times the price paid by Bush and his partners in 1989. The other members of the Rangers partnership had fattened Bush's payout six times over, by awarding him additional shares in the team that brought his 1.8 percent share up to 12 percent. The then Governor made about $15 million on the sale.

When George W. Bush declared his candidacy for President in 1999, hundreds of his wealthiest supporters pledged to raise at least $100,000 each for his campaign. For a time their names were kept confidential, but eventually the Bush campaign—meaning finance chairman Donald Evans—released the names of the first 115 Pioneers to meet their dollar quota, even as hundreds more unnamed backers were reportedly collecting checks. Listed among the founding group of successful Pioneers were R. Steven Hicks, Hicks lobbyist Tom Loeffler, three partners in Vinson & Elkins—the law firm that has served as counsel to UTIMCO, Enron, and many other crony firms—along with Charles Wyly and Lee Bass, whose partnerships received substantial investments from UTIMCO.

Of all the beneficiaries of UTIMCO's investments, however, the Carlyle Group is by far the most interesting and powerful. Carlyle may be the world's most influential and successful company based on crony capitalism. On March 1, 1995, two months after George W. Bush was sworn in as Texas Governor, the University of Texas regents voted to place $10 million with Carlyle, a Washington-based merchant bank that until recently was chaired by Frank Carlucci, a former Secretary of Defense in the Reagan administration.

The Carlyle fund that received the UTIMCO money was called Carlyle Partners II. The firm's Web site described it with exquisite delicacy as pursuing "an investment strategy focused upon the intersection of government and business." That's the polite definition of cronyism.

Among Carlyle's partners are numerous former Reagan and Bush administration figures, including Richard Darman, economic adviser to President Bush, and James Baker III, the polished former White House Chief of Staff, Secretary of State, Bush-Quayle campaign chairman, and chief attorney for George W. Bush in the contest for Florida's electoral votes in November 2000. That same month, coincidentally, the Texas teachers pension fund—whose board was appointed when

George W. Bush was Governor—gave Carlyle another $100 million to invest.

That a firm involving his father and his father's closest associates was awarded Texas public investment contracts at the beginning and the end of his term as Governor was unseemly. But George W. Bush also had his own long-standing and lucrative ties to Carlyle. Among his more obscure business activities was a corporate directorship at Caterair, one of the nation's largest airline catering services, which was acquired by Carlyle in 1989. A seat on the company's board was arranged for George W. by former Nixon White House aide and long-time Bush associate Fred Malek, then a Carlyle adviser.

In recent years, the elder Bush has enjoyed a lucrative relationship with Carlyle. Soon after leaving the White House, George Herbert Walker Bush began to deliver speeches at events sponsored by the secretive merchant bank. The ex-President joined up with Baker, Carlucci, and Darman on a more formal basis in 1998, when he became a "senior adviser" to Carlyle Asia Partners, a fund set up to buy distressed businesses in the Far East. He is also reportedly an investor in Carlyle. Over the past several years he has given many speeches in Asia and the Middle East, where he remains highly popular among politicians and government officials. Inevitably, his companions on these trips are Carlyle representatives.

The Bush White House was mortified when news reports revealed that Carlyle's investors included members of Osama bin Laden's wealthy family in Saudi Arabia—where Carlyle serves as a defense adviser to the kingdom for a reported contract of $50 million annually.

Ironically, on September 11, 2001, bin Laden family representatives were sitting with Carlucci, Baker, and other Carlyle officials at the firm's annual investor conference in Washington's luxurious Ritz-Carlton Hotel. Members of the bin Laden family in the United States were swiftly whisked back to Jidda after the terrorist attacks, without suffering the indignity of questioning by the FBI. To avoid further embarrassment, the bin Laden investment was bought out by Carlyle.

On several occasions, reports have surfaced of Carlyle's broad, pervasive interests "intersecting" with the actions of the Bush administration. The instance that drew the most attention involved a long-standing deal between the Pentagon and United Defense, a Carlyle subsidiary that is among the Army's five biggest contractors.

In a move that led to open warfare within the Pentagon and on Capitol Hill, Secretary of Defense Donald Rumsfeld terminated the Army's multibillion-dollar procurement of the "Crusader" artillery vehicle built by United Defense. While Rumsfeld was praised for a principled decision that hurt the interests of Carlucci, his old Princeton wrestling team buddy, observers noted that the decision wasn't announced until after Carlyle took United Defense public in December 2001—and pocketed more than $200 million. And the Crusader program wasn't really terminated. Instead, United Defense received a consolation prize when $475 million was budgeted to redevelop the artillery vehicle as a cannon.

The immediate interests of Carlyle were likewise aided in the fall of 2002 when the Bush administration intervened in a labor dispute on the West Coast docks. For months, the investment firm had quietly been trying to purchase a majority stake in CSX Lines, a domestic-flag ocean shipping subsidiary of the CSX railroad conglomerate.

The Carlyle-CSX deal was almost scuttled, however, when the dock employers locked out members of the International Longshore Workers Union in an effort to win contract concessions. A prolonged work stoppage on the docks made CSX Lines a far less attractive investment. Both the Department of Labor and the Defense Department sought to force the union to return to work, warning that the labor dispute was undermining "national security." With the administration's help, the employers won a judicial injunction in late October that forced a settlement. Within six weeks, the sale of CSX Lines went through, with Carlyle paying $240 million in cash and $60 million in securities. Meanwhile, in yet another remarkable coincidence, CSX chief executive John Snow was selected as the Bush administration's new Treasury Secretary.

No matter what the President may promise to do about "corporate reform," he is as likely to challenge cronyism and corruption as to join the Democratic Party. Some crooked businessmen may be sent to prison in the corporate bankruptcy aftershocks—but as Michael Kinsley once observed, the true scandal isn't what's illegal. The true scandal is what's legal. That includes the worldwide operations of Bush, Inc., which continue unabated and unembarrassed while George W. occupies the Oval Office. The awarding of billions in federal contracts in Iraq to such Bush-friendly firms as Halliburton and Bechtel was all too typical.

What the Bush family's protean worldwide network of political and financial connections symbolizes is a system where insiders almost always win and investors often lose. It is a system that encourages neither good government nor responsible business. It's a system that results in wasted capital, squandered or purloined assets, and busted companies. It mocks the conservative notion that free enterprise can operate transparently and fairly in the absence of government regulation.

The story of Bush, Inc., is also a warning against a government run by the same insiders whose political and financial fortunes have been built not on free enterprise or "compassionate conservatism," but on the infectious greed of crony capitalism.

9 FAITH, CHARITY, AND THE MAYBERRY MACHIAVELLIS

"George W. Bush is a compassionate conservative."

"I am a fiscal conservative and a family conservative. And I am a compassionate conservative, because I know my philosophy is optimistic and full of hope for every American." So George W. Bush described himself and his beliefs on the eve of his first campaign for President. With that speech, the Texas Governor hoped to finesse a paradox of national politics. To win the nomination of the Republican Party, he had to be acceptable to every kind of conservative, from the libertarian to the fundamentalist; to win the presidency itself, he also had to embody an alternative to the angry conservatism that Americans had found increasingly repellent during the Clinton years.

Now, after observing his first few years in the Oval Office, we have a clearer understanding of what his words meant on that auspicious day in New Hampshire. Being a "fiscal conservative" meant passing lopsided tax cuts for the wealthy few, and leaving the federal budget in deficit for the foreseeable future. Being a "family conservative" meant looking after certain families, particularly if their annual incomes are higher than $200,000 and their estates are valued at more than $2 million. And so far, being a "compassionate conservative" appears to mean nothing very different from being a hard-hearted, stingy, old-fashioned conservative. It always helps to smile, though.

No cheerful grin can brighten the dismal record of compassionate conservatism since George W. Bush's presidential inauguration. His budgets prove that he still emphatically prefers cutting the taxes of wealthy individuals and corporations to maintaining living standards for poor and working-class families. States and localities, their economies soured and their budgets overstrained, are unable to maintain services for their neediest citizens. Food deliveries to many of the helpless elderly will end. More than a million Americans, most of them children, are losing their Medicaid health coverage in what the National Governors Association describes as "the worst fiscal crisis since World War II." For the first time in a decade, the rate of poverty is rising again, with 1.3 million Americans falling below the poverty line in 2001.

The most vigorous response of the Bush White House to these grim prospects is to propose abolishing "double taxation" of stock dividends. "That is very much pro-poor," according to R. Glenn Hubbard, the former chairman of Bush's Council of Economic Advisers, even though the poor won't get any of the benefits.

It's the unfair burdens on the rich that always cause George W. Bush deep concern, a caring that seems strangely absent from his approach to the problems of the poor. When the welfare reform legislation enacted in 1996 was reauthorized during the summer of 2002, Bush insisted on raising the number of weekly hours worked by mothers on public assistance without increasing payments for child care. Against the advice of governors who have made those 1996 reforms work, White House officials also sought to make work requirements more rigid, creating unnecessary obstacles to education and training—all so that the President could appear "tough" on welfare mothers. The Congressional Budget Office has indicated that the President's proposed work requirements should include up to $11 billion in new child-care funding. But Bush has actually proposed to cut child-care and after-school programs as well as vocational education and job training.

And while he is fighting to allow the highest income class to pay nothing on investment earnings, he is tightening the requirements for those who seek the earned income tax credit—meaning the working poor. Wage labor will be taxed, but dividends will be tax-free. The earned income tax credit, or EITC, is one of the most successful government initiatives directed toward Americans who work full-time but cannot earn enough to keep their families above the poverty line. Essentially a refund of a portion of regressive payroll taxes paid by low-income workers, the EITC began under Reagan and was greatly expanded by Clinton, who believed that nobody who "plays by the rules" should live in hunger and squalor.

In 1999, at the zenith of his compassionate phase, Bush stood up as a defender of the EITC against mean-spirited congressional Republicans who were trying to reduce it. He quite rightly denounced the scheme pushed by his fellow Texan Tom DeLay, a professing Christian, as an attempt to balance the federal budget "on the backs of the poor." For that he won praise from Clinton and vitriol from the *Weekly Standard*, which accused him of using "liberal buzz words" for "Clintonesque" purposes. But having since legislated mammoth tax cuts for the wealthy and run up a record deficit, Bush won't defend EITC from conservatives in the White House and Congress who are seeking to cut it, eliminate the funds that help workers apply for it, impose harsher audits on families that claim it—or even eliminate it.

Even the small break provided to working poor families in Bush's 2001 tax cut—which was otherwise a bonanza for the wealthiest 1 percent—was designed so that many wouldn't be able to claim it. The tax bill made the $600 child tax credit "partially refundable," which in theory meant that low-income households could receive part of that sum even if they owed little or no federal income taxes. But the confusing and complex methods required to claim the credit left many families bereft, through either ignorance or confusion. Economists at the Progressive Policy Institute blamed the bad design of new tax forms by the Internal Revenue Service and "poor drafting of the law by Republican tax writers in Congress and the Bush administration, whose hostility to tax breaks for low-income workers seems pretty evident." Poor people unlucky enough to lack an accountant were unlikely to obtain that measly six hundred bucks.

Originally, the twin centerpieces of Bush's compassionate conservatism were his ambitious education plan, known as "No Child Left Behind," and his "faith-based initiative" to direct federal funds toward an assortment of private charities, including religious institutions. Owing to the deficits caused by the recession and his tax cuts, however, the education bill he negotiated with Senator Edward Kennedy fell far short of the funding he had originally promised. Although his budget proposal increased education spending, the proposed rise was the lowest in several years. He cut a billion dollars from programs specified in his own bill. One statistic summed up Bush's priorities: his tax cuts for the richest Americans amounted to more than fifty times the total amount he requested for new education spending. At that rate, millions of schoolchildren will be left far behind.

As President, Bush has proved himself a master of photo opportunities and public ceremonies designed to emphasize, as his father once said so plaintively, "Message: I care." The reality beyond the TV cameras often belies the kinder and gentler image, however. Sometimes these showbiz events are stunningly shameless, such as his visit to a Wilmington, Delaware, Boys and Girls Club in April 2001 to announce that he would donate book royalties from *A Charge to Keep* to the Boys and Girls Clubs of America. He and his wife would be hailed for their charitable generosity at tax time. "Because I believe so profoundly, I believe so strongly in mentoring," he said. "And I believe so strongly in helping children understand somebody loves them." At the same time, his budget proposed the complete elimination of $60 million in federal funding for the Boys and Girls Clubs. Royalties from his book sales fell somewhat short of that amount. Where's the love?

The realities of George W. Bush's compassion have certainly turned out to be quite distant from the photo opportunities. But it must be admitted that no American politician has so deftly transformed his party's image since Bill Clinton first ran as a "New Democrat" in 1992. By then, the Democrats had lost three presidential elections because the majority of Americans considered them unfit to govern. Moving himself and his party toward the center on such burdensome issues as crime and welfare, the Arkansas Governor fashioned a message appealing to the moderate independents whose votes were essential to victory.

Eight years later, Bush, too, seized the leadership of a party with a problem. The Republicans had lost two presidential elections, and although they had gained control of the House of Representatives, the large majority they had won in 1994 was shrinking fast. Moderate, suburban voters were alienated by the angry partisanship, self-righteous hypocrisy, and antigovernment extremism of Newt Gingrich's Republican "revolutionaries." By 1999 the House Speaker's colleagues had immolated him, but his brief tenure and the impeachment fiasco he sponsored left behind a cloud of acrid smoke.

The answer devised by Bush and his political adviser Karl Rove — their version of "New Democrat" — was "compassionate conservatism." So deft was this gambit that it left journalists gawking and scratching their heads, as if they had witnessed the candidate literally running in two directions at once. That was the trick: Bush and Rove knew that he could ill afford his father's mistake of alienating the far right. At the same time, they knew he had to prevent himself from being isolated politically on the right.

Distinguishing son from father was a process that began during his second gubernatorial campaign in 1998, with a massive wave of television advertising created by Mark McKinnon, formerly a top Democratic consultant in Austin. McKinnon honestly believed that George W. Bush was a "different kind of Republican," a bipartisan leader who cared about the poor, and that belief showed in his advertising. Later, McKinnon, Rove, and other advisers developed the same themes into a more sophisticated strategy that drew from the two most successful politicians of the postwar era, Bill Clinton and Ronald Reagan.

From Reagan, the Bush advisers borrowed the friendly optimism, the down-home cowboy boots, and the lavishly produced, musically manipulative Morning in America style of advertising, which they retitled "Fresh Start." (If that sounded like a name for a breakfast cereal or a deodorant, it was entirely appropriate.) From Clinton, they adopted the supple tactics of repositioning their rhetoric toward the center and rephrasing issues to neutralize any partisan disadvantage.

In a long profile for the *Washington Post Magazine*, E. J. Dionne marveled at Bush's capacity to convince moderates of his moderation and conservatives of his conservatism, his chameleon talent for "getting people of very different views to believe he is one of them." Combining compassion with conservatism, putting a new face on the old elephant — these were brilliant strokes of marketing that hinted movement toward the center without abandoning the right. Dionne wasn't the only seasoned reporter who wondered whether the Texan's "philosophy" was anything more than a clever feint.

Certainly Bush lacked Clinton's ambition to actually reshape his party. Unlike the New Democrat, Bush pushed no reform of the reigning Republican ideology or agenda. When opportunities arose to challenge the assumptions of the Republican establishment, he pandered instead. Although he loudly disdained "Warshington, D.C." and all its pencil-neck paper-pushing, Bush was very much the creature of a Beltway coalition that united corporate lobbyists with conservative activists. It was a nexus embodied by Bush campaign consultant Ralph Reed — the smooth, boyish founder of the Christian Coalition who went on to chair the Georgia GOP (and to lobby for Enron). Tough politicians like Reed accepted Bush's compassion-speak for one reason only: they assumed it would help him win.

This wasn't the first time, of course, that attractive branding had sold the nation a phony product. After two years of skewed tax cuts, destructive deregulation, and social regression, nobody doubts Bush's conservatism. But where's the compassion?

To paraphrase a famous man, it depends on what the meaning of that word is.

Americans normally understand *compassion* to mean caring for the ill, homeless, hungry, unemployed, destitute, and defenseless. *Compassionate* softens *conservative*, a word that tends to be associated with smug stinginess rather than benevolence or mercy. *Compassionate conservative* acknowledges that unfortunate stereotype, indicating a person of right-wing inclination who nevertheless feels an obligation to lift up the downtrodden. In the modern context, the term also suggests acceptance of government responsibility — since private charity has never been sufficient to relieve social distress.

A simple statistic demonstrates how ridiculous it is to think that private charity can replace the public sector in maintaining the social contract. According to a study prepared several years ago by the Century Foundation, the total *assets* of America's 34,000 foundations (not the annual income from their endowments) add up to around 10 percent of current government expenditures for social welfare and related domestic programs. There is no reason to believe that ratio has changed much, particularly after plunging equity values decimated the foundation portfolios. Charitable groups lack the resources to sustain the nation's poor at even the most minimal level of survival — let alone to help them escape poverty.

All that should be utterly obvious. But the ideological authors of Bush's "philosophy" have devised their own definition of *compassionate conservatism*, which isn't obvious at all. The phrase itself is right-wing wonk-speak. It usually refers to the policy prescriptions of Marvin Olasky, a professor of journalism at the University of Texas who also publishes *World*, an ultraconservative, fundamentalist Christian newsweekly. With the assistance of the Heritage Foundation and other think tanks on the right, Olasky has written three books extolling religious charity as a moral alternative to the sinful welfare state.

Campaign publicity presented compassionate conservatism as a break with discredited politicos and their harsh attitudes. The reality was a happy-sounding sound bite for the same reactionary agenda that has defined Republicanism since the Reagan era. Whatever benign ambitions Bush may once have nurtured for his "philosophy," their scope was soon reduced by recession, war, and tax cuts that left the Treasury bare.

But compassionate conservatism was a deception with many layers, not just another bogus slogan.

On the most superficial level—where presidential campaigns reach the broad public—Bush had pasted a smiley face over the alienating scowl worn by Republicans during the Clinton years. "I like to joke that a compassionate conservative is a conservative with a smile, not a conservative with a frown," Bush explained in an unintentionally funny passage in his 1999 campaign biography, *A Charge to Keep*. "Some who would agree with a conservative philosophy have been turned off by a strident tone."

Bush didn't mention Newt Gingrich by name in his book because there was no need to. Any American who had been paying attention for the past decade knew which strident conservative was a turn-off. As a rhetorical instrument, compassionate conservatism served to distinguish Bush from the nasty, hard-hearted House Republicans and their unlamented leader. The conservative journalist Byron York noted bitterly that Bush had set Gingrich up as a "straw man," then knocked him down to impress a fickle public.

The former Speaker wasn't even invited to address the Republican Convention that nominated Bush and Cheney, where strategist Karl Rove staged a colorful, multicultural pageant. At Dubya's convention, amid all the optimism and uplift, a Gingrich appearance would have been a serious downer.

How ironic then, as York and others pointed out, that it was Gingrich who introduced *compassionate conservatism* into the Republican lexicon with his typical relentless enthusiasm. It was Gingrich who first appreciated how such a simple phrase could paint an ethical, Christian gloss on a program of social Darwinism like his Contract with America's draconian reduction in funding for the poor, children, and the elderly. And it was Gingrich who, in an inspiring speech immediately after he was elected Speaker, vowed to alleviate poverty (and then of course did the opposite).

For once, Gingrich was too far ahead of his time. In early 1996, the House Speaker had written a gushing introduction to *Renewing*

American Compassion, one of several books by Olasky, the prolific author, editor, and college professor billed as "the godfather of compassionate conservatism." Not incidentally, Gingrich had also directed generous financial support from his privately funded Progress and Freedom Foundation to Olasky, whom he compared to Alexis de Tocqueville.

Three years later, Bush contributed the introduction to Olasky's next volume, *Compassionate Conservatism: What It Is, What It Does, and How It Can Transform America*. The author's appreciation could scarcely have been clearer. *Christian Century*'s reviewer called it "less a book than an advertisement for Bush's presidential campaign, published to coincide with his anointing as the Republican nominee." Portions of the text resembled a Bush campaign pamphlet, including several gratuitous swipes at Al Gore, a proponent of "faith-based" charity whose concern about government support for religious proselytizing infuriated Olasky.

Olasky's connections to the Bush political machine were direct and authoritative. His patron was none other than Karl Rove, the candidate's closest, most powerful adviser, who had sensed the propaganda potential of Olasky's work as early as 1993. An autodidact who never graduated from college, Rove read widely and thought of himself, with some justification, as an intellectual. Olasky's tendentious, pseudo-scholarly writings impressed him (even if Bush could hardly be bothered to read them). Rove brought Olasky to Bush's attention and approved the appointment of Olasky as chairman of the Bush-Cheney campaign's subcommittee on religion in 1999.

With Gingrich in exile, Bush could boast that "compassionate conservatism" was "the brand name my philosophy now wears. I didn't invent the phrase, but I adopted it, and I have made it my own." It was, he said, "ingrained in my heart." When he made his initial campaign stops in Iowa and New Hampshire in June 1999, he spoke in the tones of a courageous dissident. "I am a compassionate conservative. I welcome the label. And on this ground, I will make my stand."

Although Bush used rhetoric about compassion to distance himself publicly from Gingrich, their overlapping relationships with Olasky showed how little ideological space really existed between them. Both had endorsed the rebranding of conservatism with a human face. Both had done favors for this idea's "godfather" and accepted favors from him. Both were determined to dismantle the programs of the New Deal and the Great Society, from Social Security to Medicare.

But Gingrich couldn't redecorate his threatening image in comforting pastels. He wasn't sufficiently nimble to move in two directions at once. Bush, having entered the national consciousness as an unknown figure marked only by his father's famous name, had no need to remake a damaged image. He rolled himself out as the "conservative with a heart," and profited by contrasting himself with the disgraced former Speaker. And if Bush's differences with Gingrich were a pretense — as they surely were — that easy deception only reflected the more profound dishonesty of the "compassion" strategy.

On closer inspection, there is nothing moderate about compassionate conservatism or its pious godfather. Marvin Olasky is a former Communist reborn as a radical fundamentalist, whose attraction to ideas on the authoritarian or totalitarian fringe has remained a lifelong constant. He may have been the only young American who actually signed up with the Communist Party in 1972, during the rather uninspiring Brezhnev regime.

Nor is there anything innovative or visionary about Olasky's approach to poverty, which contemplates a return to the miserable treatment meted out to society's unfortunate in centuries past. His notions can be traced to Victorian-era views about the undeserving poor, and his radical goal is to replace government assistance with private (and preferably church-based) charity. His insights are no more original than they were when neoconservative historians and pundits framed the same argument decades ago, blaming poverty entirely on the moral, mental, and social inferiority of the poor themselves.

The privileged President has occasionally articulated his own quite similar outlook. When E. J. Dionne interviewed Bush about compassionate conservatism in 1999, Bush insisted that poverty is the result of personal, individual shortcomings rather than social and economic circumstances. "Oftentimes people are poor because of decisions they make," he said. "Oftentimes people are poor because they didn't get a good education . . . [and aren't] making right choices and staying in school and working hard in school." (Presumably their parents failed to usher them into Andover and Yale as "legacies," where they could earn mediocre grades while chugging beer in the frat house.)

Bush's answer sounds like a less polished version of the finger-wagging banalities that fill conservative magazines. But his guru Olasky draws inspiration from sources more arcane—and considerably more extreme—than the *Weekly Standard* or the *National Review*. The media coverage introducing him as the new Republican avatar of compassion has generally ignored his ideological pedigree—except for repeated references to his spiritual migration from his family's Judaism through Communism and atheism to his rebirth as a fundamentalist Presbyterian. That's when his story actually becomes interesting and disturbing.

In *Compassionate Conservatism*, the book featuring Bush's introduction, Olasky offers clues to the real roots of his ideology. To a knowledgeable reader, the text reveals his longstanding financial and intellectual connections with Christian Reconstructionism—a small but influential fringe of the religious right. While liberals sometimes mockingly liken Jerry Falwell and Pat Robertson to the repressive Muslim fundamentalists of the Taliban, it is the Christian Reconstructionists whose vision of a purified America most closely resembles that of radical Islam.

The Reconstructionists despise American democracy, the First Amendment, and the separation of church and state. Their ideal society would be ruled by Christians like themselves, according to a literal interpretation of Old Testament biblical law, which prescribes the death penalty for such offenses as homosexuality, abortion, atheism, juvenile delinquency, adultery, and blasphemy. They openly advocate the suppression of other religions, including that of Christians who don't share their interpretation of God's will.

Among the leading financial supporters of Olasky's work is Howard Ahmanson, an Orange County banking heir who has spent millions funding Republican and ultraright candidates and causes in California. Ahmanson is also a generous benefactor of Christian Reconstructionism who once declared that his life's purpose was "integrating biblical law" into American society. Toward that end, he spent more than twenty years as a board member and funder of the late Reverend R. J. Rushdoony's Chalcedon Institute, the most important center of the Reconstructionist movement.

Olasky has always avoided any explicit endorsement of Christian Reconstructionism, but some of his obsessions overlap with those of Rushdoony and Ahmanson, their mutual backer. Like them, Olasky seems to think public education ought to be abolished (although for some reason he hasn't resigned his position teaching journalism and history at the University of Texas, one of the largest public universities in the United States). And also like them, Olasky believes that the poor should be consigned to the mercies of Christian charity, and that the only true solution to such social ills as addiction, poverty, and homelessness is religious conversion. Indeed, the only people deserving of assistance are those who have repented and accepted Jesus as their savior.

Even though Olasky doesn't espouse Rushdoony's most outlandish precepts, he has endorsed the late reverend's loony writings as "important" and "useful." In an earlier work on the "anti-Christian bias" of the American media, for example, Olasky quoted Rushdoony respectfully as an authority on the Ninth Commandment ("Thou shalt not covet thy neighbor's wife"). He has also cited such Reconstructionist authors as George Grant and Gary North (a widely published writer in conservative publications who regards stoning as the biblically correct form of capital punishment).

Olasky gratefully acknowledges the assistance of George Grant in another of his books, *The Tragedy of American Compassion* (which Gingrich put on his syllabus for Republican House members in 1995). He has frequently published book reviews by Grant—another outspoken advocate of the death penalty for homosexuals—in *World*, the weekly religious right newsmagazine that is edited by Olasky at his Austin headquarters.

What does this fanatical ideology have to do with compassionate conservatism, which was meant to help Bush sound moderate? After all, neither Olasky nor his Republican patrons advocate Rushdoony's "dominion" theology, which would place society and government under the thumb of a repressive theocracy. Moreover, Olasky has revised his original insistence on privatizing all forms of public assistance. He now supports government aid to private religious charities and programs, under the Bush administration's "faith-based initiative."

But the mean, bone-ignorant essence of Rushdoony's teaching about poverty—with its indictment of the poor as moral miscreants who are responsible for their own misery—appears to have strongly influenced Olasky, who in turn influences Bush. Compassion is reserved for those who accept their moral failure and cease questioning authority. Only such humbled sinners merit the assistance of their social and theological betters.

Such punitive attitudes are closer to Puritanism and even feudalism than to modern American values of the last hundred years or so—or for that matter to the beliefs of the nation's founders. When Olasky writes that America's moral decline commenced with the Progressive Era at the beginning of the twentieth century, he isn't just spouting hyperbole. He deeply believes that public provision for the benefit of workers and the poor is an affront to God, even if he must tolerate such programs for temporary partisan expedience.

The ideology that shapes the political outlook of Bush and Rove as well as Olasky is an unwholesome stew of libertarian economics and religious orthodoxy. It exalts church and corporation over the modern democratic state. It condemns democratic initiatives to constrain corporate power or regulate economic activity. It defines the wealthy as God's elect, even if, like George W. Bush, they have inherited wealth and power that made their lives easy from the beginning.

Right-wing sages like Olasky and Rove fret constantly that welfare,

Medicaid, and food stamps will corrupt generations of the poor—but they never seem to worry that inheriting millions of tax-free dollars might encourage idleness, dependency, and indulgence among the children of the rich. Indeed, their ideology brusquely rejects almost any gesture by government to improve the condition of the poor, even when the beneficiaries are the sinless children of churchgoing, hard-working, inner-city families that subsist on the minimum wage, which Olasky believes should be abolished anyway.

A philosophy with these characteristics could be called miserly, mean, mindless, self-righteous, ruinous, twisted, archaic, addled, absurd, shallow, or sterile; perhaps some would call it harsh or hard-headed. Certainly such a philosophy would qualify as conservative in current parlance. In my view, it should be called un-American. To call it compassionate, however, is a perversion of language and a political fraud.

There is little recognizable as compassion in the regime of the "compassionate conservative." Bush has spoken often of "mercy" and "love" as the foundations of American life. Like his father, who talked about "a thousand points of light," Bush envisions "armies of compassion" to uplift the suffering. But speeches are cheap, and helping the poor is costly—especially when the poor don't really deserve to be helped, and all the revenues are already reserved for the affluent.

The meager quality of Bush's mercy began to be revealed years ago in Austin. Among his most widely criticized policy choices as governor was a decision to deprive 200,000 children from poor working families of subsidized health insurance. Democrats wanted the program, which combined federal and state funding, to cover children whose families earned incomes up to 200 percent of the poverty level.

Bush insisted that the state wouldn't help any family with an income higher than 150 percent of the poverty level. Although the state treasury was then flush with revenue, Bush claimed to be worried about commitments that might be unaffordable in the future. At the same time, he was handing out almost $2 billion in tax cuts to the state's most affluent families and a little lagniappe of $45 million in corporate tax breaks to the petroleum interests. "These are tough times for the oil and gas industry," he explained.

So those 200,000 children got no medical insurance. The rich suburbanites and the oil companies cashed big checks. The state treasury of Texas was stuck with an enormous budget gap when the recession eventually struck. George Bush left those problems behind and went to the White House. That episode illustrated his priorities: lavish compassion for Big Oil and affluent Texans, strict conservatism for low-wage workers and their kids.

The oil industry survived. When Bush left for Washington, however, the number of uninsured low-income children in his home state was by far the highest in the nation at 1.5 million.

The impoverished children of Texas—whose innocence of any blame for their condition should be obvious even to the sternest "Christian"—had not seen their lives improved by Bush's compassion. Compared with the rest of the nation, there was a far higher percentage of children living in poverty there, including more than 70 percent of the state's black and Hispanic children. More than one of every nine children under age six lived in what the federal government defined as "extreme poverty." A Texas child had a considerably higher risk of dying from abuse or neglect than those elsewhere in the nation, perhaps because the state authorities were less likely to investigate child abuse cases. The same child was among those in the nation least likely to receive immunization against disease.

Despite the governor's professed concern for the unborn, those still in the womb didn't necessarily fare so well, either. When he was governor, only four states provided less prenatal care than Texas. The rates of malnutrition were the third highest, after New Mexico and Mississippi. Funding for food stamps in Texas declined precipitously as a result of Bush's welfare "reform."

Spending on public health in Texas was among the lowest in the nation. The state's poor were among the least likely to receive Medicaid benefits, because the state government spent not a dime in federal funds to ensure that eligible families were enrolled. An appropriation of $11 million during Bush's final year as Governor would have brought another $18 million in federal matching funds to provide poor children with dental care. The legislature didn't bother.

Other statistics attested to how little compassionate conservatism meant to the underclass of the Lone Star State. Nearly 17 percent of the population subsisted on incomes below the federal poverty line, a figure that compared poorly with the national average, which was then under 14 percent. Contrary to the stereotype of laziness and dependency popularized by the likes of Marvin Olasky, more than 72 percent of the poor families in Texas derived most of their living from work. To those struggling people, neither Olasky nor Bush had much to offer—except an admonition to come to Jesus.

As the nation entered the holiday season in 2002, shortly after the Republican victory in the midterm elections, a stunning demonstration of feckless brutality proved that compassionate conservatism remained a hollow promise. Intent on securing his homeland security bill, Bush pressed hard for a set of special-interest amendments that would help ensure its passage.

One outrageous provision, of which nobody on Capitol Hill or in the White House would admit authorship, protected Eli Lilly Pharmaceuticals—a firm with close ties to Bush family members and the White House budget director—from lawsuits over a vaccine additive suspected of causing brain damage to children. Another amendment repealed government sanctions against U.S. companies that relocated offshore to evade federal taxes. With little debate, the package was rammed through Congress in a matter of days.

What Bush and his party's leadership in the House could not be bothered to complete during the lame-duck congressional session, however, was a bill that would have extended unemployment benefits for hundreds of thousands of jobless Americans. The Senate had approved a bipartisan plan to extend benefits until March 2003, in the forlorn hope that economic recovery would take hold by then. The House version was far stingier, providing only five weeks of additional benefits. Ignoring a plea from Democratic leaders, Bush did nothing to break the stalemate. Nearly a million families sat down to Thanksgiving dinner knowing that their benefits would end three days after Christmas.

The bad news brought a not-so-compassionate but typically conservative response from *Weekly Standard* editor Fred Barnes, a born-again Christian and ardent Bush admirer. "Now a lot of people are going to have to go get jobs," he smugly told his Fox TV audience. "People always wait until the very end of their unemployment benefits, and then when it runs out, then they go get work." (Early in the new year, at the insistence of a bipartisan group of legislators, Congress reinstated benefits for about 800,000 unemployed workers. But another million more whose benefits had already expired were left to seek help from churches and food banks.)

A few weeks after the unemployment fiasco, Bush got a lump of coal in his own Christmas stocking from John DiIulio, the former director of the White House Office of Faith-Based and Community Initiatives. The University of Pennsylvania professor, a prominent specialist in domestic policy, is probably the leading neoconservative exponent of compassionate conservatism. As a devout Catholic and lifelong Democrat, he didn't share Marvin Olasky's religious or social views, but he joined the Republican administration because he hoped to create innovative programs to assist the poor.

After eight months, DiIulio left the White House and returned to teaching and research in February 2002. Several months later, he discussed his frustrations with journalist Ron Suskind. By early December, the glossy pages of *Esquire* magazine were filled with his complaints about Bush's domestic policy.

In a devastating, emotional seven-page letter that Suskind quoted heavily, DiIulio depicted a White House dominated by partisan cynicism and devoid of competent policymakers. Karl Rove and his aides dominated every discussion of domestic issues, always emphasizing media and political strategy at the expense of substance and analysis. DiIulio told Suskind that when he objected to a proposal to kill the earned income tax credit—the landmark program that allows millions of working families to escape poverty—he suddenly realized that he was arguing with libertarians who understood little about the workings of government and had no interest in learning.

"There is no precedent in any modern White House for what is going on in this one: a complete lack of a policy apparatus," he said. "What you've got is everything—and I mean everything—being run by the political arm. It's the reign of the Mayberry Machiavellis."

That was DiIulio's unflattering nickname for Karl Rove and his political aides, "who consistently talked and acted as if the height of political sophistication consisted in reducing every issue to its simplest black-and-white terms for public consumption, then steering legislative initiatives or policy proposals as far right as possible."

The result is that the President's "faith-based initiative" has been transformed into a patronage operation. During the 2002 midterm election campaign, administration officials suddenly showed up at inner-city churches, seeking to entice African-American ministers politically with federal funding. A half-million-dollar grant was quickly slated for Pat Robertson's quasi-charitable Operation Blessing International Relief and Development Corporation, which the Christian Coalition founder has in the past used to advance his diamond-mining ventures in the Congo region. For conservatives to misuse tax dollars to finance the religious right is hypocritical and constitutionally unsound. For the Mayberry Machiavellis, perverting the President's program is great politics.

In John DiIulio's view, their narrow approach has ruined any opportunity to pass the kind of legislation that originally attracted him to Washington. For their own reasons, he said, the White House staff "winked at the most far-right House Republicans, who, in turn, drafted a so-called faith bill that . . . satisfied certain fundamentalist leaders and Beltway libertarians but bore few marks of compassionate conservatism. . . . Not only that, but it reflected neither the president's own previous rhetoric on the idea nor any of the actual empirical evidence."

The worst obstacles to progress, according to DiIulio, were the "Republican base constituencies, including Beltway libertarian policy elites and religious-Right leaders," who relied on Rove to prevent Bush from moving toward the political center. The predictable outcome was stagnation. There was no domestic policy, which suited the conservatives very well. It was better to do nothing than to permit an ideological deviation that might actually help the poor.

"Besides the tax cut, which was cut-and-dried during the campaign," DiIulio concluded in his letter, "and the education bill, which was really a Ted Kennedy bill, the administration has not done much, either in absolute terms or in comparison with previous administrations at this stage, on domestic policy. There is a virtual absence as yet of any policy accomplishments that might, to a fair-minded non-partisan, count as the flesh on the bones of so-called compassionate conservatism."

"So-called compassionate conservatism." That phrase, written by a man who said he still loved and admired George W. Bush, resounded with disillusion. Still, John DiIulio held out hope that someday in the years to come, his ideal of a spirited movement to uplift the poor might be realized. There was no domestic policy, but in two years, or six years, something might happen.

The saddened professor couldn't quite admit that this President is unlikely ever to fulfill the expectations he raised — because in a White House ruled so thoroughly and ruthlessly by pious conservatives, there is so little room for compassion.

10

"DEAD OR ALIVE" — OR MAYBE JUST FORGOTTEN

"Conservatives are tough on terrorism, while liberal Democrats are soft."

After terrorists attacked New York and Washington on September 11, 2001, liberal Democrats on Capitol Hill eagerly lined up with conservative Republicans to pledge their support for the President's war against al-Qaeda and the Taliban. No one mentioned the hesitancy of George W. Bush's initial response to the terror strikes. No one said or did anything that might hint at dissension in a time of national crisis. When Bush showed up at a joint session of Congress nine days after the fall of the World Trade Center to deliver a rousing speech, he won standing applause across the bitter partisan divide left by the 2000 election.

That evening, the Democratic leaders in Congress for the first time declined the television networks' standard offer of free airtime to answer a Republican presidential address. "We want America to speak with one voice tonight and we want enemies and the whole world and all of our citizens to know that America speaks tonight with one voice," explained Richard Gephardt, the House Democratic leader. Without knowing any specifics of Bush's plan for military action, Gephardt pledged, "We have faith in him and his colleagues in the executive branch to do this in the right way."

At a press conference after the President's address, Senate Democratic leader Tom Daschle stood with his Republican counterpart, Trent Lott, to demonstrate joint support for the President. "Tonight there is no opposition party," said Lott. "We stand here united, not as Republicans and Democrats, not as Southerners or Westerners or Midwesterners or Easterners, but as Americans." Agreed Daschle, "We want President Bush to know—we want the world to know—that he can depend on us."

Even many of Bush's harshest critics on the left praised his eloquence that evening and expressed their support for him. "He hit a home run," said Representative Maxine Waters, the firebrand Los Angeles Democrat. "We may disagree later, but now is not the time."

Left politely unmentioned by Waters was the indelible fact that in the hours following the attack, Bush had failed to reassure and rally the nation. Under the extraordinary circumstances, he was rightly afforded an opportunity to recoup his credibility with very little negative comment. (That this was more than most Republicans had ever done for Bill Clinton didn't matter. The Democrats were not inclined to trim their patriotism to match the opportunism of their adversaries.) In the wake of an act of war, liberal journalists as well as politicians voiced strong support for the President as a national symbol and as commander in chief.

"He was very shaky at first, but I resisted the urge to write a piece saying that, because I didn't think it was appropriate," said Jacob Weisberg, the *Slate* magazine writer whose specialties included regular mockery of Bush's gaffes and language problems. "I think he's now emerging as a very effective wartime leader." Weisberg explained his forbearance in terms that any American would understand. "Bush deserves the benefit of the doubt to an enormous degree. He needs to rally the nation. I want to contribute to that effort to the extent that I can."

In Bush's sudden surge of popularity, his political adviser Karl Rove saw an immediate opportunity. Midterm elections would be coming up in the fall of 2002, which meant the Republicans could exploit wartime patriotism and the President's newfound power to gain seats

in Congress and retake the Senate. The need for bipartisan cooperation didn't matter. Neither did the fact that the Democrats had been
just as supportive of the war effort and security measures as the Republicans.

The inspiring presidential rhetoric that unified the nation would
soon be discarded. The memory of politicians of both parties gathering
on the steps of the Capitol to sing "God Bless America" meant nothing.
The slogan of a nation at war that blossomed on billboards, bumper
stickers, and storefronts — "United We Stand" — was no longer convenient. Less than four months after Bush's September 20 address to the
joint session of Congress, Rove spoke behind closed doors at the Republican National Committee's winter conference in Austin, Texas.
There he revealed his plan to regain control of the Senate and retain
control of the House by turning the war on terror into a partisan
weapon.

"We can go to the country on this issue, because they trust the
Republican Party to do a better job of protecting and strengthening
America's military might and thereby protecting America," Rove explained. Those remarks, although provocative in departing from the
bipartisan unity of September 11's aftermath, were considerably
blander than the vicious line put out by Republicans and conservatives
ever since.

For Rove, terrorism served as the universal solvent of national politics. The response to terror raised President Bush's sagging poll numbers and, for a while, gave him the kind of political Teflon armor once
worn by Ronald Reagan. The war on terror excused Bush's enormous
deficit spending, his attacks on public employees, his curtailment of
traditional freedoms, his unilateralist foreign policy, and his drive to
wage "pre-emptive" war on Iraq. The threat of terror gave him a sword
against any and all opponents, foreign or domestic, which he used to
cut down Democrats in the midterm elections.

Rove's electoral strategy could only function effectively, however, if
the press and the public, as well as Congress, were discouraged from
examining what the Republicans in power had done to combat ter-

rorism in the months before the catastrophe. Any such inquiry would inevitably clash with the themes of Republican strength and Democratic weakness that Rove intended to promote.

Only one problem on the political horizon might complicate Rove's strategic use of terrorism: an independent investigation of the circumstances leading to the September 11 catastrophe. Americans wanted answers to important questions about how the Bush administration confronted the terrorist threat before the fall of the World Trade Center. Were the seasoned Republican officials who took office nine months before the attack as tough as their talk? Were they alerted to the impending threat? Did they heed the warnings?

Why did U.S. intelligence and security agencies fail to thwart the al-Qaeda plot?

The nation remains far from reaching any conclusions about those issues — and others of equal importance — because the White House obstructed the investigation for more than a year. Bush and Cheney didn't want Congress to investigate the causes of the disaster, and they certainly didn't want any snooping by an independent commission. So determined was the White House to conceal any embarrassing facts that when the Democrats took control of the Senate in spring 2002, Vice President Dick Cheney tried to intimidate Majority Leader Tom Daschle from undertaking a serious investigation of the September 11 catastrophe. Both *Newsweek* and the *Washington Post* reported that Cheney had called Daschle to warn against the investigation.

The prospect of public hearings particularly disturbed Cheney. He told Daschle that any such inquiry would be stigmatized as partisan interference with the war on terrorism. The President later echoed Cheney's bluster, in milder terms, at a breakfast with congressional leaders. In the months since those pleas and threats were issued, the White House and its political surrogates have repeatedly sought to exploit the campaign against terrorism for cheap advantage. (The Republicans sold pictures of the commander in chief on Air Force One, for example, while demanding immunity from public scrutiny.) But conservative Republicans such as Alabama Senator Richard Shelby were as bemused and troubled as the Democrats by the administration's attempt to cover up lethal incompetence.

What seems clear, even now, is that the President and his associates are not eager to see those troubling issues examined by any independent authority—out of reasonable fear that the findings will not flatter them.

Seeking to scuttle any probe before it could begin, the President's aides and his allies on Capitol Hill continued to stall the investigation by appealing to fear (and, rather brazenly, to patriotism). National Security Adviser Condoleezza Rice argued that an investigation would endanger the country still further. "In the context of this ongoing war, it is extremely important to protect the sources and the methods and the information so that we can try and disrupt further attacks," she claimed. "The problem is that this is an act that is not finished. It is ongoing. We are still fighting a war on terrorism." Tom DeLay dove into the gutter immediately: "We will not allow our president to be undermined by those who want his job during a time of war." It was quite revealing that DeLay assumed a full investigation would undermine Bush.

Propelling the demand for an independent investigation were continuing pressures from organizations representing the families of the September 11 victims, combined with slowly leaking revelations about the incompetence of the FBI. The inconclusive results of an investigation by a joint congressional committee likewise gave momentum to that demand, which the public had supported from the beginning. Finally, in September 2002, the administration agreed to an independent commission, created by an amendment to the bill establishing the Department of Homeland Security. During intense negotiations with the amendment's sponsors, Senators John McCain and Joseph Lieberman, the administration fought to gain control over the naming, staffing, and powers of the commission.

To the extent that they succeeded, the independent commission became a strange bipartisan hybrid that cannot issue a subpoena without approval of its chairman—who happens to be a presidential appointee. In many respects, the commission as constituted is far less independent than similar entities set up after earlier national disasters such as Pearl Harbor, the Kennedy assassination, and the *Challenger* explosion. Or the independent counsels who probed every corner of the Clinton administration.

To make matters worse, the President immediately cast doubt on his own good faith when he appointed former Secretary of State Henry Kissinger to chair the commission. The predictable reaction was outrage. Within weeks, the alleged war criminal, international corporate fixer, and inveterate liar resigned under a withering blast of editorial fire. Kissinger didn't want to reveal the corporate clients that might raise questions about conflict of interest. To replace him, Bush named a far blander choice: former New Jersey Governor Thomas Kean. Nine months after the passage of the independent commission amendment, little apparent progress had been made. And the commission's meager funding was being held up by the White House.

To distract attention from the Bush administration's evident failure in dealing with al-Qaeda, conservatives have pursued two separate but related offensives: defaming liberals and Democrats as "soft on terror" and blaming Bill Clinton for the September 11 attacks. Both are integral parts of Republican political strategy, but as a White House adviser, Rove leaves that kind of dirty work to others.

Naturally, Ann Coulter didn't let him down. In the first few pages of *Slander*, this is what she says on the subject of the war on terror: "Here the country had finally given liberals a war against fundamentalism and they didn't want to fight it. They would have, except it would put them on the same side as the United States." Who didn't want to fight the war against terror? The Democrats who unanimously (with one exception) voted to support Bush's military action against the Taliban? Coulter also claims that "liberals urged compassion and understanding toward the terrorists," again without citing a single name or quotation.

Joining her in the smear campaign was former ultraleftist David Horowitz, the author of various articles and pamphlets counseling Republicans on political strategy. At least one of his booklets carried a personal endorsement from Rove, who had introduced Horowitz to George W. Bush. (In 2000, the Bush political guru had blurbed Horowitz's *The Art of Political War,* a little handbook for vilifying Democrats and liberals, as "the perfect guide to winning on the political battlefield.")

In *How to Beat the Democrats,* which appeared in 2002, Horowitz emphasized the supposed culpability of Democrats, particularly in the Clinton administration, for the September 11 catastrophe. He claimed that "mainstream Democrats [were] . . . significant players in the debacle of 9/11. And no one is more singularly responsible for America's vulnerability on that fateful day than the Democratic president, Bill Clinton, and his White House staff."

Like so much of what he feels compelled to say, Horowitz's advice was stark, simple, and demagogic. He told voters that their very lives could be endangered if they voted the wrong way: "This is a story the Republicans must tell the American people if they are to be warned about the dangers of putting their trust in the party of Bill Clinton by casting their votes for Democrats come November." Among conservatives rallying around Bush, there was little doubt that Clinton had known about al-Qaeda's potential for destructive aggression and had "simply refused to do anything serious about the threat." Or so they said.

What these right-wing critics really knew about the years of American effort devoted to tracking and destroying al-Qaeda was considerably less than they affected to know. The Republican attacks on Clinton—at a moment when the nation was supposed to be unified and bipartisan—gave off a peculiar smell. It was the odor of cover-up, as if spraying Clinton with bile were the only way to ensure that no one sniffed around the policy and administrative bungling of the Bush administration.

The Republican reputation for security prowess and patriotic strength demonstrates the political value of muscular-sounding bluster matched with a profligate purse at the Pentagon. No less a warrior than Dwight D. Eisenhower warned the nation decades ago that excessive military spending was creating its own powerful constituencies, with malignant political consequences.

Republican aversions to big government and federal waste rarely affect their addiction to defense pork. Millions are recycled back from defense industry executives into the party's treasury, and millions more end up in the bank accounts of former GOP elected and appointed officials who work for the industry.

Whether any of those lucrative activities makes the nation safer is debatable. Every year Senator McCain, a distinguished former military officer and the son and grandson of Navy admirals, rises on the Senate floor to recite a list of Defense Department items that he indicts as useless waste. According to the Arizona Republican, his colleagues suffer from an incurable habit of spending enormous sums on weapons systems that don't work and that the Pentagon doesn't want.

Just as some liberals once viewed welfare spending as the definition of compassion, many conservatives regarded the bloated defense budget as proof of the nation's vigilance and strength. As military strategy this approach has severe defects, but as political propaganda it is almost unbeatable.

The most generous assessment of the Republican record in fighting terrorism is "mixed." Again, rhetoric obscures reality, with the assistance of the complaisant "liberal" media. Stereotypes of tough Republican daddies and soft Democratic mommies are irresistible to weak-minded journalists, who reinforce such clichés continuously. But recent history shows that it is conservatives, not liberals, whose attitude toward terrorism can turn squishy soft for political expediency.

The most notorious example is the Iran-Contra scandal, first exposed in 1986. At the center of that bizarre episode in conservative statesmanship was a scheme to sell high-tech missiles to the theocratic dictatorship governing Iran—in exchange for that government's assistance in obtaining the release of American hostages by their kidnappers, the Iranian-controlled Hezbollah terrorists in Lebanon.

Approved by President Ronald Reagan and his national security staff, this lunatic plan clearly violated U.S. laws prohibiting arms sales to Iran, one of several nations officially listed by the State Department as a sponsor of terrorism. Reagan's public attitude toward Iran and Islamic terrorists sounded tough, but turned out to be pseudotough. He lied repeatedly to the American people about the arms-for-hostages transactions. "We did not trade arms for hostages" was about as candid as "I did not have sex with that woman."

Obviously Clinton was fibbing about matters of grave national importance, namely his extramarital dalliance with an intern. The saintly Reagan misled the people and Congress about nothing worse than presidential violations of federal arms control laws, covert conspiracies involving the White House with a terrorist state, and the ruin of constitutional traditions.

Thanks to his popularity with the press and public, Reagan escaped impeachment and, in a broader sense, responsibility for those crimes. He claimed not to have known what his subordinates were doing. Yet Oliver North, the Marine lieutenant colonel responsible for carrying out the Iran-Contra deals, confessed in his 1991 memoir that everyone knew what Reagan had ordered: "At the time, it seemed that selling a small amount of arms to Iran was worth the risk to make it all work. But a quid pro quo arrangement of arms for hostages? This placed all of us in a moral quandary. Human life is sacrosanct, but making what people would inevitably see as concessions to terrorists was a terrible idea — especially since it violated our prohibition on arms sales to Iran." (North has gone on to a career as a conservative television commentator. Even more amazing than his continuing popularity on the right, after calling Reagan a liar, is that he still dares to criticize Democrats and liberals for not being tough enough on terrorism.)

Vice President George H. W. Bush, too, endorsed the theory that giving advanced weapons to the Iranians would convince them to behave more moderately. Well over a decade later, the ruling mullahs in Teheran remain sponsors of terrorism. They are charter members of what President George W. Bush calls "the axis of evil."

The damage done to American credibility abroad by the Iran-

Contra fiasco was incalculable. It suggested a craven willingness to do business with terrorists that didn't sit well with our allies, who had listened to many lectures from the United States about their own dealings with rogue groups and governments. Had the wrongdoing ended at selling missiles to mullahs, that would have been sufficiently sickening. But in their eagerness to please the Iranian mullahs, North and his superiors agreed to persuade the government of Kuwait to free seventeen Shi'ite terrorists imprisoned there.

Known as the Dawa'a prisoners, they weren't just any random assortment of murderous fanatics. They were members of the Hezbollah movement who had been convicted of car-bomb assaults on the American and French embassies in Kuwait City only two years earlier. The group demanding their release included the perpetrators of the October 1983 bombing of the Marine barracks in Beirut that had killed 241 American servicemen. Poindexter and North reportedly met with the Kuwaiti officials to seek the release of the Dawa'a prisoners.

Reagan's bumbling military and political engagement in Lebanon, and his hasty retreat after that atrocity, had encouraged terrorists to view the United States as fickle and feeble. Osama bin Laden has cited America's flight from Lebanon more than once as proof of our national cowardice. How much respect did America forfeit when the world learned that the "tough" Reaganites had asked to free seventeen terror bombers in order to "facilitate better relations" with Iran? (Incidentally, the Dawa'a terrorists were eventually freed — by Saddam Hussein after his army invaded Kuwait in 1990.)

Equally irresponsible was the Reagan administration's secret policy of encouraging American allies in the Gulf, such as the Saudis, to finance Saddam Hussein's war against Iran. Simultaneously, the Reagan White House was overseeing American and Israeli shipments of weapons to Iran. While pretending to seek a negotiated end to the Iran-Iraq war, which led to a million deaths and horrific atrocities, the United States was playing both sides. When Bush succeeded Reagan in the Oval Office, U.S. regional policy tilted sharply toward Baghdad, until Saddam invaded Kuwait.

Unlike the Iranians, Iraq wasn't cited by the State Department as a terror sponsor between 1982 and 1989. But as Richard Perle observed in a 1987 article warning against the incipient U.S. alliance with Saddam, "Iraq has protected terrorists Abu Nidal and Abu Abbas. That Iraq has been deleted from the list of terrorist nations that our law requires us to publish says more about the list makers than about Iraq."

In the same essay Perle, now a top Bush defense adviser, noted Saddam's criminal use of chemical weapons. Yet George Herbert Walker Bush and James Baker III pursued a policy of arming and appeasing the dictator who would eventually be denounced by George Walker Bush as the world's archterrorist. A Senate investigation in 1994 found that between 1986 and 1990, the United States licensed companies to export $600 million worth of advanced technology and materials used by Iraq to make mustard gas, VX nerve agent, anthrax, and other biological and chemical weapons. Those shipments continued for years after the United States learned about Saddam's use of chemical weapons to wipe out the Kurdish town of Halabja in 1988.

In short, Republican policymakers during the Reagan and Bush years were constantly wheeling and dealing with terrorists and their sponsors in both Iran and Iraq. The tough-minded conservatives weren't merely soft on terrorism; they aided and abetted terrorists in a manner that would have caused shrieks of treason if Democrats had done likewise.

(Ironically, it was President George W. Bush's desire to expunge his father's foreign policy errors that led him to exaggerate the case for war against Iraq more than a decade later. The evidence that Saddam had rebuilt the forbidden weapons dismantled by the United Nations inspectors, or reconstituted his defunct nuclear program, was thin and vague before the war. After a swift invasion that deposed the dictator, the American expeditionary forces had great difficulty finding any concrete confirmation of those suspicions. Nevertheless, the White House chose "preventive" war against the wishes of many traditional American allies and in the face of strong Arab and Muslim protests.

Whether that decision will ultimately enhance or enfeeble the international war on terrorism remains to be seen.)

Both the Reagan and Bush administrations were capable of coddling terrorists for ideological reasons or domestic political considerations as well. One of the first actions taken by Reagan's State Department in 1981 was to lift sanctions against the Chilean dictatorship of General Augusto Pinochet. The Carter administration had imposed economic and military sanctions in 1979, to retaliate for Pinochet's refusal to cooperate with the American prosecution of a lethal terrorist bombing that had occurred on the streets of Washington three years earlier.

A car bomb planted by agents of Pinochet's secret service had killed exiled Chilean diplomat Orlando Letelier and an American associate, Ronni Karpen Moffitt, in 1976 as they drove down a Washington thoroughfare. This bold atrocity was carried out with the connivance of three Chilean officials whom Pinochet refused to extradite. The sanctions followed, according to the State Department's official announcement, because the Chilean authorities had "in effect condoned an act of international terrorism."

That was exactly what Reagan and Alexander Haig, his first Secretary of State, did when they lifted the sanctions. As enablers of the Chilean fascist government, they didn't mind that Pinochet's goons were escaping responsibility for a bloody act of terror in the American capital.

The same dangerous double standard that condoned right-wing terrorism emerged again several years later, in a strange decision by President George Herbert Walker Bush that fostered the Florida political career of his son Jeb. The beneficiary was Orlando Bosch, a militant Cuban exile leader implicated by the Justice Department in more than thirty terrorist actions. The worst of Bosch's suspected crimes, according to U.S. government officials, was his involvement in the 1976 bombing of a Cubana Airlines flight from Venezuela to Havana that killed seventy-three civilians, including the Cuban Olympic fencing team.

Confident that the Bush family would look favorably on him despite his homicidal reputation, Bosch sought political asylum from Washington after he beat the rap for the Cubana bombing in Venezuela. As Ann Bardach reports in *Cuba Confidential*, her 2002 book investigating Cuban-American relations over the past four decades, the Justice Department rejected Bosch's asylum application in January 1989. "For thirty years Bosch has been resolute and unwavering in his advocacy of terrorist violence," wrote the Assistant Attorney General in his decision against Bosch. "He has repeatedly expressed and demonstrated a willingness to cause indiscriminate injury and death."

But the following year—although the first President Bush's Attorney General called Bosch "an unreformed terrorist," and although the FBI and other law enforcement authorities described him as "Miami's number one terrorist"—Jeb Bush and the family's friends in the Cuban exile community obtained what amounted to a presidential pardon for Bosch.

Technically, the President's action wasn't a pardon, but it might as well have been; the effect was the same. The President ordered Bosch's release from prison and two years later granted him permanent residency in the United States. (Aside from Jeb, among those who had spent years lobbying on behalf of the terrorist Bosch was Otto Reich, George W. Bush's rejected nominee as Assistant Secretary of State for Latin American Affairs.)

The conservative Republicans of the Reagan-Bush era spoke loudly about "fighting international terrorism." Their record was outstanding for its ineptitude, hypocrisy, and politically motivated leniency: conniving in arms deals with the Iranian sponsors of Hezbollah and Islamic Jihad; sponsoring secret attempts to secure the release of the Dawa'a terrorist prisoners from imprisonment in Kuwait; lifting sanctions on Chile despite the regime's refusal to extradite the perpetrators of a terror bombing in Washington, D.C.; favoring a Cuban terrorist mass murderer with presidential favors for domestic political reasons. Their record was an international disgrace. And they still have the gall to call their opponents "soft on terror."

When terrorists first tried to take down the World Trade Center with a truck bomb in February 1993, there was no organized outcry of recrimination against George Herbert Walker Bush, although he had left the Oval Office a scant six weeks earlier. Neither the incoming Clinton administration nor the Democrats who controlled both houses of Congress tried to blame Bush for the intelligence failures that had allowed the perpetrators of that atrocity to conspire undetected for more than three years.

No liberal commentator pronounced the former President guilty of "criminal negligence," as conservatives immediately did in blaming Bill Clinton for the September 11 attacks. Using fabrications, falsehoods, and half-truths, the opportunists of the right compiled an indictment of Clinton and the Democrats. Calling for "national unity" in one breath, they angrily assaulted Clinton in the next. To make their case, they had to erase his administration's extensive record of action against terrorism.

Still caught up in their Clinton compulsion nearly a year after he had left the White House, his conservative critics could scarcely resist the chance to blame him for the worst national disaster since Pearl Harbor. As Mark Steyn warned, only half-jokingly, in the *National Review*: "If we members of the Vast Right-wing Conspiracy don't get back to our daily routine of obsessive Clinton-bashing, then the terrorists will have won."

The tenor of this journalistic prosecution was epitomized by a deceptive account in the *Washington Times* of a Clinton speech at Georgetown University almost two months after the attack. By cutting and pasting from Clinton's text, the Moonie daily falsely reported that the former President had blamed America for the terrorist attack. "Clinton calls terror a U.S. debt to past," blared the front-page headline on November 8. Yet there was nothing in the speech—or even in reporter Joseph Curl's misleading story—to justify that headline. Clinton's speech had made passing references to American slavery and to the brutality of the Crusades against Islam. But the thrust of his speech was that "we have to win the fight we're in." And he went on to say, "I am just a citizen, and as a citizen I support the efforts of President

Bush, the national security team, and our allies in fighting the current terrorist threat. I believe we all should."

The *Washington Times* report was instantly regurgitated on talk radio and right-wing Web sites, which distorted his remarks into an assertion that "America got what it deserved." Among the many mindless parrots was Andrew Sullivan, who then read the text of the Clinton speech and had to grudgingly admit that the Moonie paper's version had been "appallingly slanted." But that was only the beginning of a continuing effort to transform the tragedy of 9/11 into "Clinton's legacy."

Any honest examination of the roots of the September 11 attack would necessarily begin several years before Clinton was elected President—when the Central Intelligence Agency provided up to a billion dollars in aid to the Afghan mujahideen. Those resources, controlled by the Islamist generals who ran Pakistan's Interservice Intelligence agency, were used to build the militant jihadist movements that later formed the Taliban and al-Qaeda. According to Yossef Bodansky, former director of the Congressional Task Force on Terrorism and author of *Bin Laden: The Man Who Declared War on America*, U.S. taxpayers unwittingly financed the training of Islamist terrorists under Pakistani auspices.

None of that ancient history was of much concern to conservatives who had supported Reagan's Afghan adventure. For them, the history of Islamist terror began with the first attempt to bring down the World Trade Center. That was when Clinton supposedly ought to have declared war on Osama bin Laden and al-Qaeda, as Sullivan and others insisted, because "the investigation found links to Osama bin Laden."

In fact, however, no clue to the Saudi millionaire's alleged involvement with the WTC bombing emerged until at least three years later. In 1993 U.S. authorities were scarcely aware of bin Laden's existence. Conservative journalists, such as the *New Republic*'s Fred Barnes, were then suggesting that the likeliest perpetrator of the World Trade Center bombing was Iran. Hard evidence linking bin Laden to that attack still remains scanty.

The indictment of Clinton by Sean Hannity, Sullivan, and other conservatives relies heavily on a fable about attempts by the government of Sudan to "hand over bin Laden to the United States" in 1996. That story, attested by an American businessman who represents Sudanese interests, is designed to expunge the Khartoum regime's many atrocities against its own people as well as its close relationship with Islamist terror organizations. Authoritative reporting in the *Washington Post* and in *The Age of Sacred Terror* by Daniel Benjamin and Steven Simon shows that the Sudanese offered only to "arrest Osama bin Laden and place him in Saudi custody."

Post reporter Barton Gellman detailed the efforts by the Clinton White House and the State Department to induce the Saudis to accept custody of bin Laden, a request that the authorities in Riyadh adamantly refused. There was no offer to hand bin Laden over to the United States before the Sudanese deported him back to Kabul.

The Sudanese have always had their own agenda, by the way, which Clinton's antagonists never mention. They promised to cooperate against terrorism only if the United States ended economic sanctions imposed to punish their genocidal campaign of bombing and enslavement against black Christians. Frequently during those years, Sudanese officials would promise copious intelligence about the Islamist terror network. But after many meetings, neither the FBI nor the CIA believed that Khartoum was providing anything valuable on bin Laden or al-Qaeda. In their eagerness to indict Clinton and their inexperience in dealing with matters of foreign intelligence, propagandists like Hannity have served as useful idiots in a disinformation gambit by the Sudanese intelligence service.

The Clinton critics like to dismiss his administration's efforts to stop bin Laden as a couple of missiles fired at an empty tent. Yet there was no lack of zeal in Clinton's hunt for the Saudi terrorist. In 1998 Clinton signed a secret National Security Decision Directive that authorized an intensive, ongoing campaign to destroy al-Qaeda and seize or assassinate bin Laden. Several attempts were made on bin Laden's life, aside from the famous cruise missile launches that summer, which conservatives falsely denounced as an attempt to deflect attention from the Lewinsky scandal. (It never seems to occur to the conservatives who snicker about *Wag the Dog* that they are also smearing ranking intelligence and military officers such as retired General Anthony Zinni, more recently Bush's Mideast envoy, who encouraged Clinton to take that shot in the dark.)

In 1999, the CIA organized a Pakistani commando unit to enter Afghanistan on a mission to capture or kill bin Laden. That operation was aborted when General Pervez Musharraf seized the Pakistani government from Nawaz Sharif, the more cooperative civilian Prime Minister. A year later, bin Laden was reportedly almost killed in a rocket-grenade attack on his convoy. Unfortunately, the missiles hit the wrong truck.

Simultaneously, the White House tried to persuade or coerce the Taliban regime into expelling bin Laden from Afghanistan. Clinton signed an executive order freezing $254 million in Taliban assets in the United States, while the State Department kept the Taliban internationally isolated. But there was nothing the United States could have done, short of full-scale military action, to separate al-Qaeda from the Taliban. And there was also no guarantee that such action would lead to the apprehension of bin Laden, as the Bush administration discovered when American forces helped to overthrow the Taliban after September 11.

On Clinton's watch, the CIA and the National Security Council instituted a special al-Qaeda unit that thwarted several deadly conspiracies, including a scheme to blow up Los Angeles International Airport on Millennium Eve, and plots to bomb the Holland and Lincoln Tunnels in New York City as well as the United Nations building. Timely American intelligence also prevented a deadly assault on the Israeli embassy in Washington. Meanwhile, the State Department and the CIA neutralized dozens of terrorist cells overseas through quiet prosecutions, extraditions, and executions undertaken by allies from Albania to the Philippines.

A month before Clinton left office—and nine months before the planes hit the World Trade Center and the Pentagon—the nation's most experienced diplomats in counterterrorism praised those efforts. "Overall, I give them very high marks," said Robert Oakley, former Ambassador for Counterterrorism in the Reagan State Department. "The only major criticism I have is the obsession with Osama, which has made him stronger." Paul Bremer, who had served in the same post under Reagan and later was chosen by congressional leaders to chair the National Commission on Terrorism, disagreed slightly with his colleague. Bremer told the *Washington Post* he believed that the Clinton administration had "correctly focused on bin Laden." (He has since been chosen to lead the Bush administration team in Iraq.)

Following the 1993 attack on the World Trade Center, the new President sent stringent antiterrorism legislation to Congress as part of his first crime bill. The passage of that legislation many months later was the last time he would enjoy real cooperation against terrorism from congressional conservatives. When he sought to expand those protections in 1995 after the bombing of the federal building in Oklahoma City, he was frustrated by a coalition of civil libertarians and antigovernment conservatives, who argued that his "overreaction" posed a threat to constitutional rights. Among that bill's most controversial provisions were new powers to turn away suspect immigrants, swifter deportation procedures, and a new deportation court that could view secret evidence. (During his 2000 campaign, George W. Bush won support from American Muslims by denouncing that provision.)

Thanks to an increasingly obstreperous Republican majority on both sides of the Capitol, law enforcement officials were denied new authority for roving wiretaps and new powers to monitor money laundering. All that would have to wait until after September 11, when the Republicans suddenly reversed position with a vengeance.

Indiana Representative David McIntosh, a leading conservative ideologue in Congress, enunciated the typical partisan reaction to Clinton's counterterror proposals. McIntosh insisted on steering the debate back to a phony White House scandal. "We find it very troubling that you're asking us for additional authority to wiretap innocent Americans," he declared, "when you have failed to explain to the American people why you abuse their civil liberties by having FBI files brought into the White House."

The recalcitrant Republicans later defeated another potentially important White House initiative. Led by then Senator John Ashcroft and computer industry lobbyists, they rejected proposals to tighten controls on encryption software and to ensure that law enforcement officials could crack the kind of coded messages found on the laptop owned by Ramzi Yusef—the mastermind of the 1993 World Trade Center bombing. Intelligence experts believe that the September 11 plotters probably used encrypted computer links to communicate with their commanders in al-Qaeda.

Among the most conspicuous opponents of counterterrorist action was former Senator Phil Gramm, who blocked an administration bill to close loopholes that let terrorist groups launder money through offshore banks. The Texas Republican denounced that legislation, since endorsed by the Bush White House as essential in dismantling al-Qaeda, as "totalitarian."

Clinton persevered, even as his adversaries on Capitol Hill prosecuted the right-wing harassment campaign against the White House. While politicians and journalists fanned the scandal frenzy, he and his appointees tried to prepare for the serious threats they anticipated. After the Oklahoma City bombing in 1995, they began a nationwide initiative to improve home front security.

Between 1996 and 2001, federal spending on counterterrorism increased dramatically, to more than $12 billion annually. The FBI's counterterrorism budget rose even more sharply, from $78 million in 1996 to $609 million in 2000, tripling the number of agents assigned to such activities and creating a new Counter-terrorism Center at the Bureau's Washington headquarters.

Whether FBI Director Louis Freeh properly used that gusher of funding is another question. In retrospect, Clinton must be blamed for appointing Freeh, a truly inept administrator. The Republican Freeh, always favored by conservatives in Congress, never concealed his contempt for the President who had appointed him, and after he aligned himself with Clinton's adversaries in Congress and in the media, the President had no real power to remove him. But the degree of the Bureau's deterioration didn't become clear until near the end of Clinton's second term.

Besides strengthening law enforcement, the Clinton administration sponsored a series of sophisticated simulations to improve the response of local, state, and federal officials to possible assaults with nuclear, chemical, or biological weapons. The President himself became obsessed with the potential threat of anthrax and other biological weapons.

Before he left office, the federal Centers for Disease Control issued a $343 million contract to manufacture 40 million doses of smallpox vaccine, as part of a wide-ranging research and development program of defense against biological weapons. Altogether, spending on "domestic preparedness" rose from $42.6 million in 1997 to more than $1.2 billion in 2000. The foresight represented by those appropriations gave Bush an important head start, though the White House press corps will never hear about that from his press secretary.

None of this means that Clinton's record is free of blemish. Could he have done more to reform the intelligence and law enforcement bureaucracy? Did he fail to resolve the ongoing rivalries that fractured the FBI, the CIA, and the other intelligence services? Was he distracted by domestic concerns and scandals, including the Lewinsky affair that he so foolishly and selfishly brought upon himself?

The answer to all those questions is yes. But instead of smearing Clinton, his antagonists might ask themselves what they and their political allies did in the early years of the war against terrorism. Sullivan, for one, would have to scour his own scribblings in vain for any mention of Osama bin Laden or al-Qaeda before September 11. He was hardly alone in his obliviousness and obstructionism. With few exceptions, the record of Clinton's critics on this issue compares poorly with that of the man they vilify.

But the campaign undertaken by Hannity, Sullivan, Horowitz, and other conservatives to arraign Clinton for September 11 has a more sinister, explicitly political aim. Their rhetoric is redolent of the old stab-in-the-back theories once used to discredit FDR and JFK. And of course they are attempting to deflect blame from Bush (whose vow to get bin Laden, "dead or alive," has been consigned to the same White House memory hole as the balanced budget).

Does George W. Bush deserve responsibility for the failures that led to September 11? The independent commission that the President so reluctantly approved in late 2002 is likely to provide complex and nuanced answers to that question. Perhaps the commission will explain why members of the bin Laden family were spirited out of the United States on orders from the White House before they could be questioned by the FBI. Perhaps the commission will explore why FBI terror expert John O'Neill, who died in the World Trade Center conflagration, believed that the Bush administration was soft on Saudi cooperation with al-Qaeda.

What is clear already from the public record is that the Bush administration received ample warning from Clinton's national security officials—and from CIA Director George Tenet, a Clinton holdover—that al-Qaeda posed the most significant, immediate threat to American security.

Departing National Security Advisor Sandy Berger and the National Security Council's counterterrorism chief, Richard Clarke, who was held over by Bush, gave Condoleezza Rice a series of urgent briefings on terrorism during the presidential transition in January 2001. "You're going to spend more time during your four years on terrorism generally and al-Qaeda specifically than any issue," Berger told his successor. Clarke delivered similar emphatic briefings to Vice President Cheney and to Stephen Hadley, Rice's deputy. But the supposedly competent national security managers in the new administration, including Rice, Cheney, and Defense Secretary Donald Rumsfeld, were too preoccupied with other matters (such as national missile defense) to pay heed to the most serious threat since the end of the Cold War.

The failure of Bush's national security team to recognize the threat of al-Qaeda, even after they were clearly warned, will rank among the most serious mistakes ever made by U.S. government officials. They had billed themselves as "the grown-ups," condescending to the Democrats they replaced and asserting that their experience would return steady guidance to American policy. Instead, these veterans of previous Republican administrations fumbled and fooled around with ancillary issues while an elusive new enemy prepared to strike. They weren't prepared. They had no plan. They hadn't seen what was coming. They had ignored the warnings. Their judgment was as deluded as their self-image.

Long before Bush acquiesced to the independent commission, hints of that incompetence and arrogance emerged in the media, despite the administration's effort to conceal its mistakes. On August 6, 2001, the CIA had warned the President and other top officials of an active plot by al-Qaeda operatives to seize civilian aircraft. During the same period, FBI special agents in Phoenix and Minnesota had warned their own agency of activity by suspected al-Qaeda operatives at U.S. flight schools. The FBI was essentially leaderless during that time because Freeh had resigned. Nobody at the FBI, the CIA, the National Security Council, or any other government intelligence agency managed to connect those warnings until after the disaster.

The credibility of the White House on all these matters is low. That is why many of the events of 2001 must be reexamined for additional evidence of what the Bush administration knew or should have known. One such event is the international economic summit in Genoa, Italy, in late July 2001. In the weeks preceding the G8 meeting, the Russian federal police warned about an al-Qaeda plot to assassinate Bush. The threat was considered sufficiently serious to keep the President away from the luxury cruise ship that housed his fellow heads of state.

Furthermore, U.S. and Italian officials were warned, according to a *Los Angeles Times* report, that Islamic terrorists might try to hijack an airplane and crash it into the summit location, with the intention of killing Bush and others. The Italian authorities responded by setting up rocket batteries around the ancient port to thwart an aerial assault. An Italian ministry of defense officer explained that the missile deployment was meant "merely to act as a deterrent against any aerial incursion." Just before the summit opened, the *Times* of London reported that the CIA station chief in Rome had warned Italian secret services of a possible "suicide attack" by al-Qaeda.

Almost simultaneously, on July 26, 2001, Attorney General John Ashcroft abruptly stopped flying on commercial airfcraft, reportedly due to a "threat assessment" by the FBI. The White House now claims that this had nothing to do with al-Qaeda and was related to concerns about a possible attempt against the Attorney General's life. At the time, however, CBS News reported "a senior official at the CIA said he was unaware of specific threats against any Cabinet member."

Perhaps it is a sign of paranoia to ascribe grave meaning to any of those incidents. It is also apparent, however, that warnings and portents were flying around the globe in the months before September 11. Until a plausible verdict from the independent commission arrives, the nation's conservatives should forget about blaming Bill Clinton and the Democrats. Their own record on terrorism stands up poorly by comparison.

INTRODUCTION

Hundreds of books, thousands of essays, and millions of words in periodicals of every description have been written about the meaning and history of liberalism. The books that have influenced my own views range from Thomas Paine's *Rights of Man* to Charles Lindblom's *Politics and Markets*, John Rawls's *A Theory of Justice*, and Thorstein Veblen's *Theory of the Leisure Class*. That scarcely begins to enumerate the immense and diverse list of journalists, historians, economists, activists, and politicians whose ideas have shaped modern American liberalism.

On the percentage of Americans who identify politically with liberalism, see the National Election Studies Guide to Public Opinion and Electoral Behavior tables on Liberal-Conservative Self-Identification 1972–2000 (found on the Internet at http://www.umich.edu/~nes/nesguide/toptable/tab3_1.htm). In the text I cite the sources of survey research on American attitudes on issues such as health care, taxation, Social Security, government spending, environmental protection, and so on. The Pew Research Center, the Gallup Organization, the Economic Policy Institute, and many other sites on the Internet provide copious data on these questions.

Rush Limbaugh's January 8, 2001, remarks about the 2000 election results can be found (in audio) at the Web site called Rush versus Reality (http://groups.msn.com/RushversusReality/rvr2001.msnw).

On voting patterns, see *The World Almanac and Book of Facts 2003*, which includes results from every U.S. presidential election and many details on the 2000 election. Statistics on candidate spending in 2000 compiled from Federal Election Commission data by the Center for Responsive Politics can be found on that organization's Web site, www.opensecrets.org.

Copious examples of David Horowitz's attitude toward liberals can be found on his Web site (www.frontpagemag.org). Likewise, Ann Coulter's columns on the subject can be found on hers (www.anncoulter.org), along with some very nice pictures.

1: LIMOUSINE LIBERALS AND CORPORATE-JET CONSERVATIVES

Theodore Roosevelt first complained about the "malefactors of great wealth" and their opposition to regulation of industry in a speech he delivered in Provincetown,

Massachusetts, on August 20, 1907 (*American Heritage Dictionary of American Quotations*, p. 324).

The best account of the Bush administration's attack on mine safety, while the President put his arms around the Quecreek miners, appeared in David Corn's August 6, 2002, column in the *Nation*. Cuts in the Mine Safety and Health Administration were noted in the April 10, 2001, editions of *Congress Daily* and GovExec.com. The most useful newspaper coverage of mine safety issues in the Clinton and Bush administrations has been published by the *Charleston* (West Virginia) *Gazette*, which reported remarks by the Mine Safety and Health Administration director on February 23, 2001.

For biographical references to George W. Bush, including his schooling, see *First Son: George W. Bush and the Bush Family Dynasty* by Bill Minutaglio (Times Books, 1999), especially chapters 4 and 5, and his own campaign biography, *A Charge to Keep* (William Morrow, 1999), pp. 21–22. His quote about attending San Jacinto High School appeared in the May 1994 issue of *Texas Monthly*.

Comprehensive analysis of the Bush administration's tax policy—and its effects on individuals, states, income categories, the President and his wife, and major corporations—may be found at Citizens for Tax Justice's excellent Web site (www.ctj.org) and in Robert McIntyre's articles for *The American Prospect*. Cheney is quoted on the dividend tax cut in the *Los Angeles Times*, January 11, 2003.

The pioneering research of Nolan McCarty, Howard Rosenthal, and Keith T. Poole is available on the Internet (http://voteview.uh.edu/c46105.htm) and in print: *Income Distribution and the Realignment of National Politics* by McCarty, Rosenthal, and Poole (AEI Press, 1997); and *Congress: A Political-Economic History of Roll-Call Voting* by Poole and Rosenthal (Oxford University Press, 1997).

In Ann Coulter's *Slander*, see pp. 30–35 regarding rich liberals. The *Cigar Aficionado* profile of Rush Limbaugh appeared in March 1994. Coulter expressed her preference for Kansas City in the *New York Observer*, August 26, 2002.

Analysis of the Chao proposal appeared in the *Hartford Courant*, April 4, 2003.

Jonathan Chait's comprehensive account of Clinton administration tax policy appeared in *The American Prospect*, December 6, 1999. The *Wall Street Journal* editorial urging higher taxes on low-income citizens appeared November 20, 2002. The *Los Angeles Times* reported the White House's $250 million tax break for Enron, along with the rest of its skewed stimulus package, on October 25, 2001. Citizens for Tax Justice (www.ctj.org) detailed the tax history of CSX Corporation under Treasury

Secretary John W. Snow on December 9, 2002. *The New York Times* revealed former IRS chief Charles Rossotti's aborted congressional testimony on November 5, 2002.

2: PEROXIDE PARADOX: THE BLONDE MISLEADING THE BLIND

Among the important sources and inspirations for this chapter are two remarkable Web sites that monitor media coverage: the Daily Howler (www.dailyhowler.com), managed by the incomparable Bob Somerby; and Spinsanity (www.Spinsanity.org), run by Brendan Nyhan, Ben Fritz, and Bryan Keefer, whose even-handed critiques have included my work on occasion.

The quotes from *Slander* about the "left's media dictatorship" and its alleged machinations are on pp. 96 and 114. References to Coulter's TV appearances, reviews, and other print coverage of her book can all be found on Lexis. She gave her account of *Slander*'s cancellation by HarperCollins in the *New York Observer*, August 26, 2002. Howard Kurtz reported her firing by *National Review* (and her "girly boys" retort) in the *Washington Post*, October 2, 2001.

Geoffrey Nunberg's analysis of assertions in Bernard Goldberg's *Bias* appeared in the May 6, 2002, issue of *The American Prospect*. Bill Kristol's confession appeared in *The New Yorker*, May 22, 1995. Limbaugh's November 20, 2002, gloat was recorded on his Web site, http://www.rushlimbaugh.com/home/daily/site112002/content/cuttingedge.guest.html, although unfortunately the links aren't permanent. The Bond quote first appeared in the *Washington Post*, August 20, 1992.

Much useful information on the Smith Richardson, John Olin, Sarah Scaife, and Lynde and Harry Bradley foundations, gleaned from IRS documents and annual reports, can be found in the database compiled by www.Mediatransparency.org. That database also breaks out conservative foundation funding for Media Research Center, Accuracy in Media, and the Center for Media and Public Affairs.

Reed Irvine's fulminations about Vince Foster and many other topics are available on Accuracy in Media's Web site, www.aim.org. Brent Bozell's worldview and details about his organization can be found at www.mediaresearch.org. Information about the Center for Media and Public Affairs can be found at its Web site, www.cmpa.com. The Center's early fundraising is described in a May 14, 1992, FAIR research memo (http://www.fair.org/reports/lichter-memo.html).

The Adam Meyerson quote appears on p. 385 of *Unreliable Sources* by Norman Solomon and Martin A. Lee (Lyle Stuart, 1991). *Editor & Publisher* published its endorsement survey on November 6, 2000, and its survey of the most widely syndicated columnists on May 8, 1999. The earlier studies were cited in a FAIR research memo dated January 2, 2000, available from www.fair.org.

Biased coverage of the Clintons in the mainstream media is examined in my previous book (with Gene Lyons), *The Hunting of the President: The Ten-Year Campaign to Destroy Bill and Hillary Clinton* (St. Martin's Press, 2000). The most thorough analysis of media bias against Al Gore is available in the archives of Bob Somerby's invaluable Daily Howler Web site (www.dailyhowler.com); the same topic is also covered thoroughly in *What Liberal Media?* by Eric Alterman (Basic Books, 2003).

Bush's prevarication about living in Washington was reported by the Daily Howler, January 24, 2003. His exaggerations about his health-care record in Texas were examined in the *New York Times* (on p. A16), March 20, 2000. The Project for Excellence in Journalism study of media bias against Gore can be found at http://www.journalism.org/resources/research/reports/campaign2000/lastlap.

James Warren's remark about "sucking up" to Bush by the media was reported in the *Hill*, May 9, 2001. Dana Milbank explained the media's attitude toward Gore on CNN's *Reliable Sources*, August 10, 2002. Joe Scarborough mentioned the rough media treatment of Gore on *Hardball*, November 20, 2002.

Brit Hume made his remark about Fox News's influence on the midterm election on the Imus radio show, November 19, 2002.

Michael Savage's bigotry was examined in the *San Francisco Bay Guardian*, September 20, 2000. Don Imus's racist invective has received extensive coverage, notably in *Newsday*, February 22, 2000, and the *Boston Globe*, February 23, 2000. John Stossel's right-wing bias and distortions have also received considerable attention over the past several years, most recently in the *Nation*, January 7, 2002.

The Republican leadership's orders to boycott CNN's *Crossfire* were mentioned in *U.S. News & World Report*, April 29, 2002.

3: MALE CHEERLEADERS AND CHICKEN HAWKS

The right-wing outbursts following September 11 were emitted by, respectively: Ann Coulter (of course), as recorded on Fox News's *Hannity & Colmes*, February 7, 2002; Andrew Sullivan, in the *Sunday Times* of London, September 16, 2001 (and on his weblog, no longer available there but noted in Spinsanity, December 17, 2001); and *New York Post* columnist Steve Dunleavy, as reported in a *New York Times* profile, October 14, 2001.

Notes

The mugging of Senator Daschle by the GOP and the religious right was reported in the *New York Times*, December 21, 2001, and in the *Washington Post*, November 9, 2001. I reported John Kerry's defense of Daschle in the *New York Observer*, March 11, 2002.

The relationship between McCarthy and Nixon, as well as the latter's red-baiting of Helen Douglas, are examined in *Nixon: The Rise of an American Politician* by Roger Morris (Henry Holt, 1990). George H. W. Bush's attack on Michael Dukakis and the ACLU is thoroughly reported in *Pledging Allegiance: The Last Campaign of the Cold War* by Sidney Blumenthal (HarperCollins, 1990). On the ACLU's litigation against the McCain-Feingold bill with its conservative allies, see www.aclu.org.

The investigation of Bush operatives' rummaging through Bill Clinton's passport files was extensively reported; see the *Washington Post*, December 14, 1993. Mary Matalin's remarks were released by the Bush-Quayle '92 campaign to US Newswire, October 7, 1992.

Stephen Ambrose was quoted about Prescott Bush Sr.'s opposition to McCarthy in the *Los Angeles Times*, October 12, 1992.

The late, great journalist Lars-Erik Nelson described Newt Gingrich's GOPAC lexicon in the New York *Daily News*, September 14, 1990. Gingrich's draft deferments (along with those of his fellow hawks Dick Cheney, Dan Quayle, GOP strategist Charles Black, Trent Lott, John Kyl, Pat Buchanan, and Phil Gramm) were noted in the *Washington Post*, October 13, 1992.

George W. Bush discusses his Texas Air National Guard service in *A Charge to Keep*, pp. 50–55. The *Dallas Morning News*, September 28, 1999, reported Ben Barnes's account of his role in Bush's enrollment. The *Los Angeles Times*, July 4, 1999, and the *Washington Post*, July 28, 1999, both reported the favorable treatment of Bush by Guard officials after his enlistment. The *Boston Globe's* investigative stories on Bush's service appeared May 23, July 28, October 31, and November 1, 2000. The *London Sunday Times* reference to Air National Guard drug testing appeared June 18, 2000. His cheerleading role at Andover was reported in *Newsday*, January 4, 2001.

The military records (or lack thereof) for politicians currently serving in Congress can be found on their office Web sites (www.House.gov and www.Senate.gov). Tom DeLay's amusing explanation of his inability to serve in Vietnam appeared in the *Houston Press*, January 7, 1999. His assertions about Democrats and Scowcroft were recorded in Spinsanity, September 28, 2002. The Associated Press reported John Ashcroft's history of draft deferments, January 17, 2001. Saxby Chambliss's attacks on

Max Cleland were reported in the *Chattanooga Times,* September 2, 2002, and *Congressional Quarterly Weekly,* August 9, 2002.

The *Washington Post* examined the neo-Confederate allegiances of McCain adviser Richard Quinn and his *Southern Partisan* magazine, February 18, 2000. I wrote about Clyde Wilson's *Southern Partisan* interview in the *New York Observer,* January 24, 2000.

Eyewitness accounts of the Nazi penetration of conservative movements in the United States before World War II are found in *Under Cover* by John Roy Carlson (E. P. Dutton, 1943) and *I Find Treason: The Story of an American Anti-Nazi Agent* by Richard Rollins (William Morrow, 1941). For the Buckley family's association with America First and kindred organizations and publications, see *The Buckleys: A Family Examined* by Charles Lam Markmann (William Morrow, 1973). Regarding William H. Regnery Sr.'s activity in America First, see *Danger on the Right: The Attitudes, Personnel, and Influence of the Radical Right and Extreme Conservatives* by Arnold Forster and Benjamin R. Epstein (Random House and Anti-Defamation League of B'nai B'rith, 1964). David Frum mentions conservatives' consignment of America First to oblivion in *Dead Right* (Basic Books, 1994).

4: DÉJÀ VOODOO, ALL OVER AGAIN

The unappetizing story of America's 1980s thrift debacle is told well in *Inside Job: The Looting of America's Savings and Loans* by Stephen Pizzo (McGraw-Hill, 1989), in *Who Robbed America? A Citizen's Guide to the Savings and Loan Scandal* by Michael Waldman (Random House, 1990), and in Robert Sherrill's extraordinary, book-length article, "The Looting Decade," in the *Nation,* November 19, 1990. Ronald Perelman's donations to the Bush-Quayle war chest were reported in the *Seattle Times,* May 26, 1992, while his S&L acquisitions were reported in the *Resolution Trust Reporter,* August 26, 1991.

David Stockman's revealing remarks were reported in the *Washington Post,* November 22, 1981. He explained still more in *The Triumph of Politics: Why the Reagan Revolution Failed* (HarperCollins, 1986).

Jonathan Chait provided one of the best accounts of the Clinton 1993 deficit-reduction budget—and Republican resistance—in *The American Prospect,* September 21, 1995.

David Horowitz repeated the Republican mantra about Clinton and Gore's passage of "the largest tax increase in American history" in Salon.com, March 5, 2001. Almost seven years earlier, however, on October 26, 1994, the *Wall Street Journal* had shot down that myth and noted that the Reagan-Dole tax bill in 1982 was actually the largest ever "both in 1993-adjusted dollars and as a percentage of the overall economy." I recalled the gloomy predictions made by Gingrich, Gramm, et al., regarding Clinton's 1993 budget in Salon.com, January 26, 1999.

The White House issued statistics on Bill Clinton's economic and social achievements before his administration left office in a 45,000-word report unsurprisingly titled *Eight Years of Peace, Progress, and Prosperity* (Federal Document Clearing House, January 7, 2001). It contains many of the relevant data on employment, poverty, debt, deficit reduction, welfare, and taxes during the nineties boom.

How George W. Bush blew the Clinton surplus has been the subject of many reports by the Center on Budget and Policy Priorities (www.cbpp.org); as well as many *New York Times* columns by Paul Krugman (in particular his column of August 30, 2002) and his excellent short book titled *Fuzzy Math* (W.W. Norton, 2001). Andrew Sullivan's startling admission that Bush and his political adviser Karl Rove were lying about the federal budget appeared in the *New Republic*, May 14, 2001.

The Associated Press exposed ballooning pork expansion under Republican rule in a study published August 5, 2002. That story included Dick Armey's smirking reference to victors and spoils. Dissension among the Republicans over conservative hypocrisy regarding spending, and the case of Representative Aderholt, were reported in *The Hill*, October 2, 2002.

Slate's comparison of stock indexes during Democratic and Republican administrations (http://slate.msn.com/id/2071929/) appeared October 4, 2002. The Northwestern Mutual study and table can be found on the corporate Web site (http://ww2.northwesternmutual.com/tn/learnctr—articles—page_administrations) and is not dated.

In a September 23, 2002, article for *Mother Jones* magazine, University of California economics professor Arthur I. Blaustein examined some of the historical data on prosperity, inflation, and other indicators during Democratic and Republican administrations over the past eighty years. Bloggers Dwight Meredith (http://pla.blogspot.com/2002_10_27_pla_archive.html#83597774) and Kevin Drum (http://calpundit.blogspot.com/2002_09_29_calpundit_archive.html#82576526) have compiled data from various federal agencies to demonstrate the superior economic performance of Democratic administrations. Annual Bureau of Labor Statistics data on employment are available at ftp://ftp.bls.gov/pub/special.requests/lf/aat1.txt. Year-by-year charts in several formats displaying real GDP growth, comnsumer price index, unemployment, personal income growth, interest rates, money supply, and more so-phisticated data sets can be found at www.economagic.com.

5: WHY DICK ARMEY JOINED THE ACLU

Neal Boortz's observations about liberals and freedom appeared in his column on Newsmax.com, June 15, 2000.

Useful discussion of "political correctness" from all sides, as well as the history of that term, may be found in *Debating PC: The Controversy over Political Correctness on College Campuses* (Laurel/Dell, 1992), edited by Paul Berman. Sheldon Hackney provides an extraordinary case study of anti-PC hysteria gone amok in *The Politics of Presidential Appointment* (New South Books, 2002).

Condoleezza Rice offered her not-so-conservative opinion about "political correct-ness" in an interview with the *Times Higher Education Supplement*, June 16, 1995.

Ralph Reed's role in the appalling campaign to stir up Georgia voters over Confed-erate symbolism was reported in the *Orlando Sentinel*, November 10, 2002. His black-outreach Samaritan Project at the Christian Coalition disintegrated even before Reed left, as reported by National Public Radio, March 31, 2001.

Coulter defended Lott on *Hannity & Colmes*, December 13, 2002. Paul Weyrich was quoted in the *New York Times*, December 18, 2002. The *Washington Times* editorial urging Lott's removal appeared December 17, 2002. Weyrich was quoted in the *New York Times* on December 18, 2002. The *Washington Times* editorial appeared on December 17, 2002.

Jerry Falwell's infamous 1965 sermon attacking ministers in the civil rights movement is reprinted in *God's Bullies: Power Politics and Religious Tyranny* by Perry Deane Young (Holt, Rinehart, and Winston, 1982). The theocratic ambitions of Pat Robert-son and his colleagues are discussed in *Under God: Religion and American Politics* by Garry Wills (Simon & Schuster, 1990), pp. 173–74. Robertson's 1983 remarks are quoted in my March 1993 *Playboy* article on the Christian Coalition; his speech and others at the group's October 2002 meeting was reported in *Church & State*, Novem-ber 1, 2002.

John Ashcroft describes his Crisco ritual in *Lessons from a Father to His Son* (Thomas Nelson, 1998); it was also mentioned in the *Washington Post*, January 12, 2001. Justice Scalia's essay on God and government appeared in *First Things*, May 2002, and was noted in the *Washington Post*, August 11, 2002. The religious right's role in Ashcroft's appointment was reported in the *Washington Post*, January 2, 2001. His Senate record is described in a special report on the ACLU Web site, www.aclu.org. (The Web site also provides regular reports on organizing efforts such as the Bill of Rights Defense Committees.)

On Ashcroft's civil liberties record, also see my article in the *New York Observer*, December 3, 2001; Nat Hentoff in the *Village Voice*, September 10, 2002; Jonathan Turley, *Los Angeles Times*, August 14, 2002; and the *Wall Street Journal*, August 8, 2002.

William Safire has written several columns criticizing Ashcroft on civil liberties, including November 15, 2001, November 26, 2001, March 21, 2002, and November 14, 2002. Syndicated columnist Marianne Means ably dissected Ari Fleischer's remarks about the Constitutional Convention, February 8, 2002. Ashcroft's assault on Freedom of Information was reported in the *San Francisco Chronicle*, January 6, 2002, and on the Center for Public Integrity Web site, www.publicintegrity.org.

Senator Byrd's floor speech on the Homeland Security Act is in the *Congressional Record*, November 14, 2002.

Nat Hentoff wrote about Total Information Awareness in the *Washington Times*, December 16, 2002; the *Washington Post* reported its details, November 12, 2002.

Senator Ashcroft's statement appeared in *USIA Electronic Journal*, October 1997. Jake Tapper reported the alliance of Barr, Armey, and the ACLU in Salon.com, April 11, 2003.

6: PRIVATE LIVES AND PUBLIC LIES

Paul Krugman wrote about red versus blue states in the *New York Times*, May 7, 2002. The *New York Times* reported higher Bible Belt divorce rates, May 21, 2001.

American religious right groups provide comprehensive reports of their finances on www.ministrywatch.com, the Web site of a Christian auditing organization.

In *Blinded by the Right* (Crown, 2002), David Brock describes the colorful social lives of his former friends Ann Coulter (p. 181) and Laura Ingraham (pp. 233–35), among other right-wing luminaries. Ingraham's legal scrape with the Dartmouth minister was reported in the *New York Times*, June 7, 1986. Coulter discussed promiscuity during a June 7, 2000 broadcast of *Rivera Live*. She compared Hillary Clinton with a prostitute on May 31, 1999.

The Chenoweth press release appeared on the America 21 Web site, http://www.America21.us. Her adultery scandal was widely reported, most thoroughly in

Salon.com, September 16, 1998. Her career was profiled in the *New Republic*, April 24, 1995. The editorial on Steve Symms appeared in the *Lewiston Morning Tribune*, July 11, 1991. The *Spokane Spokesman-Review* article appeared September 13, 1998.

The Newt Gingrich campaign lexicon was described in Lars-Erik Nelson's New York *Daily News* column, September 14, 1990. Peter Smith's efforts to smear Clinton are recounted in *The Hunting of the President* by Joe Conason and Gene Lyons (St. Martin's Press, 2000). Gingrich's remarks about Susan Smith were reported in the *Madison Capital Times*, July 31, 1995. Smith's molestation by her stepfather was reported in the *Washington Post*, June 25, 1995, and in the *Los Angeles Times*, August 1, 1995. The messy Gingrich divorce was fully chronicled in the *Atlanta Journal and Constitution*, April 7, 2000, and the *Washington Post*, December 18, 1999. I learned about Gingrich's extramarital affair from reporters for the *Nation* and the syndicated TV program while they worked on the Gingrich story in 1995.

The marital troubles of Jim Bunn, Enid Waldholtz, Jim Longley, and the Christensens were reported in the *Los Angeles Times*, December 17, 1995; Jim Nussle's divorce in the Dubuque (Iowa) *Telegraph Herald*, July 3, 1996. The Christensen divorce was also covered in the *Times* of London, August 10, 1996. Tim Hutchinson's divorce, remarriage, and failing 2002 Senate campaign were reported in the *St. Petersburg Times*, October 19, 2002.

In *Sound & Fury: The Washington Punditocracy and the Collapse of American Politics* (HarperCollins 1992), Eric Alterman discussed the personal histories of George Will (p. 96n) and John McLaughlin (pp. 14, 114, 292).

Sun Myung Moon's unholy conduct was reported in the *Vancouver Sun*, June 2, 2001. Rudy Giuliani's extramarital affairs are reported in *Rudy! An Investigative Biography of Rudolph Giuliani* by Wayne Barrett (Basic Books, 2000). John Fund's baroque affairs were detailed in the *Village Voice*, May 21, 2002. The sad story of the Roche family was told in the *Charleston Gazette*, November 27, 1999. Butch Kimmerling's abuse of his foster children was reported in the *Record* (Kitchener-Waterloo, Canada), April 3, 2000. Mike Trout's adultery was reported in the *Christian Century*, November 1, 2000. Jon Grunseth's weird conduct was reported in the *Chicago Tribune*, November 4, 1990. Mike Bowers's adultery was exposed in the *Los Angeles Times*, January 10, 1999.

Dr. Laura's problems were discussed in the *Los Angeles Times*, December 24, 2002, and on *Dateline NBC*, November 19, 2000. Mark Chmura's story was reported in *Sports Illustrated*, February 12, 2001. The Thomas-Steelman affair was reported in *Indianapolis Business Journal*, March 19, 2001, and her beating by Don Sipple was revealed in *Mother Jones*, September–October 1997. Richard Delgaudio's guilty plea was reported in the *Washington Post*, April 24, 2003. Ken Calvert's prostitution bust was reported in the *Washington Post*, June 5, 1994.

Frank Rich wrote about gay right-wingers, including Arthur Finkelstein, in the *New York Times*, January 14, 1999. A revealing Finkelstein profile appeared in *Boston* magazine, August 1996. Marvin Liebman wrote about his secret life in *Coming Out Conservative: An Autobiography* (Chronicle Books, 1992). Robert Bauman's version was titled *The Gentleman from Maryland: The Conscience of a Gay Conservative* (William Morrow, 1986).

The poignant tale of John Paulk was reported in the *Chicago Tribune*, October 23, 2002. Matt Glavin's arrest record and resignation were reported in the *Atlanta Journal and Constitution*, October 5, 2000.

7: TOKENS OF THEIR ESTEEM

Many useful studies of minority voting patterns are available from the Joint Center for Political and Economic Studies. A paper on the 2000 election by David Bositis, the Center's director, can be found online at http://www.jointcenter.org/selpaper/pdffiles/blackvot/2000/analysis_00.pdf.

Reagan biographer Lou Cannon recounted the "Mr. Mayor" incident in the *Washington Post*, August 2, 1989.

George Will's column on the Thomas nomination appeared in the *Atlanta Constitution*, October 14, 1991. Anthony Lewis's column appeared in the *New York Times*, October 1, 1991.

Miguel Estrada's résumé is posted on the Department of Justice Web site, http://www.usdoj.gov/olp/estrada.htm.

The elder Bush discusses his vote against the 1964 act and his support of Goldwater in *All the Best: My Life in Letters and Writings* by George Bush (Scribner, 1999), p. 88.

Horowitz examines his work with the Black Panthers in *Radical Son* by David Horowitz (Free Press, 1997). His remarks about liberals "scaring black people" were broadcast on Fox News Channel's *Hannity & Colmes*, December 9, 1999.

J. C. Watts commented on Democrats and "poverty pimps" in the *Washington Post*, February 4, 1997. The frustration that led to his early retirement from Congress was reported in the *Post*, June 21, 2002.

Notes

Racial aspects of Goldwater's career, including his vote on the 1964 act, are discussed in *Time*, August 19, 1996. *The Buckleys: A Family Examined* by Charles Lam Markmann (William Morrow, 1973) and *William F. Buckley, Jr: Patron Saint of the Conservatives* by John B. Judis (Simon and Schuster, 1988) both address Buckley's civil rights record in depth. He "reaffirmed" his views in 1998, as reported by the Joint Center's *Focus* magazine http://www.jointcenter.org/quiz/article2.htm.

For Nixon's civil rights record, see *One of Us: Richard Nixon and the American Dream* by Tom Wicker (Random House, 1991), one of the more sympathetic biographies. Reports about the White House tapes that exposed his private bigotry appeared in the *Chicago Tribune*, January 7, 200, and the *New Yorker*, December 7, 1992.

Helms's racist appeals were reported in the *Washington Post*, November 18, 1984, and the *New York Times*, October 28, 1990. The Heritage spokesman was quoted in the *Washingtonian*, November 1995. Novak's column appeared in the *Denver Post*, August 31, 2001. Barnes's encomium was in the *Weekly Standard*, August 11, 1997.

Reagan's civil rights record, from the Neshoba, Mississippi, press conference through his first term, was examined in the *Washington Post*, December 7, 1983.

The Bell Curve's bogus "science" and its partial funding by a crackpot eugenics foundation were examined in the *New York Review of Books*, December 1, 1994. Andrew Sullivan's decision to puff the book on the *New Republic*'s cover was examined in the *Washington Post*, October 14, 1994. Loury and Woodson's joint resignations from AEI was reported in the *Washington Post*, September 20, 1995; Loury's ongoing debate with D'Souza was reported in the *Washington Times*, December 18, 1996; his personal problems were reported in the *Christian Science Monitor*, September 5, 2002.

Lott's connection with the Council of Conservative Citizens was exposed in the *Washington Post*, December 12, 1998, and Salon.com, December 22, 1998.

Ashcroft's interview in *Southern Partisan* (and his historical ignorance) were examined in the *Washington Post*, January 29, 2001. His links with the CCC were reported in the *New York Observer*, January 8 and January 15, 2001.

The Mellon Foundation's study of the effects of affirmative action was reported in the *Washington Post*, April 14, 2002.

A useful legislative history of the 1964 act, with a description of the role of moderate and liberal Republicans, can be found at http://www.congresslink.org/civil/essay.html.

8: CRONY CAPITALISM, INFECTIOUS GREED, AND THE WAY THE WORLD REALLY WORKS

Greenspan's relationship with Rand was examined in the *New Yorker*, April 24, 2000, and in the *American Enterprise*, September–October 1997. The *Wall Street Journal* editorial attacking Greenspan for his July 16 testimony appeared July 18, 2002

The long relationship between Lay and Bush, including political contributions, was examined February 7, 2002, in the *Dallas Morning News*, and in the *Washington Post*, March 24, 2002. The phony Lay-Clinton sleepover story was examined in the *New York Observer*, March 4, 2002. Bush administration ties with Enron were reported extensively, including on Bloomberg News, January 18, 2002; copious information may be found on the Texans for Public Justice Web site, www.tpj.org. The Wood episode was reported by CNN, January 15, 2002.

The Natural Resources Defense Council (see their report http://www.nrdc.org/media/pressreleases/020521.asp) obtained thousands of pages from the Department of Energy documenting Enron and other firms' special access to Cheney (whose Energy Task Force report can be read at www.fe.doe.gov/general/energypolicy.shtml). Bush's favors to Enron during the California crisis were detailed in the *New York Observer*, February 11, 2002.

Terry McAuliffe's Global Crossing windfall was examined in Salon.com, February 22, 2002.

The Silverado saga is told in *Who Robbed America?: A Citizen's Guide to the Savings and Loan Scandal* by Michael Waldman (Random House, 1990); and in the *New York Times*, July 21, 1990, and June 19, 1991. Neil Bush's involvement with JNB and Apex were reported in the New York *Daily News*, May 27, 1991.

Jeb Bush's partnerships with Codina and Recarey are well summarized in *Cuba Confidential: Love and Vengeance in Miami and Havana* by Ann Louise Bardach (Random House, 2002), pp. 312–17. Original reporting on those subjects appeared in *Newsday*, October 3, 1988, and the *St. Petersburg Times*, September 20, 1998. Jeb's Bush-El deals and business in Nigeria were extensively reported in the *Miami Herald*, October 5 and 6, 2002. The solicitation in Kuwait by Neil, Marvin, and James Baker was reported in the *New Yorker*, September 6, 1993.

George W. Bush's intertwining business and political careers (from Arbusto to UTIMCO and the Texas Rangers) were detailed in a lengthy article by Joe Conason in *Harper's*, February 1, 2000. The Soros remarks were posted on the *Nation*'s Web site, www.thenation.com by David Corn, July 17, 2002. The Harken lawyers' warning to Bush (and the withholding of their letter from the SEC) was reported in the *Washington Post*, November 1, 2002. Paul Krugman explained the Aloha Petroleum maneuver in the *New York Times*, July 7, 2002. Jim Bath's involvement with Saudi sheiks (including members of the bin Laden family) was reported in the *Austin American-Statesman*, November 9, 2001.

Arlington Mayor Greene's problems with federal regulators were reported in the *New York Times*, September 24, 2000. His thrift's "notorious" failure was noted in the *Fort Worth Star-Telegram*, January 1, 1996.

The Bush Pioneers are listed alphabetically and catalogued at www.tpj.org.

The Carlyle Group's origins, business success, and Bush ties are described extensively in *Red Herring*, January 8, 2002; the *New York Times*, March 5, 2001; the *Nation*, April 1, 2002. The September 11, 2001, meeting at the Ritz-Carlton was reported in the *Washington Post*, March 16, 2003. The Crusader controversy was reported in the *Washington Post*, May 14, 2002; and the *New York Times*, December 22, 2002. Carlyle's difficult acquisition of CSX was reported in the *Daily Deal*, October 25, 2002; and the sale was reported on *CBS Marketwatch*, December 17, 2002. The President's intervention in the dock strike (and its effect on CSX) were reported in the *Honolulu Advertiser*, October 7, 2002. *USA Today* reported on the political connections of Halliburton and Bechtel, March 25, 2003.

9: FAITH, CHARITY, AND THE MAYBERRY MACHIAVELLIS

Bush's description of his philosophy is from *A Charge to Keep*, pp. 234–35.

Accurate, timely, and detailed analyses of the effects of Bush administration budgets on states and localities, poverty, and programs such as Medicaid are available from the Center on Budget and Policy Priorities at www.cbpp.org. The National Governors Association assessment of the fiscal crisis was reported in the *Washington Post*, December 6, 2002. Hubbard was quoted in the *Washington Post*, February 9, 2003. Bush's intention to require more hours from welfare mothers without increasing child care payments was reported by Reuters, May 3, 2002.

Bush's complaint about DeLay's attack on the EITC was reported in the *Washington Post*, October 1, 1999. The *Weekly Standard* retorted on October 18, 1999. The underfunding of "No Child Left Behind" was reported in the *New York Times*, April 10, 2001.

The President's visit to the Wilmington Boys and Girls Club and his budget cuts were reported in Salon.com, April 14, 2001. Cuts in nursing home regulation were reported in the *New York Times*, September 7, 2001. Plans to suspend testing requirements on pediatric drugs were reported in the *Washington Post*, March 19, 2002.

Problems with the "child tax credit" were described in the Progressive Policy Institute's *Blueprint* magazine, May 21, 2002.

I interviewed Mark McKinnon in Austin, Texas, in the fall of 1999. He provided a reel of the "Fresh Start" commercials.

Dionne's magazine profile appeared in the *Washington Post*, September 19, 1999.

The Century Foundation study, "What Charities Can and Cannot Do," can be found on its Web site at http://www.tcf.org/publications/inequality/what_charities_can_and_cannot_do/Chapter8.html.

York's article on Bush and Gingrich appeared in the *Los Angeles Times*, October 19, 1999. Gingrich's remarks about alleviating poverty were reported by the Associated Press, January 5, 1995.

The hardcover edition of Olasky's *Renewing American Compassion* (Free Press, 1996) carried Gingrich's introduction. *Compassionate Conservatism: What It Is, What It Does, and How It Can Transform America* (Free Press, 2000) advertised George W. Bush's brief foreword with his name in cover type as large as the author's.

Rove's role introducing Olasky to Bush was noted in *National Review*, December 21, 1998, and in the *Boston Globe* Sunday magazine, July 23, 2000.

Bush's remarks in Iowa were reported by the Associated Press, June 12, 1999.

Olasky's enrollment in the CPUSA was reported in *National Journal*, May 5, 2001. His "Victorian-era" perspective on charity and poverty was ably dissected by, among others, Hudson Institute president Leslie Lenkowsky in *Commentary*, July 1996.

Bush discussed the personal shortcomings of the poor with Dionne in an interview for the *Washington Post* Sunday magazine, September 19, 1999.

The theocratic, authoritarian ideology of Christian Reconstructionism is described by Garry Wills in *Under God*, p. 174; by Walter Olson in *Reason*, November 1998; and in the *Weekly Standard*, March 26, 2001 (in an obituary tribute to the movement's founder, R. J. Rushdoony).

Ahmanson's connections with Rushdoony were extensively reported in the *Los Angeles Times*, July 8, 1996.

Olasky's views on public education and charity were probed in an interview with *Texas Monthly,* July 2000. For his praise of Rushdoony, see *Prodigal Press: The Anti-Christian Bias of the American News Media* (Crossway Books, 1998), p. 220. For Olasky's citations of George Grant and Gary North, see *Church & State,* October 1, 2000.

Bush's repeated reference to "armies of compassion" was noted in the *Weekly Standard,* March 22, 1999. His health care record as Texas governor was examined in the *New York Times,* April 11, 2000. His tax cut for the oil industry was reported in the *Dallas Morning News,* March 12, 1999.

Statistics on uninsured children, families, and poverty and other social indicators in Bush's Texas were collected in *State of the Lone Star State: How Life in Texas Measures Up,* a study published by Texans for Public Justice, September 2000 (available at http://www.tpj.org/reports/sos/index.html).

The Eli Lilly provision was widely reported, including the *National Law Journal,* November 25, 2002. The amendment repealing sanctions against offshore tax-dodging was reported in the *Baltimore Sun,* November 20, 2002. The White House and Congressional Republican failure to extend unemployment benefits was reported in the *Washington Post,* November 23, 2002. Barnes talked about the issue on *Fox News Sunday,* November 24, 2002.

DiIulio's interview appeared in *Esquire,* January 2003. The magazine posted his letter to Suskind on its Web site, http://www.esquire.com/features/articles/2002/021202_mfe diiulio_1.html.

Pre-election politicking among black ministers by the White House Office of Faith-Based Initiatives was reported in the *Washington Post,* October 24, 2002. The Robertson grant was reported in the *Daily Press* (Newport News, Virginia), October 4, 2002. The televangelist's abuse of Operation Blessing property for his African diamond ventures was reported in the *Norfolk Virginian-Pilot,* July 15, 1999.

10: "DEAD OR ALIVE" — OR MAYBE JUST FORGOTTEN

The bipartisan atmosphere that followed the September 11 attacks was noted in many publications, including the *Dallas Morning News,* September 29, 2001. The Waters and Weisberg remarks were reported in the *Los Angeles Times,* September 22, 2001. The Gephardt, Daschle, and Lott remarks were reported in the *Baltimore Sun,* September 21, 2001.

Rove's remarks to the RNC winter conference were reported in the *Fort Worth Star-Telegram,* January 19, 2002.

The attempts by Cheney (and Bush) to restrict congressional investigation of events leading to the terror attacks were reported in the *Washington Post*, January 30, 2002, and in *Newsweek*, May 27, 2002. The GOP sale of Bush's image on Air Force One was reported in the *Austin American-Statesman*, May 15, 2002. Shelby expressed his concerns on NBC *Nightly News* and CNN's *Larry King Live*, May 16, 2002.

Rice made her "war on terrorism" argument in an interview on CNN's *Late Edition with Wolf Blitzer*, May 19, 2002. DeLay's remarks were quoted in the *New York Times*, May 22, 2002.

The deal to create an independent commission, as proposed by McCain and Lieberman, was reported by the Associated Press, November 15, 2002. The dispute that led to Kissinger's replacement by Kean was reported in *Facts on File World News Digest*, December 13, 2002. The White House reluctance to provide the commission with minimal funding was reported in the *Washington Post*, March 27, 2003.

Coulter accused liberals of shirking the war on terror in *Slander*, p. 5. Horowitz explained how to "beat the Democrats" using the terror issue in NewsMax.com, July 18, 2002.

McCain's annual defense pork listings are available on his Senate Web site at http://mccain.senate.gov/index.cfm?fuseaction=Issues.ViewIssue&Issue_id=27.

The most thorough accounts of Iran-Contra are *Firewall: The Iran-Contra Conspiracy and Cover-up* by Lawrence E. Walsh (W. W. Norton, 1997); *A Very Thin Line: The Iran-Contra Affairs* by Theodore Draper (Hill and Wang, 1991); and *The Iran-Contra Scandal: The Declassified History*, edited by Peter Kornbluh and Malcolm Byrne (New Press, 1993). Reagan blatantly lied in a national address on November 13, 1986; he finally acknowledged that he had misled the public about the arms-for-hostages deal, as reported in the *Washington Post*, March 5, 1987. North's admission and his accusations that Reagan "knew everything" are in *Under Fire: An American Story* by Oliver North and William Novak (21st Century Press, 1991).

The role of Dawa'a terrorists in the Marine barracks bombing and attacks in Kuwait was reported in *Time*, December 26, 1983. Their involvement with Hezbollah was reported by the Associated Press, April 14, 1988. The effort to barter their release was reported by AP, July 23, 1987. The Reagan administration's covert assistance to both countries during the Iran-Iraq war is detailed in *Spider's Web: The Secret History of How the White House Illegally Armed Iraq* by Alan Friedman (Bantam, 1993). The release of the Dawa'a prisoners in 1990 was reported in the *Washington Post*, January 19, 1992.

Notes

Ambassador-at-Large for Counter-terrorism L. Paul Bremer III acknowledged the damage to U.S. credibility in a November 22, 1988, speech at George Washington University, reported in the *Department of State Bulletin,* February 1989.

Perle's essay on Iraq appeared in *U.S. News & World Report,* October 26, 1987. The 1994 Senate investigation was reported in *Newsday,* December 13, 2002.

Reagan's decision to cancel sanctions on Chile and the details of the Letelier case were reported in the *Washington Post,* February 21, 1981.

President George H. W. Bush's "pardon" of Bosch is detailed in *Cuba Confidential: Love and Vengeance in Miami and Havana* by Ann Louise Bardach (Random House, 2002), pp. 200–204.

Conservative efforts to blame Clinton for 9/11 are examined (by the author) in Salon.com, January 15, 2002. Steyn's essay appeared in the *National Review,* January 15, 2002. The *Washington Times* report on Clinton's Georgetown speech were debunked in the *Daily Howler,* www.dailyhowler.com, November 12, 2001.

The CIA's support for Islamists through Pakistan's ISI is examined in *Bin Laden: The Man Who Declared War on America* by Yossef Bodansky (Forum/Prima, 2001). Barnes blamed Iran for the first World Trade Center bombing on NPR's *Weekend Edition Sunday,* March 7, 1993.

Gellman's reporting on Sudan and bin Laden appeared in the *Washington Post,* October 3, 2001. The episode is covered in greater detail in *The Age of Sacred Terror* by Daniel Benjamin and Steven Simon (Random House, 2002), pp. 244–47. Benjamin and Simon also provide copious evidence of Clinton's efforts to hunt down bin Laden and al-Qaeda, and his administration's efforts to strengthen U.S. counterterror measures. Bremer and Oakley's comments appeared in the *Washington Post,* December 24, 2000.

McIntosh's remarks were reported in a transcript by the Federal Document Clearing House, August 1, 1996. Ashcroft expressed his opposition to the encryption bill in *USIA Electronic Journal,* October 1997; his alliance with the computer lobbyists was reported in the *New York Times,* December 26, 1999.

Gramm's fierce opposition to money-laundering legislation was reported in *Time,* October 22, 2001. His "totalitarian" remark was quoted in the *New York Times,* September 20, 2001.

The Clinton administration's FBI budget increases and other initiatives against terrorism are detailed in *The Age of Sacred Terror,* pp. 230–31, 247–49, 252–53, 269,

326–38, 364, 382. Clinton's well-funded efforts against biological terror are described in *Germs: Biological Weapons and America's Secret War* by Judith Miller, Stephen Engelberg, and William Broad (Simon and Schuster, 2001), pp. 247–53 and 277–83.

O'Neill's concerns about Saudi influence in the U.S. are reported in *Forbidden Truth: U.S.–Taliban Secret Oil Diplomacy and the Failed Hunt for Bin Laden* by Jean-Charles Brisard and Guillaume Dasquie (Thunder's Mouth/Nation, 2002).

On the briefings of Cheney, Rice, and Hadley by Berger and Clarke and the new administration's inattention to terrorism, see *The Age of Sacred Terror*, pp. 328–33. The Bush team's arrogant fumbling of counter-terrorism during the months leading to the September 11 attacks was examined in the *Washington Post*, January 20, 2002.

The concern among Western intelligence agencies about Islamist threats to crash an airplane into the Genoa summit was reported in the *Los Angeles Times*, September 27, 2001. The possibility of a "suicide attack" by al-Qaeda at the summit was reported in the *Times* of London, July 13, 2001. Ashcroft's sudden avoidance of commercial flights was reported by *CBS Evening News*, July 26 and 27, 2001.

Acknowledgments

Writing an argumentative book makes the normal obligations more pointed. The responsible author should try to mention everyone who helped, while clearly absolving them of the inevitable blame.

That may not be so easy in the sole case of Thomas Dunne, the independent-minded publisher who convinced me to write *Big Lies*. I am especially indebted to Sean Desmond for his ideas, his cajoling, and his careful labor on the manuscript. And I appreciate the contributions of production editor Robert Cloud; production manager Eric Gladstone; Sarah Delson, who designed the jacket; and Ellis Levine of Cowan, DeBaets, Abrahams & Sheppard, a gentle but thorough legal counselor whose judgment improved the text.

As always, I feel fortunate to be represented by the Wylie Agency, where Andrew Wylie and Jeffrey Posternak provide personal encouragement as well as wise advice.

I am thankful as well to my colleagues at Salon.com who have so brilliantly sustained the magazine (and me): David Talbot, Kerry Lauerman, Joan Walsh, Scott Rosenberg, Suzy Hansen, Ruth Henrich, Jake Tapper, Eric Boehlert, and our former colleague Anthony York.

I owe a permanent debt to my colleagues at the *New York Observer*: Peter W. Kaplan, Terry Golway, Beth Broome, Barry Lewis, and Brian Kempner—and especially to publisher Arthur Carter, whose frequent disagreement with my views has never inhibited his generosity and friendship.

Many people graciously assisted with research assistance and other useful advice: Don Babets, Bill Babiskin, Tamara Baker, Peter Bloch, David Bositis, Jason Briggs, Dan Buck, Andrew Cooper, Kristi Greco, Teddy Gross, Colin Harrison, Denny Hennessey, James Kval, Curtis Lang, Maria Leavey, Rob Levine, Michael Malcolm, Jim Naureckas, Steve Rendall, Stephen Rivers, Martin Rosenblatt, Jim Ryan, Micah Sifry, Bonnie Simrell, David Sirota, Linda Starr, Helen Thorpe, Michael Tomasky, Sean Wilentz, and Eric Witte. I wish I could thank by name all the hundreds of readers who send clips, links, and comments every week.

This project was informed and improved by the work of many writers:

Acknowledgments

Jonathan Alter, Eric Alterman, Mark Bailey, Ann Louise Bardach, Mohamed Bazzi, Sidney Blumenthal, Dan Briody, David Brock, Jonathan Chait, Alfonso Chardy, Milton Coleman, Nicholas Confessore, David Corn, Stanley Crouch, E. J. Dionne, Thomas Edsall, Barbara Ehrenreich, Thomas Frank, Barton Gellman, Robert George, Paul Glastris, Mark Green, Robert Greenstein, William Greider, Doug Henwood, Hendrik Hertzberg, Arianna Huffington, Molly Ivins, John B. Judis, Glenn Kessler, Michael Kinsley, Paul Krugman, Howard Kurtz, Robert Kuttner, Lewis Lapham, Leslie Lenkowsky, Charles Lewis, Gene Lyons, Jeff Madrick, Jane Mayer, Jeremy Mayer, Robert McIntyre, Bethany McLean, Dana Milbank, Mark Crispin Miller, Bill Minutaglio, Gretchen Morgenson, David Neiwert, John Nichols, Timothy Noah, Peter R. Orszag, Greg Palast, Robert Parry, Kevin Phillips, Walter Pincus, Ahmed Rashid, R. G. Ratcliffe, Knut Royce, Robert Scheer, Isaac Shapiro, David Shaw, Robert Sherrill, Tim Shorrock, Michelangelo Signorile, Norman Solomon, Ron Suskind, Ruy Teixeira, Michael Tomasky, Craig Unger, Carol Vinzant, Ed Vulliamy, and James Wolcott.

And the book profited from my regular attention to several astute bloggers: Atrios (http://atrios.blogspot.com/), Brad deLong (http://www.j-bradforddelong.net/movable_type/), Kevin Drum (http://calpundit.blogspot.com/), Edward Jay Epstein (http://edwardjayepstein.com/), Hesiod (http://www.counterspin.blogspot.com/), Joshua Micah Marshall (http://talkingpointsmemo.com/), Brendan Nyhan, Ben Fritz, and Bryan Keefer (www.spinsanity.org), Max Sawicky (http://www.maxspeak.org/gm/), the outstanding Bob Somerby (www.dailyhowler.com), and the *American Prospect*'s Tapped (http://www.prospect.org/weblog/). I am also a diligent reader of Buzzflash (www.buzzflash.com), the Horse (www.mediawhoresonline.com), and TomPaine.com.

I could not have completed this book without the warm support of family and friends. Among the latter I particularly wish to thank James Hamilton, a very best man, and Jeanne Levy-Hinte, whose kindness and concern are so extraordinary. Julie Conason provides both practical help and moral inspiration. And for reasons they know very well, I am profoundly grateful to Wally and Celia Gilbert, Graham and Ann Gund, John and Symmie Newhouse, and John R. Wagley, Sr.

Elizabeth Wagley is my most scrupulous critic, my most devoted ally, my partner, and my love. Every day she makes everything possible and everything better, including this book, which is dedicated to her.

Index

Abbas, Abu, 200
ABC News, 43, 49–50, 51
  political Web site, 47, 95
ABC News/*Washington Post*, poll, 5
abstinence campaigns, 111
Accuracy in Media (AIM), 36, 37, 38, 50
Adams, Samuel, 70
Adelphia, 147
Aderholt, Robert, 84
Adger, Sid, 62–63
affirmative action, 143–44
Afghanistan
  bin Laden in, 206
  U.S. support of mujahideen in, 204
  war in (2001), 81
African-Americans, 71, 128, 132, 139, 188
Age of Sacred Terror, The (Benjamin and
  Simon), 205
A. G. Spanos real estate, 18
Ahmanson, Howard, 182
Ailes, Roger, 48, 49
Akaka, Daniel, 67
Alabama, 17, 136
Aloha Petroleum, 162
al-Qaeda, 56, 190, 193, 195, 196, 204, 205–6,
  211
Ambrose, Stephen, 60
America First, 72–73
American Civil Liberties Union, 58, 90, 103,
  104, 108
American Conservative Union, 125
American Enterprise Institute, 18, 37, 139, 140–
  41
American Financial Group, 18
American International Group, 18
American Lawyer, 43
American Prospect, The, 33
American Renewal, 55
American Revolution, 69–70
Americans for Tax Reform, 84
American Spectator, 48
American Sunroof, 18
America 21, 114
Amoco, 160
Apex, 155
Arbusto, 157
Argentina, 149, 155
Arizona, 136
Arkansas, 17
"Arkansas Project," 26

Arlington, Texas, 162–64
Arlington Sports Facilities Development
  Authority, 163
armed forces, support of, liberals vs.
  conservatives, 52–73
Armey, Dick, 33, 66, 75, 85, 104, 106, 108
Arthur Andersen, 147
Art of Political War, The (Horowitz), 196
Aryan Brothers, 71
Ashcroft, John, 66–67, 98–108, 142, 208, 212
Asian-Americans, 71, 128, 132
Associated Press study, 84–85
Atwater, Lee, 58–59, 72
Axis, 72–73
"axis of evil," 198

Bahrain, 159–60
Baker, James, III, 151, 157, 158, 167, 168, 200
Baker Botts firm, 161
Bakker, Jim, 111, 124
Bandow, Doug, 54
Bardach, Ann Louise, 156, 202
Barnes, Ben, 62
Barnes, Fred, 34, 137, 187, 204
Barnicle, Mike, 34
Barone, Michael, 50
Barr, Bob, 104, 106, 108, 115, 126
Bass, Lee, 18, 166, 167
Bass brothers, 76, 159, 160
Bass Brothers Enterprises, 166
Bath, James, 157
Bauman, Robert, 125
Bechtel, 170
Begala, Paul, 51
Beirut, 199
Bell Curve, The (Murray and Herrnstein), 138–
  39, 140
Benjamin, Daniel, 205
Berger, Sandy, 210
Berman, Paul, 54
Bernstein, Tom, 159
Bertelsmann, 31
Betts, Roland, 159
Bias (Goldberg), 33–34
Bill of Rights, 3, 9, 90, 101–2, 103–4
Bill of Rights Defense Committee, 103
bin Laden, Osama, 56, 168, 199, 204–7
bin Laden family, 168, 210
*Bin Laden: The Man Who Declared War on
  America* (Bodansky), 204

Index

Biseck, Callista, 119–20, 122
Black Panther Party, 133
blacks. *See* African-Americans
Blinded by the Right (Brock), 125
Bob Jones University, 123, 137
Bodansky, Yossef, 204
Bond, Rich, 34–35
Bonior, David, 68
Boortz, Neal, 91
Booth, John Wilkes, 72
Bork, Robert, 130
Bosch, Orlando, 201
Boston Globe, 45, 66
Boswell, Leonard, 68
Bowers, Mike, 124
Boys and Girls Clubs of America, 174
Boy Scouts, 126
Bozell, L. Brent, III, 36–37
Bradley, Bill, 41
Breeden, Richard, 161
Bremer, Paul, 207
Brock, David, 125
Broward Federal, 155
Bryant, William Cullen, 144
Buchanan, Bay, 49
Buchanan, Patrick J., 7, 37, 49, 54, 61, 72,
    134, 136
Buckley, William F., Jr., 31, 36, 42, 50, 91,
    134, 135–36
Buckley family, 73
budget surplus and deficit, 6, 75–85
Bunn, Jim, 120
Burke, Edmund, 70
Burton, Dan, 115, 117
Bush, Dorothy, 157
Bush, George H. W. (41st president)
    1988 election, 58, 88, 150
    military service, 59
    political ineptness of, 14
    racial attitudes of, 131, 136
    rich friends of, 62–63, 76, 157, 166, 168
Bush, George H. W., administration, 49
    economic policy, 77
    personnel of, 167
    tax policy, 74
    and war on terror, 198, 200, 201, 203
Bush, George W. (43rd president)
    in 1988 campaign, for G. H. W. Bush, 44
    2000 election, 7, 39, 41, 44, 49, 128, 131,
        171, 207
    business career, 157–68
    compassionate conservatism of, 171–76, 189
    and Enron, 149
    media coddling of, 44–46
    political skill of, 13–17
    racial attitudes of, 145
    and September 11, 2001, attacks, 190–91

    service in the Texas Air National Guard, 62–
        66
Bush, George W., administration
    civil rights policy, 98, 107
    cuts to safety programs, 21, 24
    economic policy, 80
    favors the rich, 6
    incompetence of policy makers in, 187–88
    media coverage of, 47–48
    pretended goals of, 10
    racial policy, 129–30, 144
    social policy, 183, 187
    tax policy, 25, 26–28, 173
    and war on terror, 193, 196, 198, 211
Bush, Jeb, 155–56, 201, 202
Bush, Laura, 17
Bush, Marvin, 156–57
Bush, Neil, 154–55
Bush, Prescott, Sr., vii, 60
Bush-El, 156
Bush Exploration Oil Company, 157–58
Bush family, 19, 22, 27, 131–32, 149–50, 153–
    60, 170
Bush v. Gore, 131
Byrd, Robert, 105–6, 144

California, 152
Calvert, Ken, 124–25
Cambridge, 22
capitalism, as pseudo-religion, 87–88
Carlucci, 168, 169
Carlyle Asia Partners, 168
Carlyle Group, 167–69
Carlyle Partners II, 167
Carter, Jimmy, administration, 201
Carville, James, 51
Castle, Mike, 83
Caterair, 168
Catholics, 100
Cato Institute, 54
Cavuto, Neil, 49
CBS News, 50
CBS/New York Times survey, 6
Center for Media and Public Affairs, 37–39
Centers for Disease Control, 209
Central Intelligence Agency (CIA), 204, 205,
    206, 209, 211, 212
Century Foundation, 177
Cerf, Vinton, 44
Chalcedon Institute, 182
Chambers, Whittaker, 125
Chambliss, Saxby, 68
Chao, Elaine, 24
Charge to Keep, A (G. W. Bush), 174, 178
charity
    from foundations, 177
    private, 174, 180, 182
Chattahoochee National Park, 126

Index

Cheney, Dick, 16, 66, 80, 104, 150, 151–52, 193, 210
Chenoweth-Hage, Helen, 114–17
Chicago Tribune, 46, 150–51
"chicken hawks," 61
child tax credit, 173
Chiles, Eddie, 158
China (Communist), 88, 92, 149
Chiquita Brands, 18
Chmura, Mark, 124
Chomsky, Noam, 52
Christensen, Jon and Meredith, 120–21
Christian Broadcasting Network, 48, 110
Christian Century, 179
Christian Coalition, 94, 97–98, 115, 118, 120, 121, 123, 176
Christianization of America, 96–99
Christian Reconstructionism, 181–82
Christians, 53
Cicero, 102
Cigar Aficionado, 22–23
Citizens for Tax Justice, 17
civil liberties, defenders of, Democrats vs. Republicans, 89–108
Civil Rights Act, 131, 135, 136, 142, 143, 144, 145
civil rights legislation, 137, 142–43
Civil War, American, 69, 70–71, 144
Clark, Ramsey, 52
Clarke, Richard, 210
Cleland, Max, 67–68
Clinton, Bill
  1992 election, 66, 174–75
  1996 election, 39, 143
  in 2000 campaign, 45
  impeachment crisis, 132
  liberal label avoided by, 2
  in the liberal tradition, 3, 4
  political skill of, 175, 176
  right-wing attacks on, 42, 59, 92, 150–51, 203–4
  sex scandals, 112, 118, 127, 198
Clinton, Bill, administration
  civil rights policy, 107–8
  conservative attacks on, 36
  economic policy, 86, 152
  racial policy, 129–30, 131
  right-wing attacks on, 60
  tax policy, 25–26, 74, 77–80, 173
  and war on terror, 195, 196, 203, 205–6
Clinton, Hillary, 4, 42, 91, 112
Clinton era, mores of, 10, 110
Clinton family, 26, 36, 103
CNBC, 48–49
CNN, 51
CNN/*Time* survey, 5
Codina, Armando, 155
Cohen, Gary, 32–33

Cohn, Roy, 125
Cold War, 53
Commentary, 32
Communists and Communist Party, American, 8, 72, 91, 92, 180
"compassionate conservatism," 175–89
Concerned Women for America, 115
Confederacy, 69, 141
  symbols of, 94
Congo, 188
Congressional Budget Office, 81, 172
conservatives
  different types of (fiscal, family, compassionate), 171–89
  elitism of, 22–28
  lies of, 10–11
  media attention paid to, 29–51
  racism among, 134–42
Constitution, U.S., 70, 105
Constitutional Convention, 105
Contract with America, 77, 178
Conyers, John, 68
corporate scandals, 87, 170–71
Coulter, Ann, 8–9, 10, 20, 22, 23, 30–33, 35, 38, 47, 50, 55, 73, 91, 95, 111, 112–13, 130–31, 195
Council of Conservative Citizens, 141–42
Couric, Katie, 30
Crisco, annointing with, 99
"crony capitalism," 88, 148
Crossfire, 51, 150
Croteau, David, 40–41
Crouch, Stanley, 144
Crown Publishers, 31
Crusader artillery vehicle, 169
CSX Corporation, 27–28, 169
Cuba, 201–2
Cuba Confidential (Bardach), 202
Cubana Airlines bombing, 201–2
Cuban exile community, in Miami, 202
Cuomo, Mario, 2
Curl, Joseph, 203

Daily Howler Web site, 32
Dallas Morning News, 66
D'Amato, Alfonse, 125
Darman, Richard, 167, 168
Dartmouth Review, 111–12, 139
Daschle, Tom, 55–57, 66, 67, 191, 193
Davis, Jefferson, 141
Davis, Tom, 56
Dawa'a prisoners, 199
Declaration of Independence, 69
DeFazio, Peter, 68
Defense Advanced Research Projects Agency, 106
Defense Department, 169, 197

Index

defense spending, Democrats vs. Republicans, 197

DeLay, Tom, 18, 56, 57, 61, 66, 67, 97, 114, 117, 133, 173, 194

Delgaudio, Richard, 124

Democratic Party
1964 convention, 145
in 2000 election, popular vote majority of, 7
adoption of Republican policies, 75
civil rights policy, 143
economic policy, 80, 85–86
favors the middle class and poor, 18
founding principles of, 70
and Iraq war, 54
liberal label avoided by, 2
media attacks on, 42–44
media coverage of, 37
minority voters' support of, 128, 132
money raising by, 153
moral stance of, 110, 118
new "moderate" image of, 174–75
patriotism of, 56
racial policy, 144–45
right-wing attacks on, 20, 56
social policy, 127, 186
tax policy, 77, 78
and war on terror, 190, 196, 197

Department of Homeland Security, 194

deregulation, 75–76, 87

DeWitt, William, 158

DiIulio, John, 187–89

Dionne, E. J., 176, 180

Disney Company, 47

dividends, taxation of, 16–17, 172

Dixie. See South, the

Dixiecrats, 94, 136, 144

Dixie flag crusade, 94

Dobson, James, 42, 55–56, 126

Dolan, Terry, 125

Dole, Bob, 39, 69, 77, 137

Domenici, Pete, 20

Donahue, Phil, 30, 49

Doty, James, 161

Douglas, Helen Gahagan, 58

Dowd, Maureen, 44

Dow Jones, 86

Dow 36,000 (Glassman), 87

draft avoidance, 56, 59, 60–69

Draper, William, III, 157

Drudge, Matt, 90

Drudge Report, 150

D'Souza, Dinesh, 110, 139–40, 141

Dukakis, Kitty, 115

Dukakis, Michael, 58, 60

Duke, David, 72

Dunleavy, Steve, 55

Dyer, Jim, 83–84

earmarks (attached to congressional bills), 83

earned income tax credit, 25, 173, 187

Earnhardt, Dale, 32

economy, stewardship of, Democrats vs. Republicans, 74–88

Editor & Publisher survey, 40, 42

education, spending for, 174

Eisenhower, Dwight, 135, 197

elections
of 1956, 135
of 1960, 135
of 1988, 58, 134, 150
of 1992, 59, 66, 162, 166, 174–75
of 1994, 60, 78, 143
of 1996, 39, 40, 143
of 2000, 7, 39, 41, 43–45, 49, 128, 131, 158, 171, 207
of 2002, 7–8, 94, 113, 191–92

Eli Lilly Pharmaceuticals, 186

End of Racism, The (D'Souza), 139

Energy Task Force, 151, 152

Enron, 27, 147, 148, 149–53, 157, 167, 176

Estrada, Miguel, 130–31

ethnic whites, 143

Evans, Donald, 165, 167

Evans, Lane, 68

Fair Deal, 3

Fair Labor Standards Act, 24

Fairness and Accuracy in Reporting (FAIR), 37, 38

Fairness Doctrine, 50

Falwell, Jerry, 41, 96, 98, 100, 142, 181

Family Research Council, 110

family values, protection of, Democrats vs. Republicans, 109–27

Fauntroy, Walter, 76

Federal Bureau of Investigation (FBI), 103, 194, 205, 208, 211

Federal Energy Regulatory Commission, 151

Federalist Society, 104

Finkelstein, Arthur, 125

First Amendment, 50, 90, 104

Fleischer, Ari, 105

Florida, 7
2000 election polls, 99

Flynt, Larry, 115

Focus on the Family, 42, 124, 126

Foley, Tom, 125

Fort Worth Star-Telegram, 163

Foster, Vince, 36

foundations
charitable work of, 177
conservative think tanks, 35–36

Fourth Amendment, 90, 104

Fox News Channel, 8, 34, 35, 48, 49, 50, 137, 150

Fox News poll, 6

Index

Frank, Barney, 33, 125–26
Franklin, Benjamin, 2
free enterprise, 87–88
  support for, Democrats vs. Republicans, 146–70
Freeh, Louis, 208, 211
Frist, Bill, 18
Frum, David, 73
Fund, John, 124
fundamentalists, 98

Gallup poll, 6
Gannett newspaper chain, 39
Garrison, William Lloyd, 71
gays and lesbians, 89, 111
  in Republican party, 125–26
G8 meeting (Genoa, 2000), 211
Gellman, Barton, 205
General Electric, 27, 49
Genoa, Italy, 211
George, Robert, 100
George III, of England, 70
Georgia, 94, 136
Gephardt, Richard, 54, 190
Germany, 72
GI Bill, 3
Gilder, George, 75
Gilder, Richard, 26
Gillespie, Ed, 151
Gingrich, Marianne, 121–22
Gingrich, Newt, 26, 44, 56, 60–61, 66, 78, 111, 117–23, 125, 137, 140, 175, 178
Giuliani, Rudy, 124
Glassman, James, 50, 87
Glavin, Matt, 126
Global Crossing, 147, 153
Goldberg, Bernard, 33–34, 35, 47
Goldberg, Jonah, 31
Goldwater, Barry, 36, 131, 134, 135–36
Goodman, Ellen, 42
GOPAC, 60, 118, 121
Gore, Al, 7, 26, 39, 43–44, 45, 46, 179
  media attacks on, 43–44, 46–47
Gore, Tipper, 47
government, conservatives' hatred of, 24, 75–76
Government Printing Office, 105
Gracchi (politicians in ancient Rome), 22
Graham, Lindsey, 72
Gramm, Phil, 66, 78, 82, 208
Grant, George, 182
Great Society, 3, 180
Greeley, Horace, 71
Green, Enid Waldholtz, 120
Greenberg, Maurice "Hank," 18
Greene, Richard, 162–63
Green Mountain Power, 18
Green Party, 7
Greenspan, Alan, 146–47

Greenwich, Connecticut, 15, 22
Grunseth, Jon, 124
Guccione, Bob, 113
Gulf War (1991), 157, 161, 199

Hackney, Sheldon, 92
Hadley, Stephen, 210
Haig, Alexander, 201
Halabja, 200
Halliburton, 150, 170
Hamdi, Yaser, 101
Hamer, Fannie Lou, 145
Hannity, Sean, 47, 50, 95, 204–5, 209
"Happy Days Are Here Again," 85
Harken Energy Corporation, 45, 157, 158–62
Harkin, Tom, 67
HarperCollins, 31
Harris, John, 46
Harvard University, 19
Harvey, Paul, 90
Hastert, Denny, 66
Hatch, Orrin, 97, 125
health care, 5, 185–86
health insurance, 184–85
Helms, Jesse, 125, 134, 136
Hentoff, Nat, 103
Heritage Foundation, 18, 42, 136, 177
"Hero of the Taxpayer," 84
Herrnstein, Richard, 138–39, 140
Hezbollah, 197, 199
Hicks, Muss, Tate & Furst, 164
Hicks, Steven, 165, 167
Hicks, Thomas O., 164–65
Hill, The, 83, 84
Hillsdale College, 124
Hinchey, Maurice, 68
Hirsch, Jeffrey, 86
Hispanic-Americans, 71, 131
Hitler, 72
Hodges, Bobby W., 63
"Hollywood liberals," 91
Homeland Security Act, 105–6
Hoover, Herbert, 80
  administration, 86
Hoover, J. Edgar, 90, 125
Hoover Institution, 141
Horowitz, David, 8, 77, 132–33, 134, 195–96, 209
Horton, Willie, 131, 134
House Appropriations Committee, 83
House Bible study caucus, 120
House Progressive Caucus, 68
House Republicans, 147, 178, 188
House Republican Study Committee, 82
Houston, Texas, 22
Houston Post, 161
Hsi Lai Buddhist temple scandal, 43
Hubbard, R. Glenn, 172

Index

Human Events, 73
Hume, Brit, 48, 51
Hussein, Saddam, 55, 64, 161, 199
Hutchinson, Asa, 123
Hutchinson, Tim, 123
Hyde, Henry, 115, 117

IBM, 27
Idaho, 17
Idaho Family Forum, 115
Idaho Statesman, 116
Immelt, Jeffrey, 49
Imus, Don, 49
Indochina, U.S. involvement in, 53
information, government withholding of, in
    name of national security, 104–5
Ingraham, Laura, 49, 90, 111–12, 139
Inouye, Daniel, 67
Internal Revenue Service, 27, 28, 173
International Longshore Workers Union, 169
International Medical Centers, 155–56
Internet, 44, 106, 108
Iran, 197–200, 204
Iran-Contra scandal, 107, 197–99
Iran-Iraq war (1980s), 199
Iraq, 161, 199
    weapons of mass destruction of, facilitated by
        U.S. policy, 200
Iraq war (2003), 54, 65, 67
Irish immigrants, 133
Irvine, Reed, 36
isolationists, 69
Italian immigrants, 133
Ivy League, 129

Jackson, Jesse, 127
Japan, 72
Jefferson, Thomas, 2, 22, 70
Jeffords, Jim, 55
Jews (American)
    immigrants, 133
    prejudice against, 19, 71, 129
JNB International, 155
John Olin Foundation, 35
Johnson, Lyndon B., 3, 143
    administration, 86
Johnson, Robert Wood, IV, 18
Johnson & Johnson, 18
Joint Committee on Taxation, 77
Jones, Paula, 124
Jordan, Robert, 161
journalists, political opinions of, 39, 41
Journeys with George (film), 41

Kansas City, 23
Kassinger, Theodore W., 151
Kean, Thomas, 195
Kemp, Jack, 138, 142

Kennedy, Edward, 21, 127, 174, 189
Kennedy, John F., 22, 113, 210
Kennedy, Robert, 2
Kennedy family, 19, 145
Kentucky, 17
Kerry, John, 57, 61, 67
Keyes, Alan, 49
Kilpatrick, James J., 41
Kimmerling, Earl, 124
King, Martin Luther, Jr., 2, 113, 131, 135–36,
    137
Kinsley, Michael, 170
Kissinger, Henry, 195
kleptocracy, 148
Kohlberg Kravis Roberts, 166
Krauthammer, Charles, 50
Kravis, Henry, 166
Kristol, Bill, 34, 119
Krugman, Paul, 45, 81, 109–10
Kudlow, Lawrence, 49
Ku Klux Klan, 71, 135, 141
Kurds, 200
Kuwait, 157, 161, 199

Labor Department, 24, 169
Latin America, U.S. involvement in, 53
Latinos (American), 128, 132, 139
Lay, Kenneth L., 18, 149–50
Leahy, Patrick, 101
Lebanon, 197, 199
leftists, 52–53
"left-wing," 38
Lehrman, Lewis, 157
Lessons Learned the Hard Way (Gingrich), 121–
    22
Letelier, Orlando, 201
Lewinsky, Monica, scandal, 198, 206, 209
Lewis, Anthony, 130
Lexis-Nexis searches, 38
"liberal," fear of the word, 2, 8
liberals, 127, 213
    accused of snobbism, 13, 19–21
    attacks on, 8–11, 91
    and control of media, 29–41
    and ending racism, 142–45
    intimidation of, by conservatives, 1–2
    values of, 2–11
libertarians, 98, 147
Lichter, S. Robert, 37
Liddy, G. Gordon, 47
Lieberman, Joe, 150, 194
Liebman, Marvin, 125
Limbaugh, Rush, 7, 10, 19, 22–23, 34, 38, 47,
    50, 59, 61, 66, 90, 93, 122, 134
"limousine liberals," 13, 19
Lincoln, Abraham, 71, 135, 142
Lindblom, Charles, 213
Lindh, John Walker, 55